STARS GALORE
and Even More

OTHER BOOKS AVAILABLE FROM CHILTON — ROBBIE FANNING, SERIES EDITOR

CONTEMPORARY QUILTING

Barbara Johannah's Crystal Piecing
The Complete Book of Machine Quilting, Second Edition,
   by Robbie and Tony Fanning
Contemporary Quilting Techniques, by Pat Cairns
Creative Triangles for Quilters, by Janet B. Elwin
Fast Patch, by Anita Hallock
Fourteen Easy Baby Quilts, by Margaret Dittman
Machine-Quilted Jackets, Vests, and Coats, by Nancy Moore
Pictorial Quilts, by Carolyn Vosburg Hall
Precision Pieced Quilts Using the Foundation Method,
   by Jane Hall and Dixie Haywood
Quick-Quilted Home Decor with Your Bernina,
   by Jackie Dodson
Quick-Quilted Home Decor with Your Sewing Machine,
   by Jackie Dodson
The Quilter's Guide to Rotary Cutting, by Donna Poster
Scrap Quilts Using Fast Patch, by Anita Hallock
Shirley Botsford's Daddy's Ties
Speed-Cut Quilts, by Donna Poster
Stitch 'n' Quilt, by Kathleen Eaton
Super Simple Quilts, by Kathleen Eaton
Teach Yourself Machine Piecing and Quilting,
   by Debra Wagner
Three-Dimensional Appliqué, by Jodie Davis
Three-Dimensional Pieced Quilts, by Jodie Davis

CRAFT KALEIDOSCOPE

Creating and Crafting Dolls,
   by Eloise Piper and Mary Dilligan
Fabric Crafts and Other Fun with Kids, by Susan Parker
   Beck and Charlou Lunsford
Fabric Painting Made Easy, by Nancy Ward
Jane Asher's Costume Book
Learn Bearmaking, by Judi Maddigan
Quick and Easy Ways with Ribbon, by Ceci Johnson
Soft Toys for Babies, by Judi Maddigan
Stamping Made Easy, by Nancy Ward
Too Hot To Handle? Potholders and How to Make Them,
   by Doris L. Hoover

CREATIVE MACHINE ARTS

ABCs of Serging, by Tammy Young and Lori Bottom
The Button Lover's Book, by Marilyn Green
Claire Shaeffer's Fabric Sewing Guide
The Complete Book of Machine Embroidery,
   by Robbie and Tony Fanning
Creative Nurseries Illustrated,
   by Debra Terry and Juli Plooster
Distinctive Serger Gifts and Crafts, by Naomi Baker and
   Tammy Young
Friendship Quilts by Hand and Machine, by Carolyn
   Vosburg Hall
Gail Brown's All-New Instant Interiors
*Hold It! How to Sew Bags, Totes, Duffels, Pouches, and
   More*, by Nancy Restuccia
How to Make Soft Jewelry, by Jackie Dodson

Innovative Serging, by Gail Brown and Tammy Young
Innovative Sewing, by Gail Brown and Tammy Young
Jan Saunders' Wardrobe Quick-Fixes
The New Creative Serging Illustrated, by Pati Palmer, Gail
   Brown, and Sue Green
Petite Pizzazz, by Barb Griffin
Putting on the Glitz, by Sandra L. Hatch and Ann Boyce
Quick Napkin Creations, by Gail Brown
Second Stitches: Recycle as You Sew, by Susan Parker
Serge a Simple Project, by Tammy Young and Naomi
   Baker
Serge Something Super for Your Kids, by Cindy Cummins
Sew Any Patch Pocket, by Claire Shaeffer
Sew Any Set-In Pocket, by Claire Shaeffer
Sew Sensational Gifts, by Naomi Baker and Tammy Young
Sewing and Collecting Vintage Fashions,
   by Eileen MacIntosh
Simply Serge Any Fabric, by Naomi Baker
   and Tammy Young
Soft Gardens: Make Flowers with Your Sewing Machine,
   by Yvonne Perez-Collins
The Stretch & Sew Guide to Sewing Knits, by Ann Person
Twenty Easy Machine-Made Rugs, by Jackie Dodson

KNOW YOUR SEWING MACHINE SERIES,
   by Jackie Dodson

Know Your Bernina, second edition
Know Your Brother, with Jane Warnick
Know Your New Home, with Judi Cull
   and Vicki Lyn Hastings
Know Your Pfaff, with Audrey Griese
Know Your Sewing Machine
Know Your Singer
Know Your Viking, with Jan Saunders
Know Your White, with Jan Saunders

KNOW YOUR SERGER SERIES,
   by Tammy Young and Naomi Baker

Know Your baby lock
Know Your Serger
Know Your White Superlock

STARWEAR

Embellishments, by Linda Fry Kenzle
Make It Your Own, by Lori Bottom and Ronda Chaney
Mary Mulari's Garments with Style
Pattern-Free Fashions, by Mary Lee Trees Cole
Shirley Adams' Belt Bazaar
Sweatshirts with Style, by Mary Mulari

TEACH YOURSELF TO SEW BETTER SERIES,
   by Jan Saunders

A Step-by-Step Guide to Your Bernina
A Step-by-Step Guide to Your New Home
A Step-by-Step Guide to Your Sewing Machine
A Step-by-Step Guide to Your Viking

STARS GALORE
and Even More

SPEED-CUT QUILT DESIGNS
USING HEXAGONS AND OCTAGONS

DONNA POSTER

Chilton Book Company
Radnor, Pennsylvania

DEDICATION

To every person—everywhere—who, in the midst of daily living plucks a flower from the soul and stitches it into a quilt

Copyright © 1995 by Donna Poster

All Rights Reserved

Published in Radnor, Pennsylvania 19089, by Chilton Book Company

Cover design by Anthony Jacobson
Interior design by Stan Green/Green Graphics
Line drawings by the author
Technical drawings by The D-Group
Photography by Gary Childress

Manufactured in the United States of America

The following trademark terms have been mentioned in this book:
Fiskars® (Fiskars Oy Ab, Helsinki, Finland)
Letraset® (Esselte Pendaflex Corp., Garden City, N.Y.)
Miterite™ (Holiday Designs, Mineola, Tex.)
Pigma® (Sakura Color Products of America, Inc., Union City, Calif.)
Post-it Notes™ (3M Commercial Office Supply Division, St. Paul, Minn.)
Speedy™ (Holiday Designs, Mineola, Tex.)
Tack a Note ™ (Dennison Manufacturing, Framingham, Mass.)
X-Acto® (Hunt X-Acto, Inc., Philadelphia, Pa.)

If you are interested in a quarterly newsletter about creative uses of the sewing machine and serger, edited by Robbie Fanning, write to The Creative Machine, PO Box 2634-B, Menlo Park, Calif. 94026.

Library of Congress Cataloging-in-Publication Data

Poster, Donna.
    Stars galore and even more : speed-cut quilt designs using hexagons and octagons / Donna Poster.
        p.   cm. — (Contempory quilting)
    Includes bibliographical references and index.
    ISBN 0-8019-8615-X (pbk).
    1. Patchwork—Patterns.   2. Rotary cutting.   3. Quilting
4. Patchwork quilts.   I. Title.   II. Series
TT835.P673   1995
746.46—dc20   95-7314
                                                        CIP

1 2 3 4 5 6 7 8 9 0   4 3 2 1 0 9 8 7 6 5

CONTENTS

FOREWORD BY ROBBIE FANNING vi
PREFACE vii
ACKNOWLEDGMENTS ix
INTRODUCTION x

PART I. EXPLORING NEW DIRECTIONS IN QUILTMAKING

1. USING THIS BOOK 3
2. TAKING THE FIRST STEPS 7

PART II. GETTING READY TO MAKE YOUR QUILT

3. MAKING YOUR FIRST QUILT 11
4. DECIDING WHAT QUILT TO MAKE 13
5. SELECTING COLORS 17
6. CALCULATING YARDAGES 21
7. BUYING FABRIC, BATTING AND SUPPLIES 27
8. PREPARING AND CUTTING FABRIC 31

PART III. COMPLETING YOUR QUILT

9. PIECING 47
10. APPLIQUÉING AND EMBROIDERING 57
11. ADDING BORDERS 61
12. QUILTING AND BINDING 65
13. CARING FOR YOUR QUILT 73

APPENDICES

A. 144 HEXAGON QUILT BLOCKS 76
B. 144 OCTAGON QUILT BLOCKS 96
C. QUILT SETS AND OTHER BASICS 116
D. BORDERS AND BACKING 129
E. COPY, CUT AND PASTE FUN 132
F. 56 SAMPLE COMBINATIONS 140
G. YARDAGE TABLE FOR TEMPLATES 154
H. FULL-SIZE TEMPLATES 156

GLOSSARY 177
SOURCES 178
BIBLIOGRAPHY 179
INDEX 180

FOREWORD

I'm always amazed at how serendipity has enriched my life. For example, I've met many interesting people who later became significant in my life merely by hanging out somewhere and falling into conversation with the person next to me. One topic leads to another, and five years later we're in business together.

Such a meeting occurred serendipitously between Donna Poster and me at the Houston Quilt Market many years ago. A peppy stranger who owned a quilt store sat next to me at a breakfast. We started talking, we discussed everything under the sun, and before long, she was a writer for Chilton and I was her editor. Donna wrote two excellent books for us, especially useful for readers because she had done so many of the yardage calculations that quilters and storeowners groan about.

Meanwhile, as a person who doodles endless circles, I had started noticing wheel covers on cars—those silver disks that cover the inner part of the wheel. They are round and var-

ied and make wonderful machine-quilting designs.

One day, Donna called to say she had an idea for a new book and it came from noticing wheel covers on cars (only she stubbornly, persistently, incorrectly calls them "hubcaps"). If you had X-ray vision, you'd see the exclamation points traveling the telephone lines. ("You're kidding! That's what I've been noticing!")

It's been a pleasure to see how Donna followed this discovery in a different direction from the one I took in my machine-quilting book. And from reading her preface, you'll learn how this book showed her what it wanted to be. I think the best things in life develop that way. If you pay attention, an initial idea takes it own path, serendipitously.

Robbie Fanning
Series Editiior

PREFACE

Writing a book is like raising children. You think you know where you're headed with them, then darned if they don't go off in a different direction. I'm so glad that this book, like my children, has taken a really fine direction. But it's been quite an experience!

First was the matter of a title. I love mysterious and "kitschy" titles. You know the kind. Like—oh, maybe—"Pickle Juice and Puppy Tails." A title that would leave the reader forever scratching her head and wondering what in the world the title has to do with quilting!

Instead, I decided that this book was to have a "twenty-first-century" sort of title. Throughout history, quilts made of blocks were always done in squares, so I saw the concept of using hexagons and octagons as a great new view of quilting. But my publisher pointed out that five years from now my book would be lost in a sea of twenty-first-century titles! Oh, well.

Meanwhile, I was having another major problem. All those hexagons and octagons I was designing were turning into stars. Especially the hexagons. I'd begun to picture my hexagons as naughty little trolls jumping madly up and down, demanding loudly that I make them into stars!

One day I was moaning about this problem to a quilting pal and found that she was excited about a book that was loaded with stars. I started telling other quilters and encountered the same reaction. Amazing. I'd always considered stars rather difficult to do. That didn't matter. They all wanted my book of stars anyway.

Well, what the heck. Between my screaming hexagon trolls and my enthusiastic quilters, I gave up and started going with the stars. But I did feel as though this book were developing a mind of its own.

Now the title was clear: *Stars Galore and Even More* tells it like it is and even has a nice lilt to it.

Then I looked at the quilt models that I had. Considering the title, the book should really include a few quilts with stars in them. So I picked out some designs. I would make them . . . but I wasn't going to like doing them (stamping of feet here)! Was not! Sure enough, once I got started, I faced a lot of weird points. A lot of bias. And the first time I machine-stitched twelve points together, I felt as if I were crossing the Alps!

Strangely, by the third pile of points the Alps felt like only a bump in the road. And the points were working out just fine. And bias? Well, what's a little more bias to a quilter?

Actually, I was having a lot of fun. What's more, I loved my star quilts. Surprise, surprise! My quilters pulled me, kicking and screaming, through this book—and made a convert of me!

Stars! Yes! I love them!

Through all these efforts, I discovered a number of tips, which I've passed on to you in this book. A "new," easier way of doing set-ins. Hints on machine-stitching all those crazy points. A simple concept for calculating yardages (the "scribble" method that I've used for my customers for fifteen years).

Best of all, I devised a simple way for you to play with all these hexagon and octagon designs to produce your own, unique quilts—and have fun doing it, too! I call it COPY, CUT AND PASTE FUN. And that's really all it is. Copy. Cut. Paste. Fun.

To test this method, I passed the word around that I was setting up a basic design group for nondesigners. Anyone could sign up. No charge, no rules, no format. I had to coax, cajole and promise that no one would ever laugh at anyone else. Most people who joined were beginning quilters. One gal never sewed a thing in her life but was going through a traumatic period and needed to get out of the house!

This group met weekly for three months and turned out a flood of great designs. Several designs were even contributed by the children and grandchildren of these ladies.

This incredibly diverse group of women still meets occasionally because we have found, as quilters throughout history have, that the friendships that develop during creative endeavors carry over into the rest of our living.

These quilters made suggestions, pointed out flaws and are responsible for many of the sample combinations and quilt models shown in this book. I've presented fifty-six sample combinations, using fifty different quilt block designs. They're here only to show you the possibilities and to whet your appetite for more! Use them as they are, but do have some fun and create your own, too.

Many people who use my books eventually want the entire series. They tell me that they like the vast amount of self-help information, yardages and details in these books. For this reason, I've tried to avoid duplicating information whenever possible. The only subject matter that overlaps is the general instructions. *Stars Galore and Even More* is the third in my series of books exploring a particular phase of quilting in depth.

My first book, *Speed-Cut Quilts*, has one hundred square quilt block designs, each in three sizes and four variations, for a total of twelve hundred possible designs. A popular feature of this book is the five basic sets of square block quilts, including all the information needed for seven sizes of quilts.

My second book, *The Quilter's Guide to Rotary Cutting*, is an in-depth rotary-cutting manual. All the shapes are divided into thirty basic shapes, and the book provides instructions for speed-cutting each. Understanding my basic system will allow you to cut almost any pieced quilt with the rotary cutter. This book also contains all the yardages and information needed for making twenty quilt designs, each in seven sizes.

My fourth book is already in progress! Subject? Surprise!

If you enjoy one of my books, get them all. You'll love them!

ACKNOWLEDGMENTS

Special thanks to the following persons and companies:

Gutcheon Patchworks, Inc., Tacoma, Wash., for the fabrics used in the following quilt models: Cabbage Rose, Flying Flags, Inside Track, Primrose and Star Burst.

Hobbs Bonded Fibers, Waco, Tex., for the Heirloom cotton batting used in all the quilts made by Donna Poster.

Holiday Designs, Mineola, Tex., for the rotary-cutting templates used in DONNA'S SPEEDY CUTTING SYSTEM.

Fiskars, Inc., Wausau, Wis., for their rotary cutters.

My wonderful group of design-testing ladies for their enthusiasm, ideas, stitching and friendship. A very special thank you to Margaret Barncord, Virginia Bobbitt, Sherry Reid Carroll, Luana Hall, Nina Johnston, Elizabeth Z. Lewis, Leslie McFarlane, Sue Miller, Joni Milstead, Trina Rehkemper, Susan Saiter and Iris Waal. Special thank you to Jarod Rehkemper for his two quilt designs.

Gary Childress of Captured Images, Fort Worth, Tex. for all the photography.

Sandra Barker for a lovely Sunday in her quilt shop, Calico Cupboard, Colleyville, Tex. All photographs of our quilting ladies were taken there.

Danny Smith of The D–Group, Dallas, Tex. for the graphics.

Carol Munson for her loving care and patience in the final editing of the book.

Robbie Fanning, for being my mentor in the world of publishing and for becoming my friend in life.

Zoë and Laura Pasternack, my daughters, for their encouragement and never-ending faith in me.

Arn Poster, who, once again, cooked great meals (his trout almondine is fantastic!), walked the dog, hugged me a lot and put up with the endless bellyaching that is part of writing my books.

INTRODUCTION

It all started with hubcaps.

Have you ever studied the designs on hubcaps? They're wonderful. Normal people are dumbfounded when they learn that I study hubcaps. Not quilters, though. That's because quilters do not consider themselves quite normal.

After all, who else would go to a quilt show proudly wearing a garment she spent a year stitching—-with sneakers on her feet?

Who else would sketch the design of the tile floor while sitting on the throne in a public bathroom?

Who else would own enough fabric that if-she-started-sewing-nonstop-right-now-she'd-still-be-stitching-when-she-was-195-years-old, yet happily spends the grocery money on more fabric?

No, real quilters are never surprised at people who study hubcaps! The problem was—what could I do with all those wonderful designs? One day, staring at my thousandth hubcap, I mentally put sides on the curved edges, and there was my answer. Of course. An octagon. A hexagon. Yes! All different kinds, too. Pieced like the old square quilt blocks.

I started drawing, playing, coloring and cutting. I'd copy a dozen of each quilt block, cut them out, move them around, combine them, anything I felt like doing. When I had something I liked, I pasted it down and made a few copies.

One day I showed a group of students what I was doing. They wanted to try it, too, so I showed them how to begin.

We set up a once-a-week meeting date to share what we had done. The paper piled up, and the ideas and designs were wonderful. Most of these ladies were beginning quilters, nonartists, and they were designing beautiful one-of-a-kind quilts. This secret needed to be shared with the world.

Stars Galore and Even More shows you how it happened for us and how you can make it happen for you. Just follow my simple directions and let yourself go in your own direction. You'll enjoy endless hours and make the most exciting quilts you've ever seen.

Enjoy,

Donna

Part
I

EXPLORING NEW DIRECTIONS IN QUILTMAKING

1. Using This Book

2. Taking First Steps

USING THIS BOOK

The fun part about quilt making is that there's always something new to learn: how to use a new gadget; a hint for faster, easier quilting; another way of doing something; a great new design to master. Quilters are always looking for new directions. This book was written to provide new ideas, hints and challenges that will spark your imagination and send you in your own unique direction, no matter what your level of experience. I've included projects that are fast and easy, as well as others that are downright challenging—and some in between.

Quilters love to share ideas.

Donna's Hint

Please resist the temptation to skip this chapter—even if you're an experienced quilter. Knowing how to use the book will help you plan your quilt quickly and easily. Concentrate especially on the descriptions of Appendices A through H. You'll need the information to understand PART II: GETTING READY TO MAKE YOUR QUILT.

Like a hexagon quilt, this book has many sections that interrelate. So before you purchase any fabric or cut any templates, go through the book, page by page, and become familiar with everything that's in it—especially the cross references.

Here's what you'll find:

- Tips to help you decide what to make.
- An easy method for designing your quilt.
- 144 hexagon quilt block ideas.
- 144 octagon quilt block ideas.
- 56 quilt patterns you can duplicate.
- Tables with fabric yardages.
- A list of quilting supplies.
- Two methods for cutting fabric: the traditional scissors method and the rotary-cutting method.
- Detailed cutting information: the number of pieces needed, the grain lines and the templates needed.
- Machine-construction techniques: joining points, handling bias, setting in corners.
- Hand-piecing and appliquéing instructions.
- Tips on adding borders and backing.
- Machine- and hand-quilting techniques.
- Instructions on finishing and caring for your quilt.
- Full-size templates.

That's a lot of information! But don't be intimidated. I've given you what's needed to make hundreds of quilts, and I will explain it all. Once you know your way around the book, you'll see that planning hexagon and octagon quilts with my copy-and-play format is really a breeze.

THE CONTENTS

Our book-tour will begin with PART II: GETTING READY TO MAKE YOUR QUILT. In this section, you'll learn all about planning your quilt from selecting fabrics to figuring yardages. You'll see how to preshrink the fabric, and you'll learn my speedy ways for cutting strips, squares, triangles, hexagons, octagons and other quilt shapes. In PART III: COMPLETING YOUR QUILT, you'll find all the information you need for putting your quilt together. There are tips and techniques on piecing, pressing and quilting plus hints for storing and caring for your finished quilt.

HEXAGON AND OCTAGON DESIGNS

Now, if you will, turn to APPENDIX A: 144 HEXAGON QUILT BLOCKS and APPENDIX B: 144 OCTAGON QUILT BLOCKS for 72 exciting quilt block designs. (Each appendix contains 36 designs plus 4 variations.) Following the designs are 18 pages of detailed information, making it possible for you to duplicate any of the blocks. For each design, you'll find the following:

- A drawing of the pieced quilt block, with grain lines marked for each piece.
- An indication of the level of skill needed for constructing the quilt block. Level 1 is the easiest; level 3, the most challenging.
- Quilt block pieces labeled with capital letters (A, B, C). Each letter correlates with a template number that refers to a template in APPENDIX H: FULL-SIZE TEMPLATES. For example, for Hexagon Quilt Block 1, Whirlybird, piece A is cut with Template 150, piece B with Template 67 and piece C with Template 68.
- Four variations of the quilt block, each denoted by the quilt block number, a hyphen and a capital letter from A to D (for Hexagon Quilt Block 1, *1-A* is the first variation, *1-B* is the second variation). Beside each variation is a key showing the quantity of each piece needed to make the quilt block. For example, for Hexagon Quilt Block *1-A*, the notations *1/A*, *6/C* and *6/B* mean that you need 1 piece of

piece A, 6 pieces of piece C and 6 pieces of piece B.

• A suggested method of construction. Called *Building the Block*, this method is the fastest and easiest way to put the quilt block together.

QUILT SETS AND OTHER BASICS

Having surveyed the hexagon and octagon designs, let's move on to APPENDIX C: QUILT SETS AND OTHER BASICS. Here, you'll discover six quilt layouts, or quilt sets—three for hexagons and three for octagons. For each quilt set, you'll find:

• A drawn-to-scale diagram showing these sizes: wall hanging (W), oblong (OB), crib (CR), square (SQ), twin bed (T), double bed (D), queen-size bed (Q) and king-size bed (K).
• Information about edge pieces, corner pieces, lattice blocks and pieced lattice blocks, including template numbers.
• A table detailing measurements, the total number of quilt blocks needed and yardages.
• Special instructions.
• Construction process.

Next, look over APPENDIX D: BORDERS AND BACKING. It has designs for optional quilt borders and information on piecing the quilt backing.

COPY FUN

Remember those nostalgic grade-school days when we cut things out, pasted them onto something else and had fun doing it? As children, we were creative because we were allowed to dream and play, but through the years, many of us have learned to put aside much of our playfulness.

Since quiltmaking is a creative process, let's learn to play again. Turn to APPENDIX E: COPY, CUT AND PASTE FUN. There you'll find just what you need for playing with hexagon and octagon quilt blocks and sets—and designing a quilt.

While you're playing, forget your grownup instinct to "waste not." I know many people who make their livings in creative endeavors, and their wastebaskets are big (and usually full)! (A very famous painter once spent an entire summer painting apples just to get one perfect painting. Photographers take hundreds of shots of a model to get the one that is ultimately published in a magazine. Yet you and I expect to sit down, pick up a pencil and create a masterpiece!) And forget about "designing a quilt." Just have fun—sooner or later you'll be brimming with fantastic quilt ideas.

One more suggestion: Check out APPENDIX F: 56 SAMPLE COMBINATIONS. It has wonderful designs, created by nine savvy quiltmakers. Feel free to duplicate any of the designs. Or if you like, use one as a jumping off point for creating your own special quilt.

YARDAGE TABLE AND TEMPLATES

When you're ready to purchase fabric, take advantage of the information I've compiled for you in APPENDIX G: YARDAGE TABLE FOR TEMPLATES. The table shows you, in an easy-to-follow format, the number of pieces you can cut from $\frac{1}{4}$, $\frac{1}{2}$ and 1 yard of 42-inch fabric.

Since I know that enlarging patterns is something few quilters enjoy doing, I've drawn all 238 templates full size. See APPENDIX H: FULL-SIZE TEMPLATES.

CHAPTER 2

TAKING THE FIRST STEPS

CREATE A NOTEBOOK

Now that you know what's in this book, I'd like you to cut your book apart and put it into a three-ring binder. Don't be alarmed. This book is a tool to be used, not a coffee table decoration. A loose-leaf format will allow you to do several things:

• Remove the pages as you need them.
• Keep the pages neat and clean.
• Place a page of instructions where it is easy to see.
• Lay a page flat when you copy a full-size template.

To turn your book into a notebook, purchase a binder with 1- or 1½-inch rings. Next,

"Now let's try it this way."

remove the book's spine so the pages are separate. Many office supply stores will remove the spine for just a few dollars. They'll also punch the holes needed for inserting the pages into your binder. (This book has been designed so that the holes will not disrupt the printed area of the pages.) Or you can easily remove the spine yourself. I cut my book apart, and the entire process took only about fifteen minutes. Here's what to do:

Using a thick, sturdy ruler (like the one you use for rotary cutting) and an X-Acto (Hunt X-Acto, Inc., Philadelphia, Pa.) knife or a rotary cutter with a used blade, cut several pages at a time. Cut as close to the spine as possible ($1/8$ to $1/16$ inch).

To make the holes, use an inexpensive three-hole punch; it should be able to punch several pages at a time. If the binder has clear pockets on the outside, place the book covers there.

CHOOSE A PATH

You've previewed the book and feel comfortable with it. You've made the book into a notebook. Now you're eager to take a step—perhaps a small one or maybe a big one—in some direction.

If you're a first-time quilter, *please* do my beginner's exercises in CHAPTER 3: MAKING YOUR FIRST QUILT before starting any of the projects. The practice will help you feel comfortable about tackling your first project and will help ensure that your quilting experience is enjoyable and successful.

Experienced quilters: You may want to warm up by doing the beginner's exercises in CHAPTER 3. If not, go on to CHAPTER 4: DECIDING WHAT QUILT TO MAKE.

Part
II

GETTING READY TO MAKE YOUR QUILT

3. Making Your First Quilt

4. Deciding What Quilt to Make

5. Selecting Colors

6. Calculating Yarding

7. Buying Fabric, Batting and Supplies

8. Preparing and Cutting Fabric

MAKING YOUR FIRST QUILT

BEGINNER'S PRACTICE

If you're making your first quilt, please read this book from cover to cover. As a beginner, don't expect to understand all of it (or even much of it). Just become familiar with the contents.

Then do some practicing. You'll need to learn two techniques before you start cutting and piecing:

- How to maintain a scant ¼-inch seam.
- How to sew and press bias.

Being able to do both well is important for success in quilting and is essential when you're dealing with angles.

For your practice sessions, get some quality cotton fabric. Muslin and other fabrics on sale are acceptable, but avoid thin, sleazy fabric, which will fight you like a cranky child and make mastering any technique difficult.

These are the practice exercises I suggest following:

STEP 1. Cut. Practice cutting strips first. Then, cut simple shapes such as squares and rectangles. (See ROTARY-CUTTING, page 33.)

STEP 2. Stitch. Using the pieces you just cut, sew a scant ¼-inch seam (See THE ¼-INCH SEAM, page 49.)

STEP 3. Press. Carefully press, but don't iron, each seam. (See PRESSING SEAMS, page 51.) Good, your first seam is done.

Sue, cutting her quilt.

STEP 4. Construct. Now, try making a quilt block, such as Octagon Quilt Block 1, Going Up. (See STARTER SEAMS, page 51.) Now you're having fun!

STEP 5. Cut. Let's work with some triangles. Cut out a few pieces using Template 38. (See DONNA'S SPEEDY CUTTING SYSTEM, page 37.)

STEP 6. Stitch. To learn about handling bias, practice sewing together the triangles you just cut. (See HANDLING BIAS, page 48.)

STEP 7. Construct. Put together a quilt block, such as Hexagon Quilt Block 23, Pile of Points. (See ANGLES AND POINTS, page 53.) You're really cooking now! That was a level 2 hexagon quilt block!

STEP 8. Practice. Want to try some set-ins? Check out Octagon Quilt Block 16, Holding Hands. (See SET-INS, page 51.)

STEP 9. Practice some more. Ready to give stitching eight points a whirl? Go for Octagon Quilt Block 6, Big Wheel. (See ANGLES AND POINTS, page 53.)

Ideally, you should follow this agenda. I say ideally, because if you're anything like me, you'll want to get right to cutting and stitching a quilt. So you'll cut your fabric, sew it wrong, look at the mess you've made, and then grab the book to see what you did wrong. Well, what the heck—that method works, too, for a lot of us.

How perfect should your work be? As good as you can make it while still having fun. With each quilt you make, you'll find yourself improving. However, careful cutting and maintaining a scant $\frac{1}{4}$-inch seam allowance will make your piecing most successful and infinitely more pleasurable!

THE BASIC CONSTRUCTION PROCESS

Now that you've had some practice, let's go over the basic steps for planning and constructing a quilt. Steps 1 and 2 are covered in this part of the book; steps 3 and 4, in PART III: COMPLETING YOUR QUILT.

STEP 1. PREPARATION

Choose a design, a size and colors for your quilt.

Record all the design, size and color information on a Layout Page.

Purchase the fabric and the batting.

Gather all other quilting equipment and supplies needed.

STEP 2. CUTTING

Preshrink the fabric.

Make or tape all the cutting templates.

Cut all the pieces for the quilt top.

STEP 3. SEWING

Piece the quilt top.

Add the borders.

STEP 4. FINISHING

Mark the quilting lines.

Baste and quilt the layers together.

Finish the outside edges.

Let's plan a quilt!

CHAPTER 4

DECIDING WHAT QUILT TO MAKE

CONSIDERING TYPE, TIME AND SKILLS

As you think about the quilt you want to make, all sorts of questions come to mind: What type of quilt do I want to make? How much time can I spend on the quilt? What level of skill do I want to attempt? How big should my quilt be?

What blocks should I use? What set? Good grief.

Sometimes I believe that I could make a whole quilt in the time I spend fooling around with such questions. If you're stuck at this hurdle, too, here are some hints to help you over it:

• If you're new to using the rotary cutter, do the beginner's steps in CHAPTER 3 first, then make a small level 1 quilt.

Leslie, Elizabeth and Virginia lay out Leslie's quilt.

• To make a fast, easy quilt, select a design with one or two pattern pieces.

• If time is less of a concern, choose a project with special techniques, such as set-ins, joined points or appliqués. A complicated project will take a bit longer than straight-line piecing and joining, but if you're enjoying the project, time will pass quickly.

• If your ability to match points is not polished, consider using a busy print to help hide errors. Poorly matched points can also be disguised with added trim. Buttons and ribbons work great!

• If you love a particular quilt block but the piecing is so formidable that you know you'll never finish the quilt, use some unpieced quilt blocks in the quilt. Using solid blocks cuts the piecing time way down.

• When you need a large quilt but you're sure you'll be bored repeating the same quilt block, choose a quilt composed of three or four different quilt blocks, or create a sampler. Such quilts are slower to construct, but they're more fun.

• Even if you're a dedicated machine-piecer, consider occasionally doing some hand-stitching. I like to hand-stitch in these situations:

When I'm piecing small hexagon or octagon quilt pieces such as Hexagon Quilt Block 12, Poinsettia. I machine-piece everything up to piece A. If I were to machine-piece A, I'd have to execute six set-ins! I've tried it. The piecing takes forever. Hand-piecing or appliquéing actually requires less time.

When I'm working on a take-along project. I keep everything needed for a hand-pieced project in a small container: needles, thimble, thread, small scissors and a stack of cut pieces. I grab the container whenever I know I'll have waiting time. You'd be amazed at how much you can get done while waiting!

When I have an appliqué project under way. Appliquéing is picky work and usually too large to drag around. I do it while watching game shows and sitcoms.

• If you want to make a unique quilt that's fun to make and use, you might want to consider constructing a scrap quilt. It's easy to become hooked on scrap quilts (they're my favorites!). Once you're hooked, though, you'll find yourself buying piles of different fabric to add to your stash so that you can make great quilts from your growing pile of "scraps." Is there any drawback to making scrap quilts? Yes, they take a lot of time. You can spend hours just playing with the fabric, and the cutting, even with my speedy system, is slow. My solutions to this drawback?

Use quilt blocks with simple pieces and an uncomplicated design.

Set up an ongoing scrap quilt. I have a template taped for cutting Hexagon Quilt Block 12, Poinsettia. Every time I have scraps from something, I cut six of these pieces and add them to the box I've established for this project. When I'm ready to piece the top, the cutting will be done!

• If one quilt really jumps out and says, "Do me!"—do it! Go with your instincts. Remember, quilting is your hobby and if you make your quilts with love and happiness, others will feel it, too.

Once you've considered what type of quilt you'd like to make, how much time you want to spend quilting, and what your skill level is, you're ready to select a design.

CHOOSING A QUILT BLOCK AND SET DESIGN

I've organized this book so you can create as much or as little of your own quilt design as you wish. If you'd like to do your own designing, start by selecting a block in APPENDIX A: 144 HEXAGON QUILT BLOCKS or APPENDIX B: 144 OCTAGON QUILT BLOCKS; then proceed to the sets in APPENDIX C: QUILT SETS AND OTHER BASICS. (Or if you're one of those people who likes to start with the set first, go to

Donna's Hint

Remember to look ahead for easy ways of setting your quilts. For example, after I completed a quilt made with Octagon Quilt Block 28, Flippin' Stars (see color photograph section), I realized that if I had looked at the whole quilt instead of the octagon quilt blocks, I could have divided the project into easy-to-put-together square quilt blocks.

APPENDIX C and then to A.) Next, get out APPENDIX E: COPY, CUT AND PASTE FUN and play with the hexagon or octagon sets until you've put together just the right combo.

If one of the clever and beautiful quilts shown in the color section has your attention, then go right to the sample combinations in APPENDIX F. Follow the selected sample exactly, right down to the colors, or change it as you like.

As you review each hexagon and octagon set, please note the following about the ease and speed of construction:

> **Hexagon Quilt Set 2** is the quickest and easiest quilt set to stitch as it can be done with no set-in piecing. If this set catches your fancy, but you'd like more challenge, consider using one of the eight pieced lattice block designs that I've put in APPENDIX C.

> **Hexagon Quilt Set 1** is relatively fast.

Donna's Hint

While you're designing your quilt, think about how large you want to make it. Quilts are like wallpaper. The design on the small swatch of wallpaper will have an entirely different effect when it covers a whole room. Likewise, the same quilt design will be different on a smaller quilt than on a larger one.

The quilt blocks must be set together, but they are large and easy to stitch.

Octagon Quilt Sets 1 and 2 take a bit more time than Hexagon Quilt Sets 1 and 2 but are not difficult. Again, you might want to add pieced lattice blocks.

Octagon Quilt Set 3 looks intimidating at first, but it's not more difficult, only a bit more time-consuming than the first four quilt sets. Pieced lattice blocks look magnificent with this set, too.

Hexagon Quilt Set 3 is picky and time-consuming. Make it when you are not rushed or extremely busy. I find it is easier to appliqué the little triangles in the lattice.

DECIDING ON A QUILT SIZE

Is this your first quilting project? If it is, perhaps you want to start with a small wall hanging or an oblong. If you've already made several quilts, then you know how much fun quilting is and you're ready to stitch up a bed covering. Each quilt set shown in APPENDIX C: QUILT SETS AND OTHER BASICS can be made in eight sizes: wall hanging (W), oblong (OB), crib (CR), square (SQ), twin bed (T), double bed (D), queen-size bed (Q) and king-size bed (K). I suggest copying the page of the quilt set that you choose and cutting out the size you want to make. The cutout will show you exactly how many quilt blocks you will need.

SIZING UP BORDERS

Quilt borders are optional. You may decide that your project is simply gorgeous without one, or you may find that a border gives the quilt the perfect finishing touch. Border suggestions are included in APPENDIX D: BORDERS AND BACKING, but feel free to create your own border.

I design most of my borders after I've finished piecing the quilt. Then I can lay the quilt on the different types of fabric and see what arrangement will work best. Reminder: Buy extra fabric if you think you'll use it in a border.

Borders can be simple and still be fun! My favorite is a narrow framing strip for the first border. I use one of my darker fabrics and cut it 1½ inches wide (including a ¼-inch seam allowance) for small quilts and 2 inches wide for medium and large quilts. My last border is usually the widest, and I always use my favorite print from the quilt for it.

Other simple ideas for designing borders include the following:

• Insert quilt block pieces into the border (Fig. 4-1). Cut the border the same width as the piece used.

Fig. 4-1

• Overlap and appliqué a portion of a quilt block onto the border, using the background fabric for the first border (Fig. 4-2).

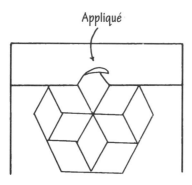

Fig. 4-2

• Float a simple stripe or set of stripes by using the background fabric for the first and third borders (Fig. 4-3).

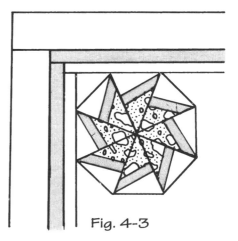

Fig. 4-3

Once you've designed your quilt and borders (if any), it's time to choose colors and fabric.

CHAPTER 5

SELECTING COLORS

Color selection is one of the most important parts of creating a beautiful quilt. It's also the scariest because the rules we've learned for clothing are not the same for quilts. Even the color experts don't agree on the rules, and to add to the confusion, some of the most beautiful quilts break *all* the rules!

So where do you start? Begin by looking at quilt magazines, books and calendars, and at nature, for color schemes that you like. Collect anything you can in which the color appeals to you: Pictures and ads from magazines. Photographs of quilts. Fabric swatches. Anything! Study these. Ask yourself *why* you like them.

Elizabeth, Sherry, Trina and Nina pinning Sherry's quilt.

What do all these have in common? You'll be surprised at what you'll discover.

If you're having trouble, ask for help from teachers, store owners and other quilters. In my classes, we have show-and-tell times to learn how colors and prints work in combinations. The following guidelines are ones that my students find most helpful.

CHOOSING A COLOR FAMILY

First, pick one or two main colors. Be flexible, though; you may change your mind when you see a fabric that you "have to have."

Start by picking a fabric with the look you want. Study it. Are the colors bright and clear? Or grayed earth tones? Whatever the colors, keep all other colors in that family. A bright sailor blue added to a pile of teal, salmon and taupe will be as obnoxious to the eye as the screech of fingernails dragged across a blackboard is to the ear. But the same blue with a bright red and sunshine yellow will look terrific.

Look at the proportions of the colors: Which stand out? Which are small highlights? Is the print so tiny that it's almost a solid? Is it a bold geometric? A frilly, fussy print? Use the answers to these questions as a starting point.

When you are putting fabrics together to create a lovely quilt, there are as many sets of rules as there are "experts." The soft, subtle quilt that warms Sue's heart is simply dull and bland to Becky. And the bold, vibrating colors that Becky enjoys are garish to Sue.

UNDERSTANDING COLOR VALUES

Value is the lightness or darkness of the fabric. The contrasts and shadings created by the values you choose will determine the character of your quilt.

Look through pictures of quilt designs and note the light, medium and dark values. Observe how these values affect the quilts. In general, high-contrast colors will produce a

strong, bold look. Use a very light value next to a very dark one and your quilt will take on the color of the darker fabric.

For a subdued, quiet look, use low-contrast colors. To create a dark but quiet quilt, use darks and mediums, but no lights. For a light but quiet look, use light and medium values but no dark values.

In a way, no medium values exist. If you put a medium fabric next to a light one, you will see a contrast. The same is true if you put a medium fabric next to a dark fabric. If you want to soften a contrast, insert fabrics that shade the two together to create the illusion of a medium value.

If you like the look of a quilt block, follow the values shown to achieve similar results. Do feel free to change them, though. Experimenting is fun.

COMBINING PRINTS, STRIPES AND SOLIDS

For an interesting quilt, use a variety of print sizes and styles, including an occasional solid color. Cut up large prints at random for an exciting sense of movement. The pieces will not be exactly alike, but the overall effect will be one of unity.

Don't worry about tiny bits of odd color in a fabric. If you're making a maroon and blue quilt and that perfect navy print has tiny rust-colored bits in it, use it. When the quilt is done, your eye will perceive the rust color as maroon.

When working with stripes, carefully plan the cutting of even the smallest pieces. They should end up in the finished quilt in an orderly fashion not a hodge-podge. Stripes are also very effective in borders. For conventional borders, cut one stripe or set of stripes to go around the quilt. For a fun kind of border, cut the outer border across the stripes so they appear to "run off" the edge of the quilt. Sew mitered corners on both types of borders.

Some prints create illusions of stripes when viewed from a distance. These usually require no special cutting for small pieces. But for borders and lattice strips, the stripe effect should line up with the long edge. To achieve this, cut the long edges parallel to the selvage and the design will fall into line.

You may find a design with areas or motifs that you would like to highlight. Cut these individually. (Be sure to buy extra fabric to account for waste.) Be aware of the top and bottom of this motif in relation to your finished quilt. (Transparent templates are perfect for centering these special prints.)

Generally, these guidelines hold true:

• Medium-to-small prints will give your quilt an old-fashioned, "quilty" look.

• Large prints are fun to use but tend to stand out in the quilt block. You'll want to plan your color scheme around such a print.

• Solids used with prints will add a nice bit of flash to your quilt. The solids will catch your eye, so you may want to use them as highlights.

• Quilts created with just solids have a clear, clean-cut look. By using dark and bright colors, you can create a boldly modern, flashy quilt. Or with pastels, you can achieve something soft-looking for a baby quilt.

Select prints because they look good together. The overall design of a fabric that is ugly on the bolt may be just the thing you need to make your quilt gorgeous.

DEVELOPING COLOR SCHEMES

Black can add excitement to a quilt. Use it to set off brilliant splashes of color to make them positively vibrate. (My biggest problem in picking the colors for my own quilts is that, no matter what scheme I start with, I always seem to end up with some black in it!)

Be a little daring. Try an accent of an odd color for a really striking look. Tuck a bit of lavender into a blue quilt. Or a bit of teal into a beige project.

Don't try to overcoordinate everything. Study nature and you'll see all sorts of colors together. Part of the beauty of a forest is the many shades of green, mixed with the highlights of sun and shadows. A beautiful sunset will include yellow, magenta, brilliant blues, purple and white! Wouldn't those colors look magnificent in a quilt?

After selecting several fabrics, place them on a counter, walk away, turn and take a fast look. Did any color stand out? If so, use this as either your main color or in small amounts as a highlight. Did any colors blend together? They'll perform as one color and you'll lose the effectiveness of both. Did your fabric choices please you? Then, buy them!

Don't forget your backing fabric. A really smashing print will make your quilt interesting and reversible. If you choose a large print, buy an extra repeat per seam so you can match design elements. (See APPENDIX D: BORDERS AND BACKING to determine the number of seams your backing will have.)

Rely on your intuition. It's fun to play with fabric colors with someone, but for a final choice, you are the one who knows best what you like.

Try not to form a set picture of your finished quilt. Visualizing it will be virtually impossible. Pick fabrics that work well together, then enjoy watching your quilt grow.

Schemes for Scrap Quilts

Developing a color scheme for a scrap quilt can be somewhat intimidating. Through the years, I've developed several guidelines for my own use. Eventually, you'll want to make your own list, but here are my ideas to get you started:

• Include lots of contrast. My light colors are so light that even my mediums look dark.

• Keep color family unity. I rarely mix clear, bright colors with gray-tone, earthy ones. A bright color would be too loud in a gray-tone quilt and a gray tone would look dirty in a bright quilt.

• Again, don't overcoordinate. This is probably the hardest thing to keep from doing in a scrap quilt—and it really separates the right-brain people from the left-brain ones.

STAYING FLEXIBLE

When you're making a quilt, unexpected events happen along the way: You need more of a certain fabric and it's no longer available; your cousin had a baby boy not a girl; Aunt

Ruth wants a purple quilt and you hate purple. The list of reasons for change is endless.

Relax. Let's consider some alternatives. That fabric you need: Could you substitute something similar? Use a coordinating fabric rather than a matching fabric in the border? Make a lap throw, pillow or tote bag of this piece and start over on another quilt?

Parents might use a blue quilt for a baby girl, but they rarely want pink for a boy. Put the pink quilt away for the next baby girl, find the quickest quilt in the book and whip up a new (blue) one.

You can't imagine sewing a whole purple quilt? Try to convince Aunt Ruth that a tiny accent of purple would be much more dramatic than a whole quilt of purple. If she insists on lots of purple, plan a fast-to-make quilt. After all, the project should be enjoyable to you, too.

If everything in the project has gone wrong and you simply hate it, fold it up neatly, put it in a box and hide it on the top shelf of a storage closet. Then forget about it and start something else. A small project that's a guaranteed success will have you quilting again. Someday you'll want to give that boxed project another try. If it still isn't workable, give it away.

CALCULATING YARDAGES

Before you purchase any fabrics, you obviously need to know how much to buy. Higher mathematics wasn't one of your best subjects in school, you say? Don't worry. I've developed an easy-to-use Layout Page so you can do your figuring in small manageable steps.

Exactly what is a Layout Page? Put plainly and simply, it's a master plan for your quilt. On it you'll record everything from fabric colors and template numbers to border widths and batting selection. You can then use that information for calculating fabric amounts.

Joni, Leslie, Nina and Susan designing with PLAY PAGE.

Before you start your layout page, ask yourself these basic questions:

• How many pieces do I need to cut with each template?
• Which fabric should I cut them from?
• How wide do I cut my borders?

Let's look at the decisions you must make to answer those questions:

• What quilt block design or designs will I use?
• How large will my quilt be?
• How will I set the quilt blocks to make the quilt?

Guess what? If you've been following this book from the beginning, you've already made those decisions.

Now, turn to APPENDIX C: QUILT SETS AND OTHER BASICS. There, you'll find the number of quilt blocks that you'll need for popular quilt sizes. You'll also find the template numbers and cutting information for edge pieces, corner pieces and lattice blocks, along with cut widths for borders and backing yardages.

Let's write down this information in a way that makes sense.

First, remove the following pages from your notebook (or turn to them as you need them).

• The pages for the hexagon or octagon quilt block design or designs that you want to make. (See APPENDIX A: 144 HEXAGON QUILT BLOCKS, or APPENDIX B: 144 OCTAGON QUILT BLOCKS.)
• The pages for the quilt set you'll be making. (See APPENDIX C: QUILT SETS AND OTHER BASICS.) You'll need to copy, or trace, the diagram of your quilt set and cut it to the correct size, if you haven't done so already.
• The pages for the pieced lattice blocks you'll be using (if any). (See APPENDIX C: QUILT SETS AND OTHER BASICS.)
• The SAMPLE LAYOUT PAGE on page 26.

RECORDING THE BASICS

Now you're ready to prepare a Layout Page. Referring to my SAMPLE LAYOUT PAGE (page 26), do the following:

STEP 1. Get one sheet of unruled 8½ x 11-inch paper for each quilt block design. For each, at the top of the sheet, record the following information from the appropriate page in APPENDIX A or B (Fig. 6-1):

Number of the quilt block
Name of the quilt block
Shape of the quilt block (hexagon or octagon)

Draw a line under this information.

#16. HOLDING HANDS - OCTAGON
Fig. 6-1

STEP 2. Paste the following diagrams (from the appropriate page in Appendix A or B) on your Layout Page (Fig. 6-2):

Lettered graphic
Variation and key
Template numbers
Building the Block

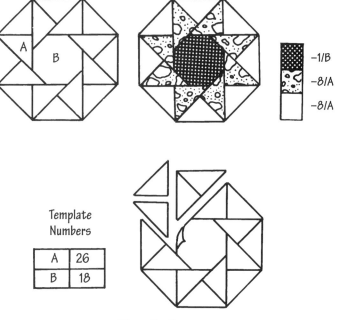

Template Numbers

| A | 26 |
| B | 18 |

Fig. 6-2

CRIB—49"X63"
18 Quilt Blocks
3 across
4 down

Octagon
Quilt
Set #2
Pieced Lattice
Block #3

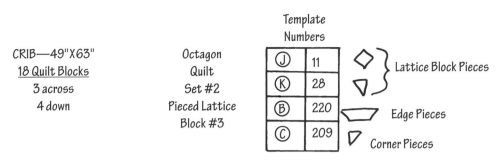

Fig. 6-3

Under these diagrams, draw a line across the page.

STEP 3. Record the following information from the appropriate page in APPENDIX C (Fig. 6-3):

Quilt size
Number of quilt blocks across
Number of quilt blocks down
Total number of quilt blocks needed
Quilt set number
Pieced lattice block number (if applicable)

Template information for lattice block pieces, edge pieces and corner pieces

Under this information, draw a line across the page.

STEP 4. Down the left side of the paper, but indented a bit, draw one rectangle for each fabric and number the rectangles. (Later, you'll paste small swatches of fabric into these rectangles.) Write the template letter for each piece of the quilt block next to the appropriate

rectangle. Leave space so that you can add more letters. Do the same for the lattice block pieces, the edge pieces and the corner pieces, but circle each of these template letters to indicate that they are not pieces of the main quilt block (Fig. 6-4).

STEP 5. For each fabric rectangle, record the number of template pieces needed. To do so for the quilt block pieces, look at the key next to the quilt block variation (e.g., 1/B, 8/A, 8/A). *Multiply the number of template pieces needed by the total number of quilt blocks composing the quilt.* For example, if you need 8 pieces of piece A for each quilt block and the whole quilt is composed of 18 quilt blocks, you need 144 pieces of A (8 x 18 = 144) (Fig. 6-5).

To determine the number of edge and corner pieces, see the appropriate table in

Fig. 6-5

APPENDIX C (in my example, you need 4 corner pieces and 10 edge pieces total). DO NOT multiply these numbers by the number of quilt blocks. If you're using unpieced lattice blocks, see the appropriate table in APPENDIX C. For example, for Octagon Quilt Set 2, the total number of lattice blocks needed for a crib-size quilt is 17. If you're using pieced lattice blocks, for each piece, multiply the number of pieces used in one lattice block by the

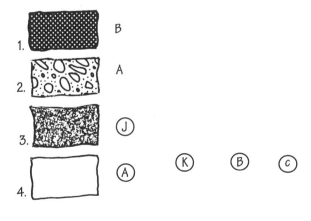

Fig. 6-4

total number of lattice blocks needed. In my example, referring to APPENDIX C, I see that Pieced Lattice Block 3 requires 4 of piece K, so I need 68 pieces of K (4 x 17 = 68) (Fig. 6-6).

Draw a line under all this information.

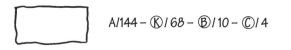

A/144 – Ⓚ/68 – Ⓑ/10 – Ⓒ/4

Fig. 6-6

STEP 6. Record the information for the borders from the appropriate table in APPENDIX C. Write "Borders—Cut Width" and below the word *Borders*, draw rectangles for your fabric swatches. Number them "1st, 2nd, 3rd" as appropriate. Below the words *Cut Width*, write the cut width of each (Fig. 6-7).

Draw a line underneath this information.

BORDERS – CUT WIDTH

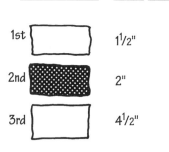

1st   1¹/₂"

2nd   2"

3rd   4¹/₂"

Fig. 6-7

That's all there is to it! Honest! Now, let's go have a cup of coffee, then we'll do the yardages.

FIGURING THE AMOUNTS

Determining the number of yards of fabric you need is now very simple. All you must do is look up the numbers. I like to work on a piece of scratch paper, then mark the totals next to the rectangles on my Layout Page.

STEP 1. On your scratch paper, write "Fabric" as a heading. Underneath, list the numbers that you assigned the fabric swatch rectangles on your Layout Page (e.g., 1., 2., 3., 4.). Turn to APPENDIX G: YARDAGE TABLE FOR TEMPLATES to determine the number of pieces that can be cut from a yard. For each template letter on the Layout Page, jot down the yardage. For example, if you needed 144 pieces of Template 26 (piece A), you'd need 1 yard because that amount would give you 156 pieces. You'd write "1" beside Fabric 2 and beside Fabric 4.

STEP 2. List the border yardages beside the appropriate rectangle numbers. You'll find these yardages in the appropriate table in APPENDIX C (Fig. 6-8).

FABRIC

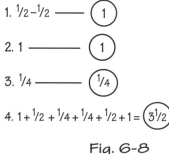

1. ¹/₂–¹/₂ ——— ①

2. 1 ——— ①

3. ¹/₄ ——— ⟨¹/₄⟩

4. 1 + ¹/₂ + ¹/₄ + ¹/₄ + ¹/₂ + 1 = ⟨3¹/₂⟩

Fig. 6-8

STEP 3. Add the amounts for each fabric and write the total to the left of the appropriate rectangle on your Layout Page. Circle the number. Add the heading "Yards" above the circled numbers (Fig. 6-9).

YARDS

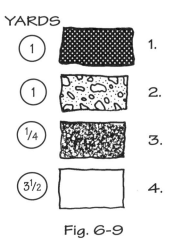

①   1.

①   2.

⟨¹/₄⟩   3.

⟨3¹/₂⟩   4.

Fig. 6-9

STEP 4. Determine the yardage for the

backing. First, from the appropriate table in APPENDIX C, locate the number of yards required for backing your quilt (make sure that you look under the correct size). Next, under the "Borders" section on your Layout Page, indent a bit and write "Backing." Under this heading, draw a rectangle for the fabric swatch. Finally, write the yardage to the left of the rectangle, circle the number and write "Yards" above it.

You're done calculating yardages!

To complete your records, attach a photograph of the finished quilt to the Layout Page. And on the back or in any leftover space, record the date the quilt was finished, who received it and a few other interesting things about your family or about current events that occurred while you were making the quilt.

To review my SAMPLE LAYOUT PAGE, turn to the next page.

Donna's Hint

When calculating the yardages, don't be afraid to juggle a bit if you need a small amount of fabric. Suppose that you need just 2 pieces, say small triangles. On checking the yardages, you see that you can get 26 of those pieces from $1/4$ yard of fabric. You can probably skip recording the $1/4$ yard and assume that you can cut the 2 pieces from the yardage needed for other pieces of the same fabric. For example, on my SAMPLE LAYOUT PAGE, you could probably eliminate $1/4$ yard of Fabric 4: One yard for piece A will give you 156 pieces (you need only 144). Instead of using $1/2$ yard for piece K, you could use $1/4$ yard, which would give you 57 of the 68 needed pieces, and cut the remaining 11 pieces from the fabric leftover for piece A.

SAMPLE LAYOUT PAGE

#16 — HOLDING HANDS — OCTAGON

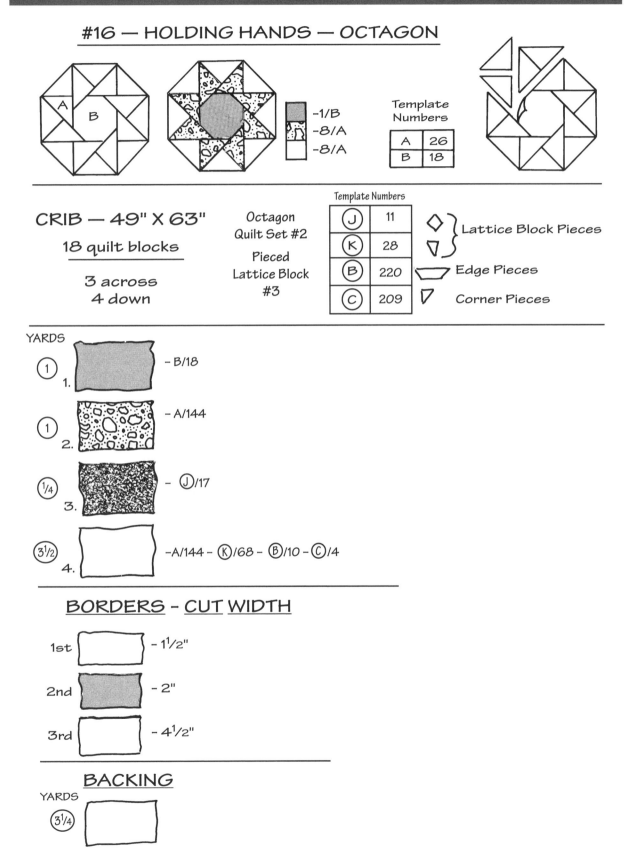

CRIB — 49" X 63"

18 quilt blocks

3 across
4 down

Octagon
Quilt Set #2

Pieced
Lattice Block
#3

Template Numbers	
A	26
B	18

–1/B
–8/A
–8/A

Template Numbers

Template Numbers	
J	11
K	28
B	220
C	209

◇ ▽ } Lattice Block Pieces

⬠ Edge Pieces

▽ Corner Pieces

YARDS

1. (1) – B/18

2. (1) – A/144

3. (1/4) – (J)/17

4. (3 1/2) –A/144 – (K)/68 – (B)/10 – (C)/4

BORDERS – CUT WIDTH

1st – 1 1/2"

2nd – 2"

3rd – 4 1/2"

BACKING

YARDS

(3 1/4)

CHAPTER
7

BUYING FABRIC, BATTING AND SUPPLIES

Are you ready to go shopping? Let's buy the fabric, the batting and other supplies.

FABRIC

Take your Layout Page to the fabric store with you, and remember these tips when selecting and buying cloth:

• One hundred percent cotton is the sturdiest, most durable fabric for quilts. It also has a slight nap, which helps keep the pieces together while you stitch.

• Fabrics can shrink. The yardages in this book are based on 42-inch-wide fabric and allow extra for shrinkage and waste.

• Stripes and directional prints require extra fabric. Be sure to buy enough.

Once home, store your fabrics neatly according to color. Put them in boxes or open crates, where they can breathe, and avoid air-

Sandy helping Sherry, Joni and Luana choose fabrics.

Stores can be "sold out" of a particular fabric overnight, and because manufacturers often produce only one run of a special color or print, the fabric may never become available again. Your best bet is to buy extra and use any leftovers for a scrap quilt. So if you see a fabric you really like, buy it. How much to buy? My rules of thumb are:

• If I'm ecstatic about a fabric, I'll buy at least 2½ yards—enough for an unpieced border.

• If the fabric will make a really super background, I'll buy 5 or 6 yards.

• If the fabric will make a nice accent piece, but a little goes a long way, I'll get 1 or 2 yards.

• If the fabric is striped, I buy an extra ¼ yard or so, depending on the width of the stripe.

tight plastic bags, which will eventually cause your fabric to deteriorate.

BATTING

What kind of batting should you buy? Each person has a preference. For hand-quilting, I like cotton blends (80 percent cotton), wool or flannel. Of these, flannel is the thinnest and nicest for clothing and table coverings; fleece also works well for such projects. Wool is the warmest but is a bit more expensive. My favorites are cotton blends and wool because they both give your quilt the cozy, "huggy" feel of old-fashioned quilts. Some very nice cotton blend battings are available. Be sure to check the label to see how close together you must place the quilting lines so the batting doesn't move and bunch up in the finished project.

For inexpensive durability, the bonded polyesters are marvelous and require the least amount of quilting. They're wonderful for children's quilts, baby blankets and lap throws, which require frequent machine washing and drying.

If you can, experiment with small pieces of batting to find your favorite. Get leftover swatches from your friends who quilt (remember to label the swatches), or buy crib-size battings to try them.

All the types of batting mentioned are good for machine-quilting; just be sure to get a "bonded" one. It'll hold up well in the washing machine and will require the least amount of quilting. Flannel is a good bet, too, if you plan to tie your quilt.

Always purchase a batting piece that's at least 2 inches larger, on all sides, than the quilt top. This extra size makes layering much easier.

When buying batting, look at the actual measurements. For example, you'll probably find that a batting labeled "Queen" is too small for your queen-size quilt. Buy, instead, the batt labeled "King."

SUPPLIES

The quilting supplies listed here are readily available in most local sewing or quilting stores. If you don't live near a store, or you prefer ordering through the mail, see SOURCES for a list of mail-order sources.

Rotary-Cutting

For rotary cutting, you'll need these items:

Cutters and Mat

• Large rotary cutter for cutting straight lines.

• Small rotary cutter for cutting curves and circles.

• "Self-healing" mat (9 x 23 inches or larger) for use with the rotary cutter.

• Spare blades for the rotary cutters.

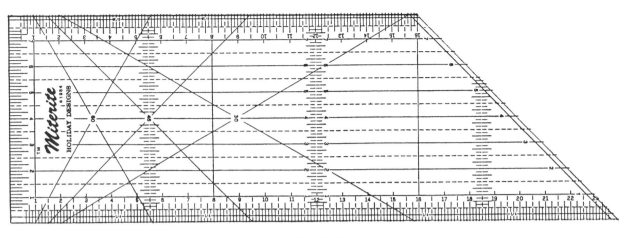

Fig. 7-1

Rulers and Templates

• Ruler for squaring corners and for cutting straight strips; bias strips; 45-, 90- and 135-degree triangles and angles; and mitered borders. I like to use my husband's Miterite (see SOURCES). A Miterite is an 8 x 24-inch clear plastic ruler with one end cut at a 45-degree angle (Fig. 7-1.)

• 12½-inch plastic square for squaring corners and quilt blocks and for cutting ½- to 12½-inch squares and rectangles.

• Speedy cutting templates for rotary-cutting. These clear, hard plastic templates, are available in a variety of sizes and shapes.

• 60-degree plastic diamond template for cutting 30-, 60- and 120-degree triangles and angles.

• Plastic hexagon template for cutting hexagons (you can also use the 60-degree diamond template).

Donna's Hint

Be sure the rulers and templates that you use with the rotary cutter are made of sturdy, clear acrylic and be a bit more than ¹/₁₆-inch thick. The edges should be straight, not rounded, so the blade will roll smoothly against them. The rulers should be at least 6 inches wide; narrow rulers are difficult to hold in place. Use the same ruler throughout a project because not all rulers are exactly alike.

General Supplies

You'll also want to have these items handy:

Needles

• Hand-sewing needles for appliquéing and hand-sewing. Buy #12 sharps or betweens.

• Embroidery needles for embroidering only.

• Large darning needle or curved upholstery needle for tying a quilt.

• Quilting needles for hand-quilting only. Get short needles called betweens, which come in sizes 8 to 10.

Pins

• Long quilting pins with large heads for pinning through thick layers. They're great—you won't know how you stitched without them.

• Safety pins for basting. Get nickel-plated, 1-inch-long pins. You'll need about 350 pins to baste a quilt for a double bed.

• Sequin pins for appliquéing. Many of my students prefer these very short pins for holding appliqués in place.

• Silk pins for pinning just two layers together. These long, extra-fine, dressmaker pins glide easily through fabric. Use them, too, when you must stitch over a pin.

Quilting Frames

• Lap frame, used for hand-quilting small areas at a time.

• Hoop or floor frame, used for hand-quilting whole quilts.

Sewing Machine Attachments

• Darning foot for free-form machine-quilting only.
• Walking, or even-feed, foot for machine-quilting. It'll feed the three quilt thicknesses (top, batting and backing) evenly.

Threads

• Fine sewing thread for hand-appliquéing. Get silk-finish or machine-embroidery thread; it should match or blend with the fabric.
• #3 Pearl cotton for tying a quilt. Pearl cotton has a sheen, is washable and is easy to handle. Use several strands at once.
•Invisible thread, used for machine-quilting.
• Quilting thread, used for hand-quilting.
• Sewing thread for piecing. My favorite is a large cone of natural-colored thread. I wind a dozen bobbins with it and I'm set to stitch for hours. You'll also need thread to match the backing fabric (for machine-quilting) and to match the outer border.

Donna's Hint

When machine-piecing, use threads that match light-colored fabrics. On the finished quilt, dark threads will be visible beneath very light-colored fabric.

Other Items

• Bicycle clips for keeping a quilt tightly rolled when machine-quilting.
• Iron for pressing seams. I prefer a steam iron; use it to press gently.
• Other sewing tools for general tasks. Be sure you have sharp scissors, a seam ripper and a tape measure.

Donna's Hint

When you're buying and using quilting needles, keep this in mind: The higher the number, the smaller the needle; the smaller the needle, the shorter the stitch.

• Permanent marking pen with a fine point for marking template plastic. My favorite is the Pigma pen, which can be used to write on muslin labels, too.
• Pliers or a piece of rubber for pulling the needle through the three layers of the quilt if you tie it.
• ¼-inch quilter's tape for hand-quilting and taping templates.
• Quilt labels for signing your quilts. You'll want several so you can sign all your quilts. Tell the world you're proud of your accomplishments!
• Quilting stencils for drawing quilting lines on your quilt. You can purchase some or create your own from lightweight plastic sheets.
* Spray starch or fabric sizing for restoring body to fabrics after prewashing. Either is helpful when you're working with a lot of bias seams.
• Template plastic or oaktag (strong cardboard) for making templates for traditional cutting and appliquéing. (Don't use with the rotary cutter; the blade cuts such material too easily.)
• Thimble for hand-stitching and quilting. Try on different ones until you find one you like. Getting a thimble that's comfortable is worth the effort.
• Water-soluble marking pen or chalk pencil for marking quilting lines. If the lines follow seam lines, a marking pen isn't needed.

Once your shopping trip is over, be sure to complete your Layout Page by pasting a small swatch of the appropriate fabric into each rectangle on the page. After that, you'll be ready to cut the pieces of your quilt! Let's get started.

CHAPTER 8

PREPARING AND CUTTING FABRIC

PREWASHING FABRIC

Before cutting your fabric, wash it to preshrink it and to remove excess sizing and dye. Another reason for prewashing: The grain will be reliable if the fabric is dried in a dryer. Here are my recommendations for prewashing:

Snip a ¼-inch triangle off each corner of the fabric. Cutting off the corners will reduce the amount of raveling and tangling.

Wash light and dark colors separately.

Avoid overdrying fabrics in the dryer.

Lightly spray each piece of fabric with spray starch or fabric sizing as you iron. Either product makes ironing out wrinkles easier, and it adds a bit of body so you can handle small pieces with less hassle. If you're working with a lot of bias cuts, a little starch or sizing is a necessity.

Trim off all selvages *after* laundering and before cutting.

Donna's Hint

Occasionally, a fabric simply will not stop bleeding dye. I washed one fabric 17 times! If this happens, discard the fabric and use something else. When I suspect that a fabric might not be colorfast, I do this: I wet a small piece or corner, then let it dry on a white paper towel. If the paper towel is still white when the fabric is dry, I use the fabric.

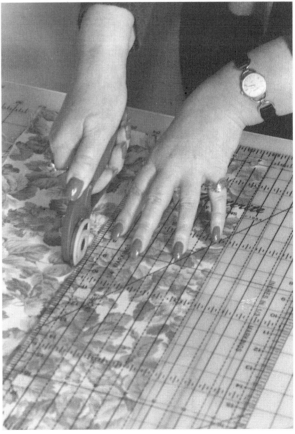

Using the rotary cutter.

CUTTING FABRIC

You can cut fabric using either of two methods: traditional cutting or rotary-cutting. Whichever you choose, keep these guidelines in mind:

General Guidelines

On the diagrams in this book, I've marked the grain lines for rotary-cutting and sewing ease. These lines indicate the direction—either lengthwise or crosswise grain—in which I would cut the strip. You may change the direction.

You'll discover that most pattern pieces can be cut without regard to layering. However, you'll need to recognize the following two exceptions:

Like pieces. These are pattern shapes that repeat in a "like" fashion (Fig. 8-1). Stack the fabric with *right* sides up.

Fig. 8-1

Mirror pieces. These are pattern shapes that repeat in a "mirror," or opposite, fashion (Fig. 8-2). Stack the fabric with like sides together, as you would if cutting out a garment.

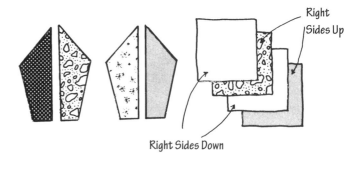

Fig. 8-2

Traditional Method

For speed and ease, especially on large projects, I strongly recommend cutting fabric by the rotary-cutting method. However, if you don't have rotary-cutting tools, you'll need to cut the traditional way—with scissors. Even if you use rotary-cutting as your primary method, there are times when traditional cutting is preferable. For example, unpieced hexagon and octagon quilt blocks are most accurately cut with scissors. Here are the basic steps in traditional cutting:

STEP 1. Trace the appropriate pattern pieces (from APPENDIX H: FULL-SIZE TEMPLATES) onto a sheet of sturdy template plastic or oaktag. Use a ruler: Accuracy is important.

STEP 2. Cut out the template pieces.

STEP 3. On the wrong side of the fabric, with the wrong side of the template up, trace around the template. Use a sharply pointed #2 lead pencil, or for dark fabrics, use a white or silver pencil. Slant the pencil point into the template to get the line as close to the edge as possible. Repeat the process until you've traced the number of pieces needed.

STEP 4. Using scissors, cut out each piece. If you have good, sharp scissors, you should be able to cut neatly through several layers.

Rotary-Cutting

The rotary cutter is to the quilter what the computer is to the writer: A tool for quicker, easier manipulation of material. No longer do we have to spend days cutting each separate piece for a quilt. And the accuracy in cutting is nothing short of a stitcher's dream. Could you hand-cut twelve layers of fabric—even with the best pair of scissors money can buy? Cutting the top and bottom layers identically would be impossible! But with the rotary cutter, they are identical. Cut edges are straight, even and precise. So how does rotary-cutting work?

Using the edge of a ruler (Miterite) or a hard plastic template (Speedy) as a guide, just roll the cutter blade through the layers of fabric to cut it.

Yes, it really is as simple as that! And there are ways to make cutting even easier. Here are a few guidelines.

Handling the Fabric

With the selvages even, fold the fabric as it was folded on the bolt. If the layers don't lie smooth, don't force them. Just lift the top layer and move it gently to one side until it automatically lies flat. Position the fabric on your cutting mat (Fig. 8-6).

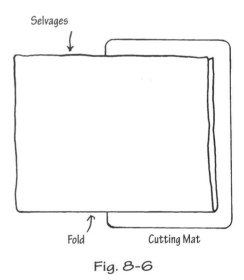

Fig. 8-6

To cut multiple layers, stack the fabric with the folds even and the selvages parallel. I can cut as many as 12 layers this way. Practice first!

Handling the Ruler

Holding your left hand like a tent, place your thumb and forefinger ½ to 1 inch in from

---

Donna's Hint

All full-size templates in this book are to be used with the *right* side of the fabric up. You must know when to position the fabric this way and when you may deviate from this rule. These examples should help explain the differences:

Example 1. All A pieces face the same direction. They must be cut right side up (Fig. 8-3).

Fig. 8-3

Example 2. A and B pieces are mirror images. Instead of using the two templates called for, you could use either of the templates and simply fold the fabric with the wrong sides together. Doing so will give you the mirror images necessary (Fig. 8-4).

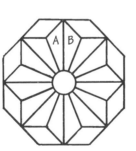

Fig. 8-4

Example 3. Some pieces can be done either way: fabric right side up or folded. This is the case only if you still get the same piece when the pattern is reversed (see piece A in Fig. 8-5).

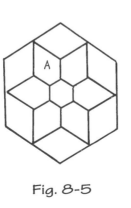

Fig. 8-5

the cutting edge. Place your remaining fingers in a comfortable position (Fig. 8-7).

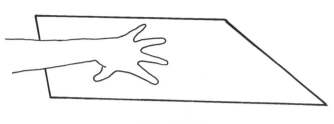

Fig. 8-7

Press down firmly to prevent the ruler from moving and to keep the layers of fabric together. When cutting across a 22-inch span, press on one end of the ruler while cutting, then carefully walk your hand to the other end and finish cutting.

Handling the Cutter

Pull the guard back to expose the blade. Hold the cutter at a comfortable angle, with the blade side next to the ruler edge (Fig. 8-8).

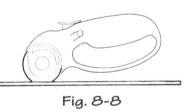

Fig. 8-8

Be sure that the blade is perpendicular to the ruler. Holding it at an angle away from the ruler will damage both the ruler and the blade (Fig. 8-9).

As you cut, press the cutter down firmly and slightly against the ruler. Always cut away from yourself so that you have the most control. Be sure to flick the guard on at the end of every cut. Rotary cutters are extremely sharp; handle yours with the same caution that you use with kitchen knives and sewing shears.

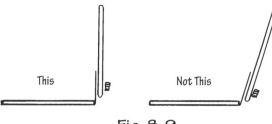

This   Not This

Fig. 8-9

Basic Strips

After reviewing the basic cutting techniques, it's time to try a few practice strips. If you don't have any scraps of good-quality cotton fabric (poor-quality fabric will be difficult to handle and will dull your rotary-cutter blade), invest in a yard or two of quality muslin. Let's get started!

Donna's Hint

Two DON'Ts when you use the rotary cutter:

• DON'T use templates made of template plastic or cardboard with the rotary cutter. The rotary cutter cuts through these materials too easily.

• DON'T cut batting with the rotary cutter. The batting fibers will embed in the cutting mat.

STEP 1. Trim the fabric (see Fig. 8-13 on facing page).

STEP 2. Place the 3-inch ruler marking on the trimmed edge (Fig. 8-10).

STEP 3. Cut! You've done it! That's all there is to cutting basic strips.

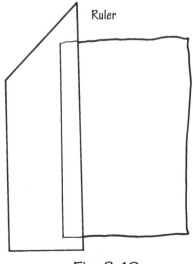

Ruler

Fig. 8-10

Donna's Hint

Here are two rotary-cutting rules of thumb (they form the basis of my *speedy cutting system* for cutting shapes, described later in this chapter):

• The portion of the ruler on the fabric will determine the size of the piece that you'll cut. For example, if you're cutting a 2-inch strip, place 2 inches of the ruler on the fabric and let the rest of the ruler hang off (Fig. 8-11).

To make the first cut, place the 1-inch cross mark of the ruler on the fold. The cutting edge is then at a 90-degree angle (Fig. 8-13).

Note: My personal preference is not to use the lines on my cutting mat, but if you use my method, you'll need to cut from both sides of the mat to make this cut (never try to cut under your arm!). I simply cut at the end of a table so that I can easily step to either side. Figure 8-13 illustrates my method. Instead, you may prefer to use the lines on your cutting mat, in which case the ruler would be positioned as in Figure 8-11. If you're left-handed, cut from the other side of the table.

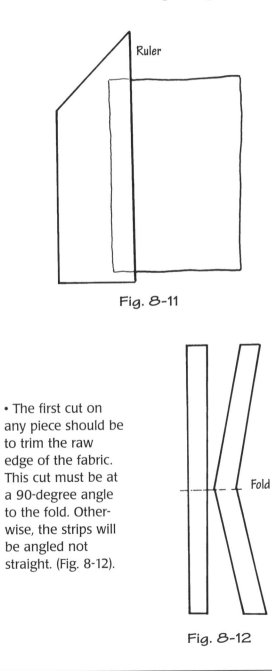

Fig. 8-11

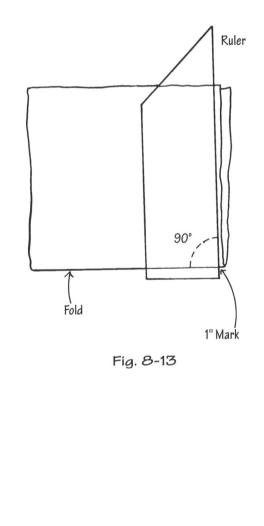

Fig. 8-13

• The first cut on any piece should be to trim the raw edge of the fabric. This cut must be at a 90-degree angle to the fold. Otherwise, the strips will be angled not straight. (Fig. 8-12).

Fig. 8-12

Multiple Strips

Here are three hints for accurately and quickly cutting lots of strips at once:

• Put a piece of ¼-inch quilter's tape on the ruler line that you're using. It's too easy to zip along, be distracted and plunk your ruler on the wrong line. The tape will catch your attention.

• Always put the tape outside the cutting line. The tape should never be on the piece to be cut (Fig. 8-14). Tape on the unprinted side whenever possible so that you don't damage the printing on your ruler.

• Every third or fourth strip, check the 90-degree angle. If it's off a bit, retrim the edge.

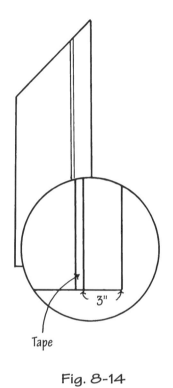

Fig. 8-14

Borders

Here's where I really love using my rotary cutter. It makes cutting borders quick and painless. A few hints I'd like to share:

• To make an unpieced border, cut strips along the length of the fabric. The length of the fabric must be at least as long as the border that is being cut.

• To end up with the least number of seams, first cut the borders, then cut the quilt pieces from the remaining fabric.

• Cut borders along the longest fabric measurement. For example:

Cut *crosswise* if you have ¾ yard (27 inches) of 45-inch-wide fabric, but cut *lengthwise* if you have 2 yards (72 inches) of 45-inch-wide fabric. Exception: If your fabric has a directional print or stripe, you may have to cut lengthwise, even if that is the shorher fabric measurement.

Bias Strips

Cutting bias strips with a rotary cutter is faster than cutting a "continuous bias tube" with scissors. And the strip method has half as many seams. Here's how to do it:

STEP 1. Trim the end of your fabric so that it forms an exact 90-degree angle (see Fig. 8-12 on previous page).

STEP 2. Open the fabric to a single thickness. Fold the cut edge of the fabric to meet the selvage (Fig. 8-15).

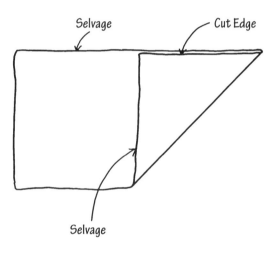

Fig. 8-15

STEP 3. If the length of the diagonal fold is longer than your ruler, fold the upper point down to the lower point (Fig. 8-16).

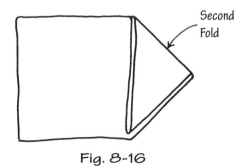

Fig. 8-16

STEP 4. Trim ⅛ inch from the diagonal (folded) edge (Fig. 8-17).

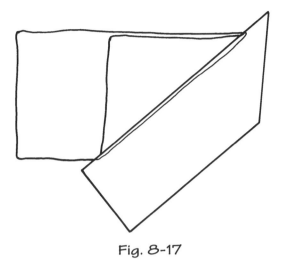

Fig. 8-17

STEP 5. Cut bias strips of desired widths (Fig. 8-18).

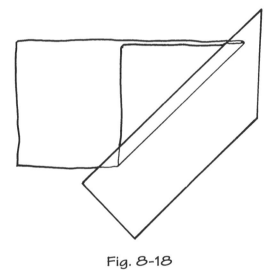

Fig. 8-18

STEP 6. With the right sides of the fabric together, sew the bias strips end to end, using a ¼-inch seam (Fig. 8-19). Press the seams open.

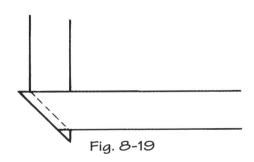

Fig. 8-19

Donna's Speedy Cutting System

Let's move on to rotary-cutting shaped pieces. In my easy-to-use speedy system, you'll tape a hard plastic template (Speedy) instead of cutting shapes from conventional template plastic and then cutting the fabric with scissors. After you've taped the Speedy, you'll simply cut a stack of strips, then chop the stacks into shaped pieces.

Here are the three basic steps in the speedy system:

STEP 1. Create two parallel lines by simply placing your ruler on one edge of the appropriate pattern piece (from APPENDIX H: FULL-SIZE TEMPLATES) and taping the parallel edge. Cut strips to this width (Fig. 8-20).

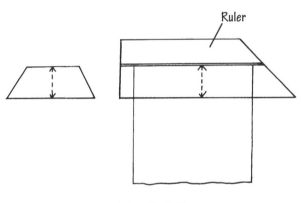

Fig. 8-20

STEP 2. Choose a Speedy or a Miterite to fit the shape of the design to be cut. (The pattern *must* include seam allowances.) Place the Speedy on the pattern piece, lining up the two outer edges of the tool with the pattern. Tape all other pattern sides on the tool (Fig. 8-21).

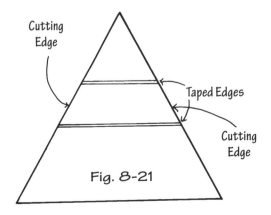

Fig. 8-21

Donna's Hint

Here are my solutions for smoothing four troublesome cutting spots:

• Rotate or flip over templates as needed. When you first do so, turning may seem awkward, but with practice, it will feel natural.

• Triangles can be cut with the straight of the grain on the short edge (Fig. 8-23).

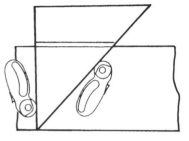

Fig. 8-23

• Or cut triangles with the straight of the grain on the long edge (Fig. 8-24).

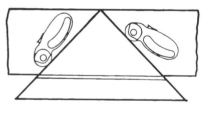

Fig. 8-24

• Use a small rotary cutter and short, choppy strokes when cutting circular edges. The chopping motion allows the layers to ease back into place.

• Use template plastic and scissors (see TRADITIONAL CUTTING METHOD, earlier in this chapter) to cut unpieced hexagon and octagon quilt blocks.

Place the tape *around* the pattern, *not inside* it. When you're taping, lean over the table so you're looking straight down on the pattern.

You now have two cutting edges and two taped edges. Use the taped edges to match previously cut edges. Make all cuts on the cutting edges.

STEP 3. Use the taped Speedy or Miterite to cut many pieces from the stacked strips (Fig. 8-22).

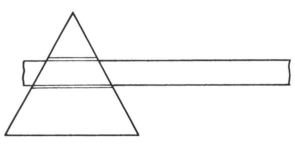

Fig. 8-22

Taping and Cutting

Next, I'll show you how to cut the shapes in APPENDIX H: FULL-SIZE TEMPLATES by using my speedy system. For each shape, there are two figures. The first shows you how to tape a Speedy or Miterites, the second, how to cut the shape from a fabric strip using your taped ruler. Here are the 16 template shapes.

SQUARE OR RECTANGLE: This shape is cut with a square cutting template.

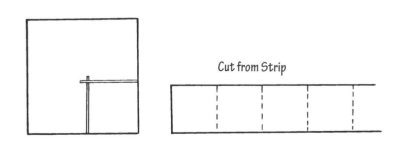

Cut from Strip

Fig. 8-23

45- OR 90-DEGREE TRIANGLE: This shape is cut with a 45-degree triangle cutting template.

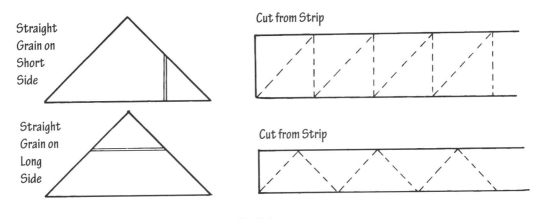

Fig. 8-24

60-DEGREE, EQUILATERAL TRIANGLE: This shape is cut with a 60-degree triangle or a 60-degree diamond cutting template.

Fig. 8-25

45- OR 60-DEGREE ANVIL: This shape is cut with a 90- or 60-degree triangle cutting template.

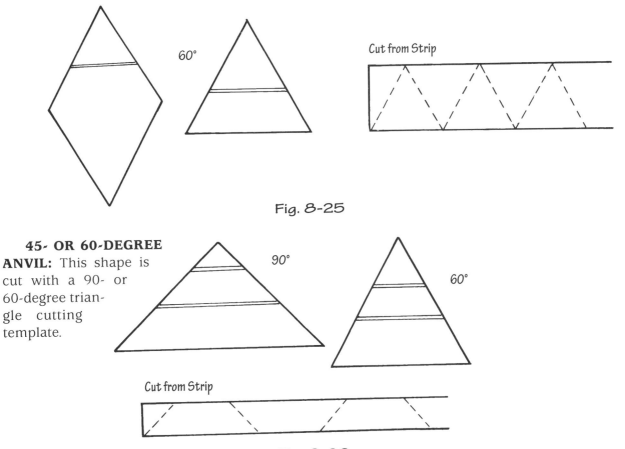

Fig. 8-26

LOP-EARED SQUARE: This shape is cut with a Miterite.

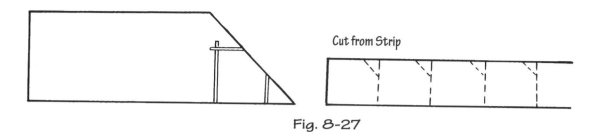

Cut from Strip

Fig. 8-27

HEXAGON: This shape is cut with a hexagon cutting template.

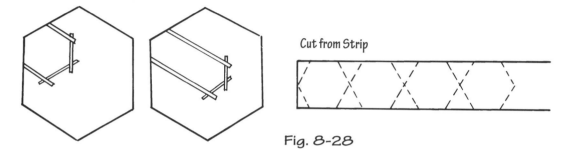

Cut from Strip

Fig. 8-28

OCTAGON: This shape is cut with a square cutting template.

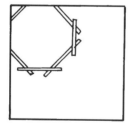

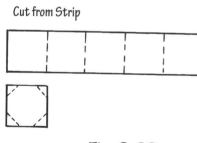

Cut from Strip   Cut from Strip

Fig. 8-29

45- OR 60-DEGREE DIAMOND: This shape is cut with a 45- or 60-degree diamond cutting template.

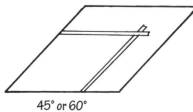

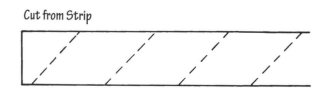

Cut from Strip

45° or 60° Template

Fig. 8-30

TWO-ENDED CANDLE WITH 90-DEGREE ENDS: This shape is cut with a 45-degree triangle cutting template.

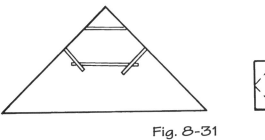

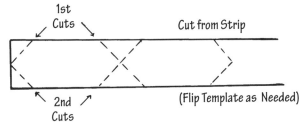

Fig. 8-31

45- OR 60-DEGREE SHOE: This shape is cut with a 45- or 60-degree triangle cutting template.

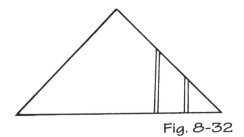

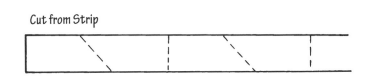

Fig. 8-32

GEMSTONE: This shape is cut with a 60-degree diamond cutting template.

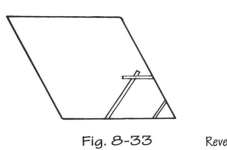

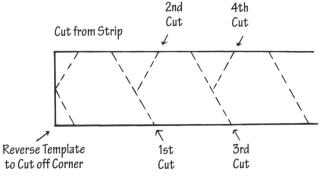

Fig. 8-33

POINTED CONE: This shape is cut with a square cutting template.

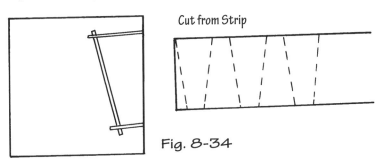

Fig. 8-34

CIRCLE: This shape is cut with a circle cutting template (no taping is necessary).

Cut from Strip

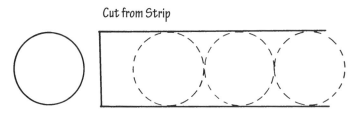

Fig. 8-35

ODD-SHAPED TRIANGLE WITH A 90-DEGREE ANGLE: This shape is cut with a Miterite.

Option 1: Straight grain on long edge of shape

Cut from Strip

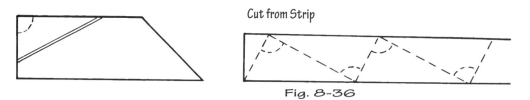

Fig. 8-36

Option 2: Straight grain on two shorter edges of shape

Cut from Strip

Fig. 8-37

ODD-SHAPED TRIANGLE WITH A 45-DEGREE ANGLE: This shape is cut with a Miterite.

Cut from Strip

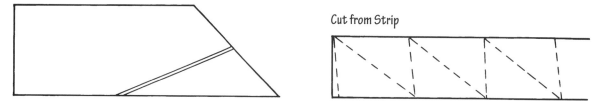

Fig. 8-38

UNUSUAL SHAPES: If no angle can be found, any piece with straight edges can be speed-cut, one side at a time. Just follow this procedure:

   STEP 1. Make one cut by cutting a strip (this will be the straight grain of the piece).

Fig. 8-39

   STEP 2. Place the template over the pattern piece and tape the template along as many straight edges as needed to cut the other sides of the shape.

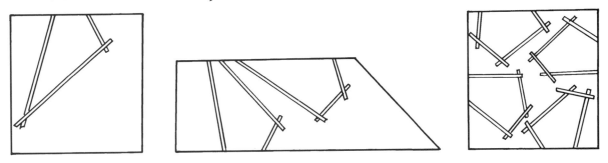

Fig. 8-40

   STEP 3. Cut the shape from the strips.

COMPLETING YOUR QUILT

9. Piecing

10. Appliquéing and Embroidering

11. Adding Borders

12. Quilting and Binding

13. Caring for Your Quilt

PIECING

All the pieces of your quilt are cut and waiting to be stitched into a gorgeous quilt. What do you piece first? How do you get everything to fit together? Following is an overview of your next steps:

STEP 1. Piece all the quilt blocks together. Then piece all the lattice blocks. For a fast and efficient piecing order, refer to BUILDING THE BLOCK in APPENDIX A: 144 HEXAGON QUILT BLOCKS or APPENDIX B: 144 OCTAGON QUILT BLOCKS. For diagrams on piecing the lattice blocks, check APPENDIX C: QUILT SETS AND OTHER BASICS.

STEP 2. Stitch the quilt blocks, lattice blocks, edge pieces and corner pieces together. For guidance, see PIECING THE QUILT in APPENDIX C.

You can piece by machine or by hand. This chapter outlines both techniques.

PIECING FUN

When my beginning students get to this stage, ready to make the quilt top, they always ask, "How do I know when to rip out a seam and redo it?" I tell them the following:

Be as accurate as you can while still having fun. Remember, this is your hobby, not your job, and your first quilts will not be hung in the Smithsonian Institute, so don't spend time ripping out every seam that's not a perfect match.

If you enjoy your first quilt, you'll make more, and as you do, you'll increase your skills.

I've examined many old quilt tops and found that "grandma" wasn't nearly as picky about her piecing as we think she was. Yet her quilts are beautiful.

Don't be afraid to do some easing. I've

Susan, piecing her quilt

found that many errors are hidden in the puffi-ness of the quilt after it's quilted!

I use three levels of neatness when I stitch. I'll be very casual about a just-for-fun quilt. It will be just as warm regardless of whether the points match. If the quilt will be part of the decor and will be displayed or spread out, I'll be a bit pickier. But I will positively suffer over any quilt I intend to hang for the world to see and judge.

Know what is important and pay attention to that. For example, learn to maintain a scant ¼-inch seam allowance. Also, careful cutting is important. Learn to adjust your sewing machine to maintain good tension. Use a small-size (70/10) sewing machine needle for piecing, and change it every time you start a new quilt. Use good-quality fabrics and thread.

Pay attention to all these factors and you'll be amazed at how easily everything fits together!

MACHINE-PIECING

In most instances, machine-piecing is faster than hand-piecing. To get accurate, dis-tortion-free results, you'll need to adjust your sewing machine, handle bias with respect, ease some pieces together and press carefully.

Readying Your Sewing Machine

Before you begin machine-piecing, check the tension balance. Your stitching should not draw up the fabric (if it does, the tension is too tight or your stitches are too long). And you shouldn't see the bobbin thread from the top side.

For piecing, use a fine- to medium-size machine needle (size 70/10 to 80/12) and a small stitch (12 to 15 stitches to the inch). Because no backstitching is necessary at the ends of most of the seams, these small stitch-es won't pull out.

For best control of your fabric while stitch-ing, replace the wide-hole (zigzag) needle plate on your machine with a single-hole plate (Fig. 9-1). And, of course, don't set your machine on zigzag!

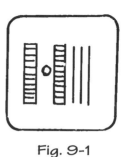

Fig. 9-1

If you don't have a single-hole needle plate, decenter the needle to the left or right, but remember that doing so changes the width of your seam allowance. Or create your own single-hole plate. Tape an index card over the needle plate and cut holes for the feed dogs. Lower an unthreaded needle into the card. Then enlarge the hole slightly.

Handling Bias

Handling bias correctly is critical to easy piec-ing. Learn to recognize bias and be aware of it: Bias is any direction other than the straight grain, which consists of the lengthwise and crosswise threads used to weave the fabric. True bias is a 45-degree angle to the straight grain (Fig. 9-2).

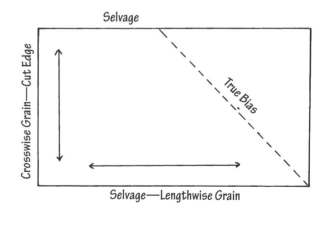

Fig. 9-2

To recognize the difference between straight and bias edges, closely examine a piece of fabric. Notice the tiny lines running in two directions? You're seeing the threads used to weave the fabric. These threads indicate the straight grain of the fabric (Fig. 9-3).

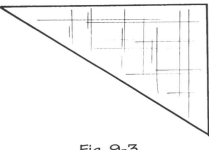

Fig. 9-3

Here are a few hints and tips for working with bias:

• When sewing a bias edge to a straight edge, try to sew with the bias piece on the bottom. If it's on top, your machine foot will stretch it by pushing the fabric ahead. If it's on the bottom, the feed dogs will help to take up any fullness. (When hand-piecing, keep the bias toward you so your thumb can work the fullness in place.)

• Always sew away from the bias, not into it. That is, sew from the wide end of a piece to the narrow end.

• When pressing a piece with a bias edge, either set the iron down and pick it up without moving it, or gently move the iron with the grain of the bias piece (Fig. 9-4).

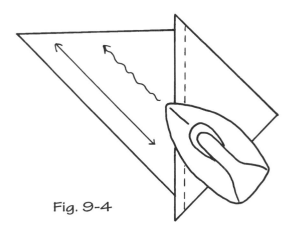

Fig. 9-4

• As your project grows in size and weight, handle it flat or folded; don't pick it up by a raw edge. Otherwise, the weight of the quilt will stretch any unstitched bias edges.

Pinning

Some people refuse to sew if they must pin. Others create metal sculptures of their seams. Most of us use pins only at key places. In general, a few well-placed pins help on any bias seam, set-in blocks, eight-point stars, long seams and matched seams.

Pin across seams, but always remove a pin before the machine needle reaches it (Fig. 9-5). Sewing across pins puts stress on the needle, weakens the seam and shifts the fabric at that point.

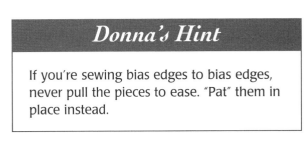

Fig. 9-5

Easing

Occasionally, you'll need to ease two pieces together to match the seams. To do so, pin or hold the two ends in place and gently pull the fabric as you sew. If possible, place the larger piece against the feed dogs. If the two pieces simply don't fit, make sure that you've cut them from the correct template patterns.

Donna's Hint

If you're sewing bias edges to bias edges, never pull the pieces to ease. "Pat" them in place instead.

The ¼-Inch Seam

Maintaining a perfect ¼-inch seam will make piecing time enjoyable. Pieces will fit together and the need to rip will become almost nonexistent. How to maintain such a picky seam allowance? Start by marking a reference point on your machine. Here's an easy way to mark it.

On a piece of paper, draw a line ¼ inch from the edge. Insert the machine needle into that line. Drop the presser foot. Then find an easy-to-use sighting, such as the side of the foot or the presser-foot opening, that lines up with the edge of the paper. If nothing lines up perfectly, place a piece of masking tape on the throat plate along the paper's edge. You can also use a seam guide.

On some machines, you can decenter the needle so that it falls ¼ inch away from the sighting that you choose. If you have a computerized machine, be sure to return to this setting every time you turn on the machine. Learn to guide the cut edge of your fabric along this sighting.

Reminder: Make your ¼-inch seams a scant ¼ inch (Fig. 9-6). There's a bit of loft in the fabric at any seam; this loft creates a shortage in the size of that piece. It may seem insignificant, but a block with eight pieced seams can end up much shorter than a block with only two seams. Using scant ¼-inch seams allows for this loft (Fig. 9-7).

A good way to test your stitching accuracy is to sew three 2-inch-wide strips together. Press the seams all to one side. If the block measures exactly 5 inches wide, your seams are perfect! If not, try again until they are. This practice is very worthwhile!

Long Strips

To sew strips evenly without pinning, match one end of the strips, sew two stitches and stop with the needle in the fabric. Without stretching the fabric, match the edges of the next 12 to 20 inches. Hold the fabric tightly at this point and, pulling slightly, stitch. Stop and repeat as necessary until you reach the end of the seam. If you simply allow the two pieces to feed through without stopping and pulling slightly, the two strips will be uneven, and the block will curve (Fig. 9-8).

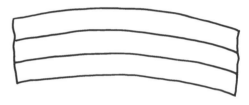

Fig. 9-8

The "Factory" Method

When sewing several identical sets of pieces, feed them through the machine without separating them (Fig. 9-9). This "factory," or chain, method of stitching is quick, and it allows you to keep your pieces in order. Later snip the pieces apart.

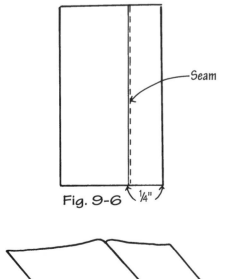

Fig. 9-6

Seam

¼"

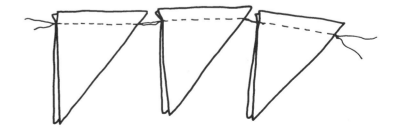

Fig. 9-9

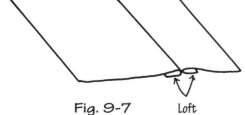

Fig. 9-7   Loft

Pressing Seams

When pressing seams, press them to one side, not open, and toward the darker fabric. The exceptions to this rule? There are two: When one seam will be matched to another, press them in opposite directions. When using the fast and easy method of stitching set-ins, press the seam open.

You can press with or without steam; however, steam can change the shape and size of a piece, so use it with caution. Press the seam gently from the underside, and use an up-and-down lifting motion. Remember that you're not ironing a pair of blue jeans!

To finish pressing, turn the fabric to the right side and press, moving the iron in the same direction in which you pressed the seam.

Matching Seams

To perfectly match seams, always press the seams to be matched in opposite directions (Fig. 9-10), and pin the seams together at the seam line. Stitch up to the pin before removing it.

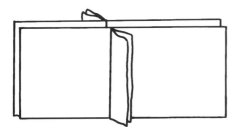

Fig. 9-10

With practice, you'll be able to match most seams quite nicely without pinning by butting them together with your fingers and holding them as close as possible while stitching.

Starter Seams

In APPENDIX A: 144 HEXAGON QUILT BLOCKS and APPENDIX B: 144 OCTAGON QUILT BLOCKS, under BUILDING THE BLOCK, you'll occasionally see something that looks like a piece with a turned-down corner (Fig. 9-11).

I call this a starter seam, and it comes in handy when you want to avoid setting in a corner.

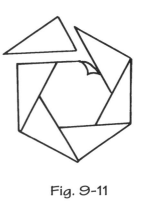

Fig. 9-11

To use a starter seam, partially sew the first in the series of seams. Partial stitching allows you to cross that seam with the next piece. When you've stitched all the other seams and return to the starter seam, finish it.

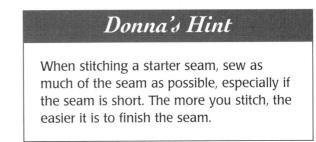

Donna's Hint

When stitching a starter seam, sew as much of the seam as possible, especially if the seam is short. The more you stitch, the easier it is to finish the seam.

Set-Ins

You can set in pieces using either the basic method or the fast-and-easy method. Directions for both follow.

Basic Method

When setting in pieces, most sewers stitch each side of the set-in piece as two separate seams. Using this method, you sew each seam *away* from the inside corner.

STEP 1. Sew the first seam with the set-in piece on the bottom (Fig. 9-12 on page 52). The first stitch should meet the end stitch of the adjoining seam. At each end of the seam, backstitch two or three stitches.

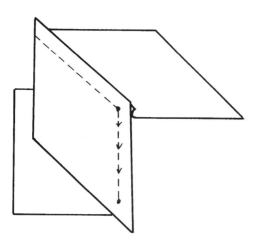

Fig. 9-12

STEP 2. Sew the second seam with the set-in piece on top (Fig. 9-13). The first stitch should meet the first stitch of the first seam. At each end of the seam, backstitch two or three stitches.

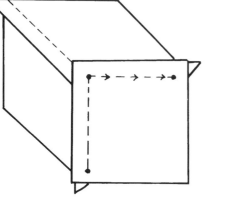

Fig. 9-13

Fast and Easy Method

While examining the backs of many old quilt tops, I found that set-in pieces were often done as one continuous seam. This method looked easier than the one I'd always used, so I decided to figure out how to do set-ins grandma's way.

Use this technique when only three pieces need to be joined. If you need to join more than three pieces, use the BASIC METHOD described above. Here's what I do:

STEP 1. Sew the seam. Start at the point, then stitch to the inner corner. Do not backstitch, but stop about ⅛ to ¼ inch before you reach the end of the seam. Leave a tail of thread at least an inch long to prevent the seam from coming apart in the next step (Fig. 9-14).

STEP 2. Press the seam open. This is pickier than pressing seams to one side (Fig. 9-15).

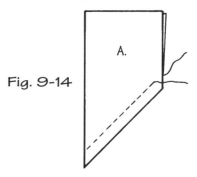

Fig. 9-14

STEP 3. Pin the inset piece to the stitched piece, matching the seams at the corner point. Fold the B piece out of the way (Fig. 9-16).

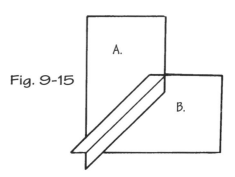

Fig. 9-15

STEP 4. With the seamed piece up, stitch from the top of the A piece to the corner point (Fig. 9-17). With the needle down and in the

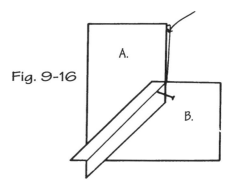

Fig. 9-16

seam (try to position the needle between the A and B pieces), lift the presser bar. Slide A to the left and up far enough for B to fall into place (Fig. 9-18).

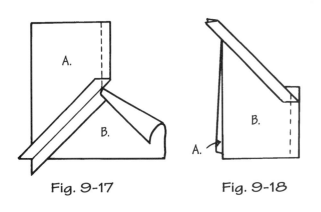

Fig. 9-17   Fig. 9-18

STEP 5. Match the end of B to the inset piece. With a pointed tool, snug seam B in place against the needle before stitching, then stitch the B seam.

Angles and Points

After a while, you'll become quite good at judging ¼-inch areas. Until then, you may want to mark a few difficult-to-judge corners with scant ¼-inch seams. I suggest marking when you'll be doing the following:

• Sewing two different angles together (Fig. 9-19).

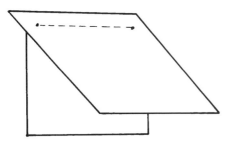

Fig. 9-19

• Sewing any seam that must end 1/4 inch from the edge, as with set-ins (Fig. 9-20).

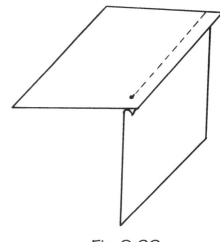

Fig. 9-20

• Matching two angled seams (Fig. 9-21).

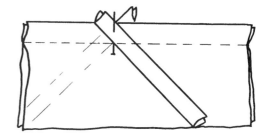

Fig. 9-21

Donna's Hint

To determine the points for matching, draw intersecting scant ¼-inch lines on the cutting template (Fig. 9-22). Don't draw these lines directly on the fabric because the bias edges will stretch.

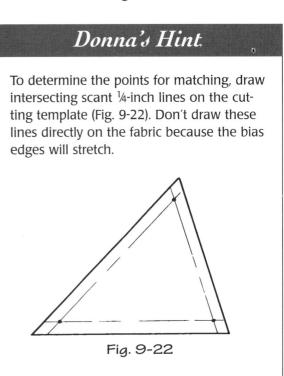

Fig. 9-22

Donna's Hint

Important: When you're sewing points together, be certain the sewn point is at least ¼ inch from the seam that it is pointing to. If the point is less than ¼ inch away, the crossing seam will lop off the tip of the point (Fig. 9-23).

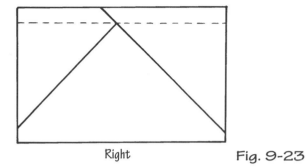

Right

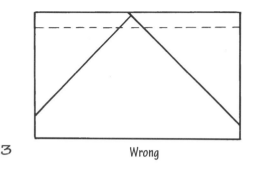

Wrong

Fig. 9-23

When you can, leave some leeway in your design. If the points are at the outer edge of a quilt block, whether they meet probably won't be important. For example, look at the color photograph of the quilt made with Octagon Quilt Block 28, Flippin' Stars. These stars are separate blocks and are independent of one another. I was casual about making these points meet. If, however, the points are an important part of the design, they need your best effort; if they don't meet, they will stand out. Look at the color photograph of the quilt made with Octagon Quilt Block 31, Fairy Blossoms. The center points matter; the outer ones don't.

Pieced hexagons and octagons are loaded with point combinations, and no single rule will cover the gamut. So here's how I suggest you approach them. For just the first few,

mark the points at the stitching line and pin the pieces together. Then take a good look at how they line up with each other, and line up the rest the same way. A second approach is to snip off the hang-off piece (Fig. 9-24) and use it to snip the same amount off the remaining similar pieces. Now you can line up the cut edges.

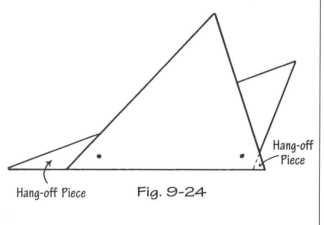

Hang-off Piece

Hang-off Piece   Fig. 9-24

Octagon Quilt Block 2, TEN O'CLOCK; Quilt Set 1; Pieced Lattice Block 5; 86 x 67
Quilt by Joni Milstead

Octagon Quilt Block 18, GOOD LUCK;
Quilt Set 1; 96 x 65
Quilt by Trina Rehkemper

Octagon Quilt Block 21,
EIGHT-POINT STAR; Quilt Set 1; 76 x 59
Quilt by Elizabeth Z. Lewis

Octagon Quilt Block 18, GOOD LUCK; Quilt Set 1; 109 x 76
Quilt by Trina Rehkemper

Hexagon Quilt Block 3,
CAMPING OUT; Quilt Set 2; 102 x 84
Quilt by Virginia Bobbitt

Hexagon Quilt Block 3, CAMPING OUT; Hexagon Quilt Block 4,
SPECIAL OCCASION; unpieced; Quilt Set 2; 64 x 51
Quilt by Iris Waal

Octagon Quilt Block 7, BOX O' FUN; Quilt Set 2; 69 x 55
Quilt by Iris Waal

Octagon Quilt Block 6, BIG WHEEL;
Quilt Set 1; 60 x 60
Quilt by Sherry Reid Carroll

Hexagon Quilt Block 2, SUNSHINE; Hexagon Quilt Block 32,
NORTHERN STAR; Quilt Set 1; 71 x 60
Portions of design overlapping first border
Quilt by Susan Saiter

Hexagon Quilt Block 1, WHIRLYBIRD; Quilt Set 1; 96 x 64
Quilt by Sherry Reid Carroll

Hexagon Quilt Block 33, DOILY;
Quilt Set 2; 108 x 98
Quilt by Nina Johnston

Hexagon Quilt Block 36, JUMPIN'
JEHOSHAPHAT!; Hexagon Quilt Block 4,
SPECIAL OCCASION; unpieced;
Quilt Set 1; 98 x 94
Quilt by Joni Milstead

Eight Points

Joining eight points is fairly easy if you take these six steps:

STEP 1. Sew four sets of two pieces each (Fig. 9-25).

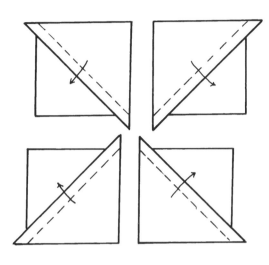

Fig. 9-25

STEP 2. Join and press these sets. If you're sewing bias pieces, be very careful not to stretch the seams or edges. Trim the extending corners at the joining points (Fig. 9-26).

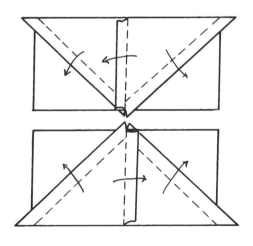

Fig. 9-26

STEP 3. Insert a pin straight through both pieces at the point where all the seams meet (Fig. 9-27). Keeping this pin straight, insert a pin on either side of the center point, ⅛ inch from the center point (Fig. 9-28). Remove the center pin.

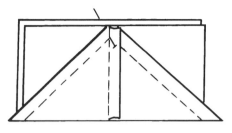

Fig. 9-27

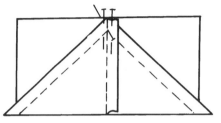

Fig. 9-28

STEP 4. Stitch the seam, being careful not to stretch the fabric. Sew over the pins slowly, gently pushing heavy thicknesses under the machine foot (Fig. 9-29). (I know, I said not to sew over pins, but this is an exception.)

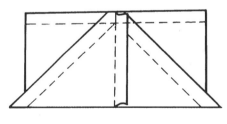

Fig. 9-29

STEP 5. Press the seam to one side.

Twelve Points

To join twelve points, use the same construction method described in JOINING EIGHT POINTS. Just start with either two blocks of three pieces or three blocks of two pieces. The important idea is this: Whichever way you join and press one half of the twelve-point block must be the same way you join and press all the halves. The seam allowances will then be evenly spread at the central point of the block.

HAND-PIECING

Hand-piecing has become popular again, not only because it makes quilting a portable hobby, but also because it's soothing. But drawing seam lines on the pieces is time-consuming and it stretches and distorts bias edges. Besides, my grandmother did wonderful hand-piecing and never had a seam line to follow. So I devised a method of training myself to hand-piece perfect $^1/_4$-inch seams by sight.

Mark the first few seams, then start making those marks lighter and lighter until you only think you can see them. Now try it with no marks. You'll discover that you've trained your eye to see the $^1/_4$-inch mark. Give it a try: It really works!

Using a size 12 sharp needle (or your favorite size) and good quality sewing thread, sew a tiny running stitch $^1/_4$ inch from the edges. Try for 16 to 18 stitches to an inch. Evenness matters.

Sew only to the seam ends, leaving all seam allowances free. Backstitch at the beginning and end of each seam (Fig. 9-30). When moving to an adjacent seam, take the needle through the seam allowances at the exact point where the seams meet. Continue stitching.

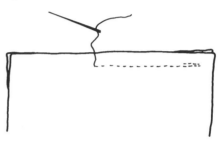

Fig. 9-30

When hand-piecing points, press the seams in a swirl fashion (Fig. 9-31).

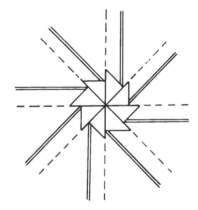

Fig. 9-31

Chapter 10

APPLIQUÉING AND EMBROIDERING

APPLIQUÉING

There are many techniques for hand- and machine-appliquéing. You may want to explore several of them and choose the one you prefer.

Hand-Appliquéing

Here's an easy-to-learn and -do hand-appliquéing technique referred to as needle turn:

STEP 1. Trace the pattern piece to be appliquéd on template plastic or lightweight cardboard. (Note: Cardboard will reduce in size if used a lot.) This piece is the actual shape; it does not include seam allowances. Cut out this piece.

STEP 2. Trace the piece on the right side of your fabric, using a pencil of any color that will show on the fabric. Do not use a pen of any kind.

STEP 3. Leaving a ⅛-inch seam allowance, cut the piece from the fabric (Fig. 10-1).

STEP 4. Pin or baste the appliqué in place. Use small pins (sequin

Fig. 10-1

pins work well), and pin from the back of your project so the pins are out of the way.

STEP 5. Select your needles and thread. For fine stitches, use a size 10 or 12 sharp or a quilting needle and good quality sewing thread (silk-finish or machine-embroidery thread

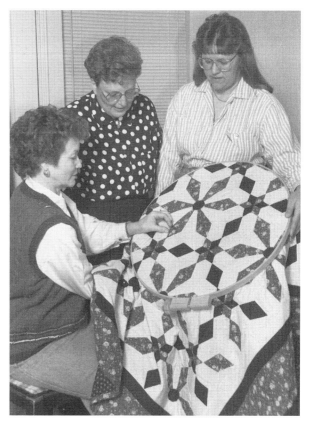

Susan shows her hand-quilting to Iris and Trina.

works well). To prevent the thread from twisting while you're sewing, use the thread in the direction that it comes off the spool (Fig. 10-2). And to prevent the thread from tangling, hold the ends of the thread and give it a sharp snap.

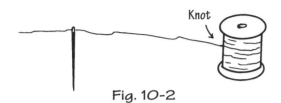

Fig. 10-2

STEP 6. Knot the thread. From the underside of the appliqué, bring the needle up on the stitching line.

STEP 7. Working from right to left (if you're right-handed) and using the needle as a tool, turn under the seam allowance. To do this, start about 1 inch to the left of the knot, and hold the seam allowance under with your thumb (Fig. 10-3).

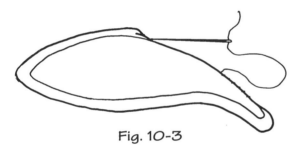

Fig. 10-3

STEP 8. For almost invisible stitches, take a small stitch in the background fabric (only two or three threads of the fabric). As you come up, catch just two or three threads of the fold on the appliqué piece (Fig. 10-4). Start the next stitch in the background as close as possible to the stitch taken in the fold.

Fig. 10-4

STEP 9. To create sharp points, stitch to the point. Take an extra anchoring stitch. With a large quilting pin, first turn under the point, then the seam allowance (Fig. 10-5). Trim the seam allowance at the point, if necessary. Continue stitching.

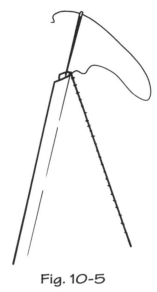

Fig. 10-5

STEP 10. Clip inside curves and points as needed (Fig. 10-6). At sharp inside cuts, take more and slightly deeper stitches.

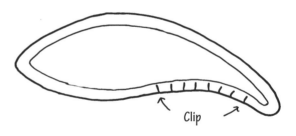

Fig. 10-6

Machine "Hand-Appliquéing"

A fast and sew-smart method for achieving the look of hand-appliqué is to zigzag the edges of the appliqué with invisible thread (Fig. 10-7). This is what to do:

STEP 1. Set your sewing machine to a narrow zigzag or blind

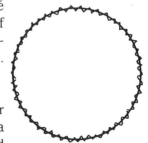

Fig. 10-7

hem stitch, matching the length and width shown in Figure 10-8.

Fig. 10-8

STEP 2. Lower the upper tension slightly so that the bobbin thread does not show on top.

STEP 3. Start and stop with ¹/₂ inch of very tight stitches (Fig. 10-9). Stitch in a continuous, unbroken line as much as possible.

1/2"   1/2"

Fig. 10-9

Donna's Hint

When machine "hand-appliquéing," cut the seam allowances ¹/₈ to ³/₁₆ inch. Turn under the edges and pin them or baste them in place.

EMBROIDERING

Depending on your project, some well-placed embroidery stitches may be the perfect finishing touch for a well-designed quilt block or appliqué. So here are a few embroidery hints, tips and instructions:

The Outline Stitch

A fast, simple stitch for the stems on the Primrose appliqué for Octagon Quilt Block 9, Primrose, is the outline, or stem, stitch. These tips should help you achieve good-looking results:

• Use 4-ply of embroidery floss. The stitches will lay more smoothly if you separate each piece of floss first, then recombine them.

• Take 12 to 14 stitches to an inch, spacing your stitches evenly.

• Work from left to right. The "back" of a new stitch should enter the same hole as the "front" of the previous stitch (Fig. 10-10).

Fig. 10-10

French Knots

To create three little dots in the center of a flower in the Primrose appliqué, use tiny beads or make French knots. There are four easy steps to making the knots:

STEP 1. Using 6-ply of embroidery floss (separate each strand first, then recombine), bring the thread up to where you want the knot.

STEP 2. Holding the thread slightly to the left of the knot site, wrap the needle around the thread twice (Fig. 10-11).

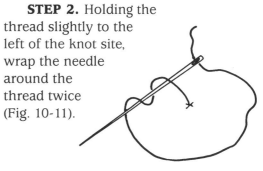

Fig. 10-11

STEP 3. Insert the needle back into the fabric, close to where the thread was brought up. (Don't use the same hole or the knot will pull through.) Holding the needle up-right, ease the "wraps" down to the fabric (Fig. 10-12).

Fig. 10-12

STEP 4. Holding the knot with your left thumb, pull the needle through to form the knot.

Chapter 11

ADDING BORDERS

Your quilt center is pieced together. If you decided that one or more borders will give your quilt the perfect finishing touch, this section will help you apply the borders and create mitered corners. If you decided not to add any borders, you're ready to bind the edges.

THE FIRST BORDER

No matter how carefully you measure, cut and stitch, your finished quilt top may not be per- fectly "square." Fortunately, you can easily square it as you add the first border. I'll show you how.

To add the first border, lay the entire pieced quilt top on a flat surface. With the right sides together, pin one border strip to a side edge.

Trim the border strip for the other side of the quilt top the same length as the first border strip. Pin that border strip to the remaining side edge. Note: If the second piece is too long, trim both pieces to the same length and ease the first side to fit the shortened border. Stitch

And a great day was had by all!

both sides in place (Fig. 11-1). Press. Use the same process to fit and attach the top and bottom border strips (Fig. 11-2).

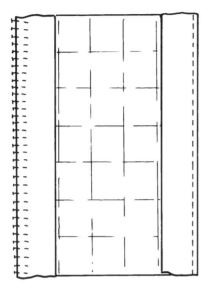

Fig. 11-1

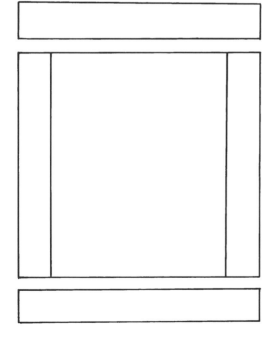

Fig. 11-2

REMAINING BORDERS

Once the first border is in place, add the remaining borders in the same sequence: sides, then top and bottom. They shouldn't require measuring or pinning.

MITERING THE CORNERS

You can miter the corners of the borders by using one of two methods: the speedy method or the traditional method. Directions for doing both follow:

Speedy Method

To miter the corners of borders with my speedy method, sew the border strips to all four sides, Leaving the ¼-inch seam allowance at the ends free and backstitching at the start and end of each seam. Place the short, lengthwise edge of the Miterite against the wrong side of the border seam line (Fig. 11-3). Using a pencil, draw a stitching line along the angled edge at the seam line.

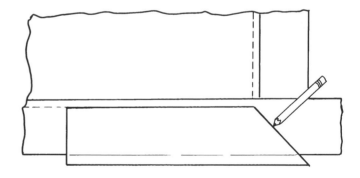

Fig. 11-3

Move the edge of the Miterite past the line that you just drew and draw a cutting line along the angled edge (Fig. 11-4). Repeat this process on all four corners.

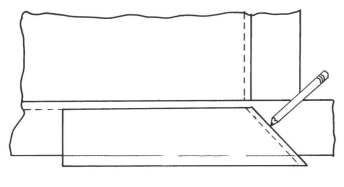

Fig. 11-4

Sew the right sides of the border strips together on the seam lines (Fig. 11-5). Trim along the cutting lines.

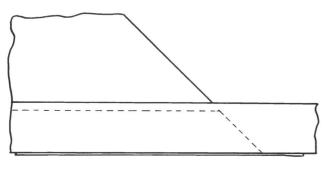

Fig. 11-5

Traditional Method

The traditional method of mitering borders includes four steps.

STEP 1. Sew the borders to the quilt, centering each strip on the quilt edge. The border strips should extend equally on both ends. Stitching must stop $1/4$ inch from the end of the quilt edge. Backstitch to secure the stitching.

STEP 2. With the wrong side of the fabric up, gently smooth the left border over the right one. Draw a diagonal line from the inner seam to the point where the outer edges cross (Fig. 11-6).

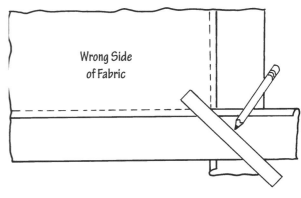

Fig. 11-6

STEP 3. Fold the quilt, right sides together, until the adjacent border edges are aligned with each other (Fig. 11-7). Stitch along the diagonal line, sewing from the outer edge to the inner seam. Do not catch the original border seams. Backstitch to secure the seam.

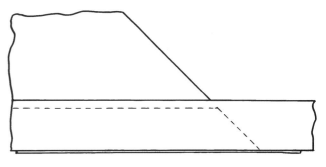

Fig. 11-7

STEP 4. Check the shape of the corner; it should form a 90-degree corner. Trim the seams to $1/2$ inch, and press them open.

CHAPTER 12

QUILTING AND BINDING

Beautiful job! Your piecing is done, and now you're ready to mark the quilt top and quilt the layers together.

MARKING QUILTING LINES

The time to mark quilting lines is just before you baste together the quilt top, batting and backing. Where you stitch on your quilt is a personal decision. Most people choose specific seam lines and follow them.

If your quilting will follow seam lines (quilting in the ditch) or appliqué edges, you won't need to mark the lines. For designs that you're creating in open areas, mark with a water-soluble marking pen or a chalk pencil. (Marks made with a lead pencil do not wash out. Be sure to test the marking pen or pencil on a piece of scrap fabric to be sure the marks really do wash out.) Mark very lightly, using a ruler for straight lines or your favorite quilting stencil for a design. Or if you want, you can draw your own free-hand design.

A popular approach is quilting ¼ inch away from seam lines, thus avoiding the excess thickness of the seam allowances. Use ¼-inch quilter's tape to mark these quilting lines.

How many quilting lines should you use? In general, the less quilting you do, the puffier the quilt; the more quilting, the flatter the

quilt. Check the batting label; it may recommend a maximum distance between lines to prevent the batting from shifting and bunching.

Iris, machine-quilting her Christmas Tree quilt.

PREPARING THE BACKING

Wash and press the backing fabric. Remove the selvages, and piece if necessary. Refer to APPENDIX D: BORDERS AND BACKING for suggestions on piecing the backing. Using ³/₄-inch seams, seam the backing. Press the seams open.

The finished backing should be at least 1½ to 2 inches larger than the quilt top on all sides.

BASTING THE LAYERS

To baste the three layers—quilt top, batting and backing—together, you'll need to work on a large, flat surface. Using a chalk pencil, mark the center of this surface and the center of your quilt backing. Matching these centers, lay the quilt backing wrong side up on the work surface. Center the batting on top of the backing. Center the quilt top, right side up, on the batting.

To be sure that there are no folds or wrinkles in the backing, pull gently on each of the four sides of the backing fabric. Repeat this every time you reposition the quilt during the basting process.

Starting at the center and working out, pin through all the layers, using 1-inch-long, nickel-plated safety pins. Position the pins every 3 to 4 inches (Fig. 12-1). Avoid placing any pins directly on a line that will be quilted.

After basting an area on the work surface,

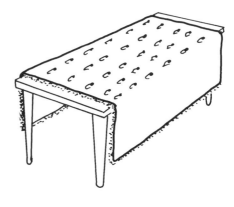

Fig. 12-1

carefully slide the quilt so that an unbasted area is now on top. Repeat the process until the quilt is completely basted.

Check the underside for pleats and wrinkles. You may want to rebaste an area.

QUILTING

There are three methods for fastening the quilt layers together:

Hand-quilting. This is the traditional method that gives your quilt a hand-finished quality. Hand-quilting is done with tiny, evenly spaced running stitches.

Machine-quilting. If you use clear nylon thread, this is a fast and easy way to quilt. It's especially effective for quilting in the ditch.

Tying. This is a quick, simple-to-do technique that produces the puffy look of a comforter.

Hand-Quilting

To hand-quilt, you'll need quilting thread, betweens (size 8 is easiest to learn with, but size 10 will give you shorter stitches), a thimble (don't give up—you'll enjoy quilting more when you learn to use one!) and some sort of frame. Start with a small lap frame. If you do a lot of quilting, check out the various hoop or floor frames available.

The quilting stitch requires practice. Start with a tiny knot. Insert the needle into the quilt top, about 1 inch from where you want the first quilting stitch. Snap the thread just hard enough to pull the knot through the top layer, catching it in the batting, and bring the needle up through the fabric close to where you want to make your first stitch (Fig. 12-2).

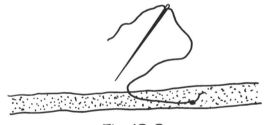

Fig. 12-2

With your free hand under the quilt, insert the needle straight down (Fig. 12-3). As soon as your finger feels the point, "rock" the end of the needle down, at the same time pushing the point up.

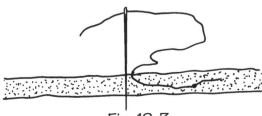

Fig. 12-3

Repeat these two motions, using the thumb of your free hand to push the fabric over the point (Fig. 12-4).

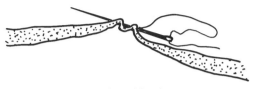

Fig. 12-4

To end the thread, take one or two tiny backstitches, then come out about 1 inch away and cut the thread short, leaving the 1-inch tail anchored in the batting.

With bonded batting, tiny stitches aren't quite as important for holding the batting in place. So, first try for even stitches, then try for shorter ones, if you want.

Machine-Quilting

The walking, or even-feed, foot and invisible, or clear nylon, thread have made today's machine-quilting easy.

When quilting over two or more colors of fabric, use the clear thread on the top. You'll need to loosen the top tension on your machine to get a perfect stitch. For the bobbin, choose a good sewing thread that matches the backing fabric.

With a walking foot, you won't have to push or pull the quilt through the machine. However, be careful that the weight of the quilt doesn't create a drag.

As I mentioned previously, your movement is limited when you machine-quilt a large item. However, sewing-machine attachments are available that allow free movement of the fabric while you stitch. You may want to experiment with these. If so, I suggest reading Robbie and Tony Fanning's book *The Complete Book of Machine Quilting*, second edition (Chilton Book Co. 1994).

To machine-quilt, use a long stitch, about 6 to 8 stitches to the inch. The quilt feeds through easier and the long stitch creates a puffier look. If you're using clear thread on top, loosen your upper tension to prevent the thread from breaking.

The trick to successful machine-quilting is handling all the bulk. Roll each side tightly toward the center quilting line. Use bicycle clips to help keep these two rolls in place (Fig. 12-5). Fold the quilt as shown in Figure 12-6 to make a manageable bundle to put in your lap.

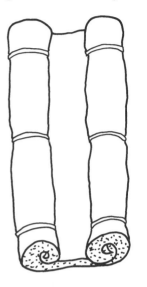

Fig. 12-5

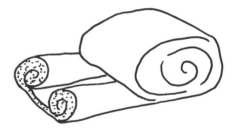

Fig. 12-6

Using a walking foot, sew the entire length of this quilting line. Reroll the quilt to the next area and stitch. Repeat until all desired quilting is done.

Tying

The fastest way to finish a quilt is to tie it. Follow the procedure for layering and smoothing the quilt; then, instead of pinning and quilting, tie the layers together. For a tied quilt, the middle layer should be either a flannel fabric or a bonded batting.

When tying, I use #3 pearl cotton (double strand) and a large darning needle or a curved upholstery needle. I've also found that a pair of pliers or a piece of rubber is helpful for pulling the needle through the layers.

These are the simple steps for tying a quilt:

STEP 1. Using a vanishing marker or chalk pen, mark the positions for the ties. The positions can be uniform or fairly random, just be certain they're evenly spaced and close enough together to keep the batting from shifting.

STEP 2. Using a long piece of thread (about 36 inches when doubled), take one stitch through all the layers (Fig. 12-7) at one of the marks.

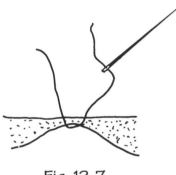

Fig. 12-7

STEP 3. Knot the thread by tying it twice (Fig. 12-8). The quilt will gather at the tied spot, but don't worry; it'll work out as it's used.

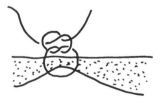

Fig. 12-8

STEP 4. Cut the tails 1 inch long. Take another stitch at the another mark and tie the thread. Repeat for the remaining marks.

BINDING THE EDGES

You've reached the last step in creating a quilt. Take time to admire your beautiful work, then move on to binding the edges. Caution: Resist the almost overwhelming temptation to rush. You'll want the edges to have the same precision as the rest of the quilt.

Straight Edges

The quickest way to bind the quilt is to turn the raw edge of the outermost border to the back and stitch it in place. To do this, you must make sure that the outer border is 1 1/2 inches wider than the finished top; this extra width allows 1 1/2 inches for turnback. All outer borders in this book include that extra width.

For straight edges, follow these steps:

STEP 1. With the right sides up, trim off any excess batting and backing so that all edges are even with the raw edge of the outer border (Fig. 12-9).

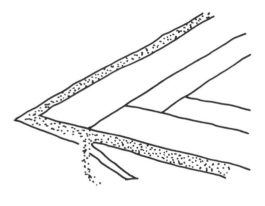

Fig. 12-9

STEP 2. With the back of the quilt faceup, trim 1 inch off the backing and batting (Fig. 12-10). Do not cut off any border fabric.

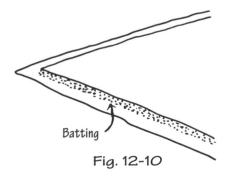

Batting

Fig. 12-10

STEP 3. Turn 1 1/2 inches of the border to the back of the quilt. You will be turning back 1/2 inch of the batting and backing, too. Turning these two layers will help retain a plump binding when the quilt is used. Turn under 1/2 inch on the raw edge of the border. Pin in place, and machine-stitch along the fold.

STEP 4. For easy mitered corners, fold the corner wrong side out (Fig. 12-11). Measure 2 1/8 inches from the point. Mark or pin.

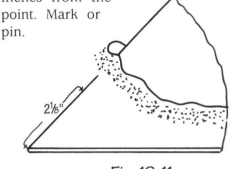

2 1/8"

Fig. 12-11

STEP 5. Fold the point at the mark, keeping the cut edges together. Mark the quilt at the fold line (Fig. 12-12).

Fig. 12-12

Stitch 1 1/2 inches from the fold. Backstitch. Trim the seam to 1/2 inch, tapering at the corner (Fig. 12-13).

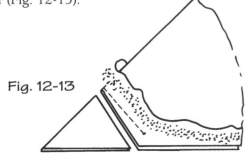

Fig. 12-13

Turn the binding to the right side. The mitered corner will fall neatly into place, and ½ inch will be free for you to turn under (Fig. 12-14).

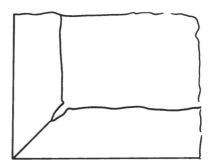

Fig. 12-14

STEP 6. Turn under ½ inch. Pin in place. Topstitch through all the layers (Fig. 12-15).

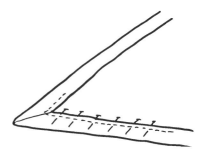

Fig. 12-15

Borderless Edges

For quilts without borders as well as those with shaped edges, follow these five steps:

STEP 1. Trim the backing and batting even with the quilt top.

STEP 2. Cut bias strips 2¼ inches wide. Sew them end to end (Fig. 12-16).

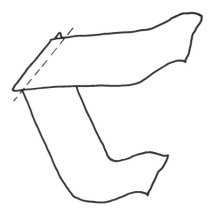

Fig. 12-16

STEP 3. With the wrong sides together, fold the strip in half lengthwise (Fig. 12-17). Press.

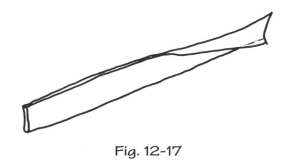

Fig. 12-17

STEP 4. Pinning both edges of the strip to the top edge of the quilt, stitch the strip to the quilt, using a ⅜-inch seam. Begin stitching along a side, not at a corner. Leave a 6-inch piece of the strip unstitched (Fig. 12-18). Pin at the corners.

Folded Edge

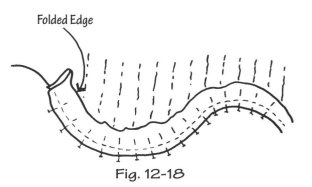

Fig. 12-18

You may at times design a quilt omitting the side and corner pieces, resulting in shaped edges rather than straight edges. Proceed in this manner:

For inside corners: Clip ¼ inch into the corner. Stitch ⅜ inch into the corner, lift the presser foot to pivot and continue stitching (Fig. 12-19). When the bias is turned to the back, make a tiny fold with the excess (Fig. 12-20).

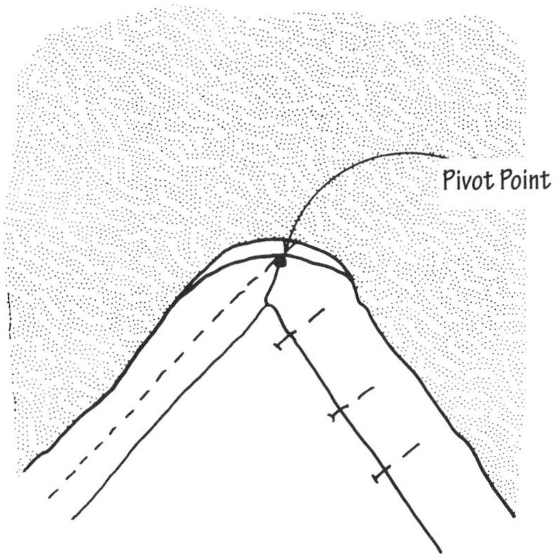

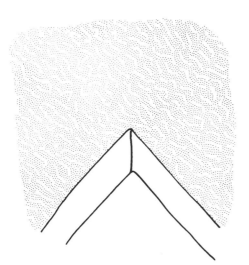

Fig. 12-19

Fig. 12-20

For outer corners: Stop stitching ⅜ inch before the corner, back tack one or two stitches and cut the threads. Lift the presser foot, and fold the bias strip (Fig. 12-21). The fold should be even with the raw edge. Begin stitching again at the fold (Fig. 12-22). When turned to the back, the bias will form a neatly mitered corner.

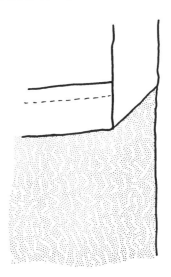

Fig. 12-21

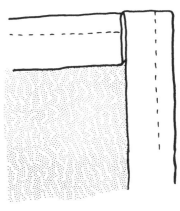

Fig. 12-22

STEP 5. Turn the bias to the back of the quilt. Hand-stitch the folded edge to the quilt, covering the machine-stitching. Use the same slip stitch that you use for hand-appliquéing.

CHAPTER 13

CARING FOR YOUR QUILT

Hurray! You did it. You took a new quilting direction and made your own special quilt! It's lovely, isn't it? Before you do anything else, take a minute to hand-stitch the quilting label to the back. Let everyone know you're the quilter.

Sometime in the future, you may to want to wash your quilt and store it. After all the time and love that have gone into creating it, proper care is a must.

Showing off our gorgeous quilts! (Back row, left to right: Elizabeth Z. Lewis, Leslie McFarlane, Sue Miller, Luana Hall, Iris Waal and Donna Poster. Second row, left to right: Trina Rehkemper, Sherry Reid Carroll, Susan Saiter and Nina Johnston. Front row, left to right: Joni Milstead and Virginia Bobbitt.)

MACHINE-WASHING AND -DRYING

You can machine-wash and -dry your quilt if you used a bonded batting and have a large-capacity washer and dryer. Use the gentlest wash cycle and a mild detergent. Set your dryer to the delicate cycle, and dry the quilt just until it's slightly damp. Remove the quilt and finish drying it flat on a blanket or a bed.

HAND-WASHING AND -DRYING

To hand-wash your quilt, fill the bathtub half full with lukewarm water. Use a mild detergent. Squeeze the quilt gently and swish it around in the water. Never lift the quilt while it's wet; the weight of the wet quilt will snap the quilting threads. Rinse the quilt several times, and squeeze out as much water as possible. Do not wring.

To move the wet quilt, fold it into a bundle and carry it in your arms. Dry your quilt on a blanket that is spread out on a large flat surface, such as the floor. You can dry the quilt outside on a sunny day, but be sure to place the top of the quilt down to prevent fading.

STORING

To keep your quilt in beautiful condition, fold it loosely and wrap it in muslin or place it in a cotton pillowcase. Never store it in plastic; allow air to circulate around the quilt to preserve it.

Part
IV

APPENDICES

A. 144 Hexagon Quilt Blocks
B. 144 Octagon Quilt Blocks
C. Quilt Sets and Other Basics
D. Borders and Backing
E. Copy, Cut and Paste Fun
F. 56 Sample Combinations
G. Yardage Table for Templates
H. Full-Size Templates

144 HEXAGON QUILT BLOCKS

1. WHIRLYBIRD

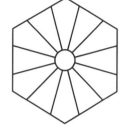

2. SUNSHINE

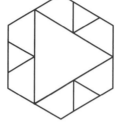

3. CAMPING OUT

4. SPECIAL OCCASION

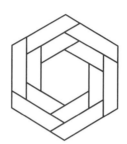

5. ROUND CABIN

6. TULIP

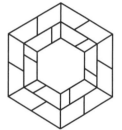

7. FREE MOTION

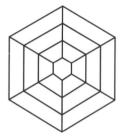

8. CABBAGE ROSE

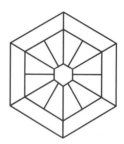

9. INSIDE TRACK

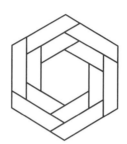

10. WAGON WHEEL

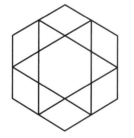

11. ROLLING STAR

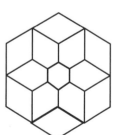

12. POINSETTIA

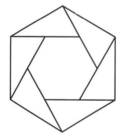

13. BLOSSOM

14. FALLING LEAVES

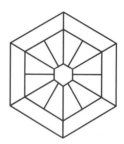

15. DELTA QUEEN

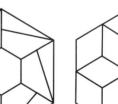

16. AWAY WE GO!

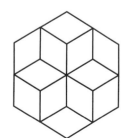

17. JUST A REAL
NICE STAR

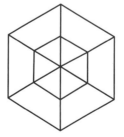

18. BITS O' FUN

19. EVENING STAR

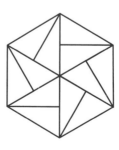

20. MAJOR STAR

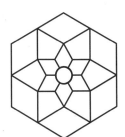

21. STARFLOWER

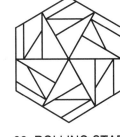

22. ROLLING STAR

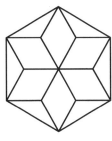

23. PILE OF POINTS

24. TRILLIUM

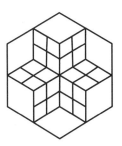

25. STAR BRIGHT

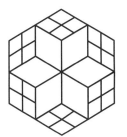

26. STAR LIGHT

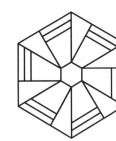

27. STARS & STRIPES

28. STROLLING ALONG

29. HIGH NOON

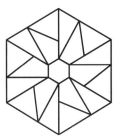

30. WINDBLOWN

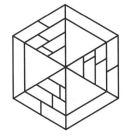

31. INDIAN SIGNS

32. NORTHERN STAR

33. DOILY

34. TALK SHOW

35. KALEIDOSCOPE

36. JUMPIN' JEHOSHAPHAT!

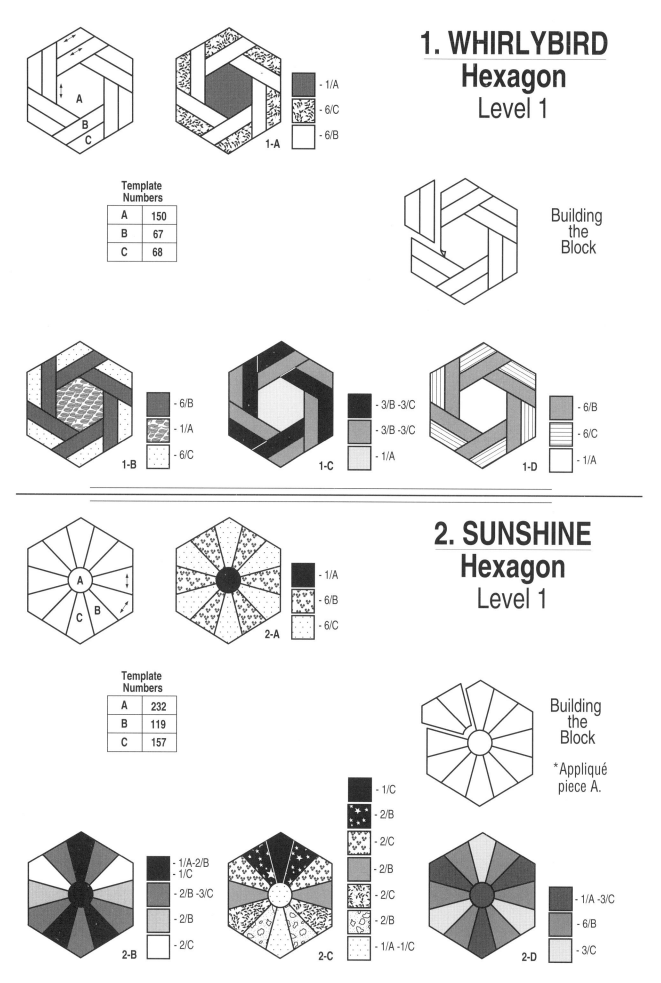

1. WHIRLYBIRD
Hexagon
Level 1

1-A
- 1/A
- 6/C
- 6/B

Template Numbers

A	150
B	67
C	68

Building the Block

1-B
- 6/B
- 1/A
- 6/C

1-C
- 3/B -3/C
- 3/B -3/C
- 1/A

1-D
- 6/B
- 6/C
- 1/A

2. SUNSHINE
Hexagon
Level 1

2-A
- 1/A
- 6/B
- 6/C

Template Numbers

A	232
B	119
C	157

Building the Block

*Appliqué piece A.

2-B
- 1/A-2/B
- 1/C
- 2/B -3/C
- 2/B
- 2/C

2-C
- 1/C
- 2/B
- 2/C
- 2/B
- 2/C
- 2/B
- 1/A -1/C

2-D
- 1/A -3/C
- 6/B
- 3/C

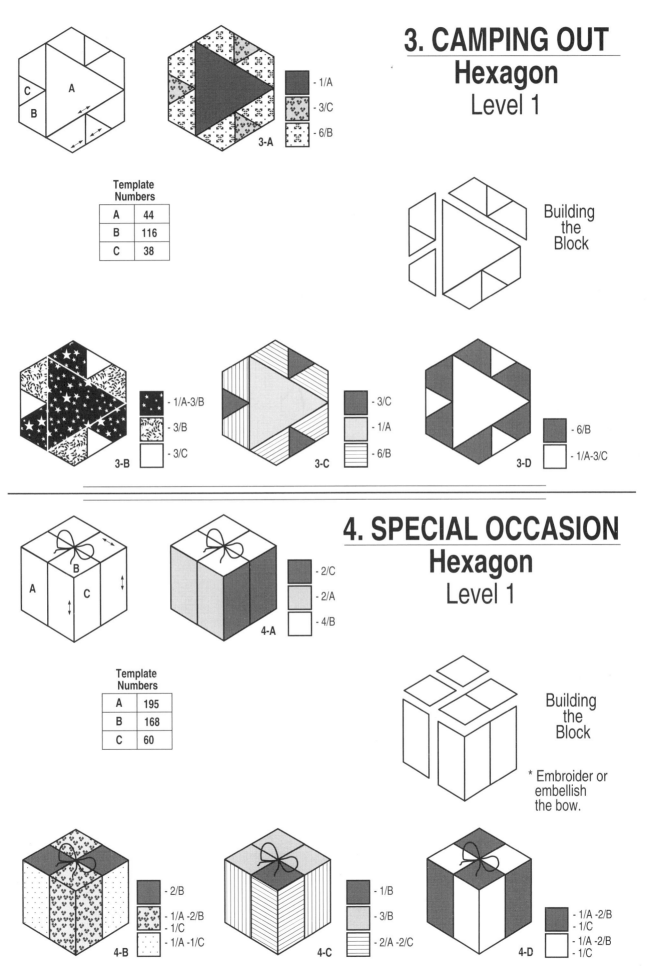

3. CAMPING OUT
Hexagon
Level 1

- 1/A
- 3/C
- 6/B

3-A

Template Numbers

A	44
B	116
C	38

Building the Block

- 1/A-3/B
- 3/B
- 3/C

3-B

- 3/C
- 1/A
- 6/B

3-C

- 6/B
- 1/A-3/C

3-D

4. SPECIAL OCCASION
Hexagon
Level 1

- 2/C
- 2/A
- 4/B

4-A

Template Numbers

A	195
B	168
C	60

Building the Block

* Embroider or embellish the bow.

- 2/B
- 1/A -2/B
- 1/C
- 1/A -1/C

4-B

- 1/B
- 3/B
- 2/A -2/C

4-C

- 1/A -2/B
- 1/C
- 1/A -2/B
- 1/C

4-D

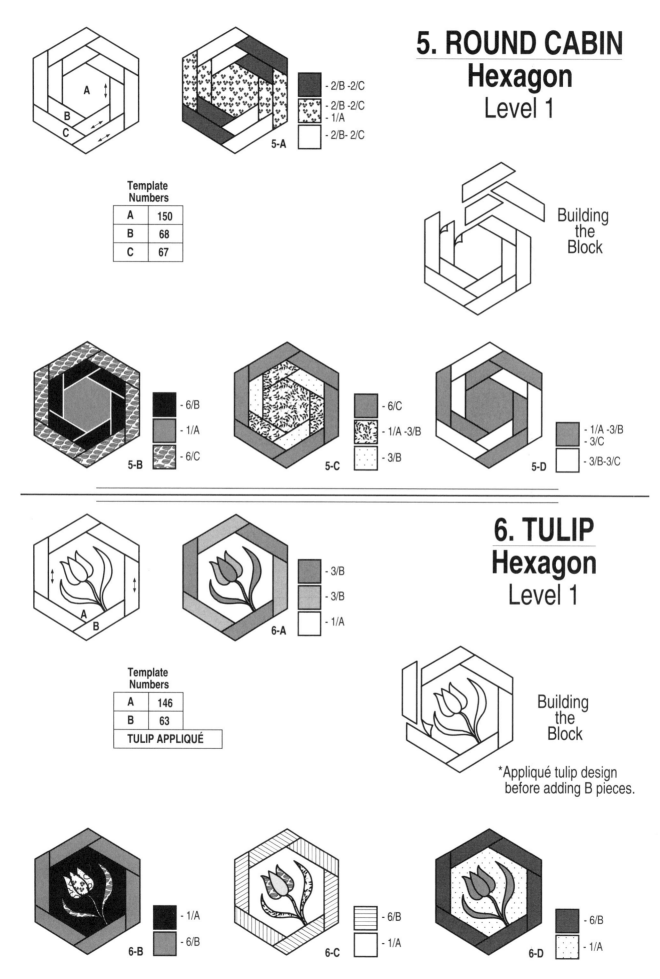

5. ROUND CABIN
Hexagon
Level 1

5-A

- 2/B -2/C
- 2/B -2/C
- 1/A
- 2/B- 2/C

Template Numbers

A	150
B	68
C	67

Building the Block

5-B
- 6/B
- 1/A
- 6/C

5-C
- 6/C
- 1/A -3/B
- 3/B

5-D
- 1/A -3/B
- 3/C
- 3/B-3/C

6. TULIP
Hexagon
Level 1

6-A
- 3/B
- 3/B
- 1/A

Template Numbers

A	146
B	63
TULIP APPLIQUÉ	

Building the Block

*Appliqué tulip design before adding B pieces.

6-B
- 1/A
- 6/B

6-C
- 6/B
- 1/A

6-D
- 6/B
- 1/A

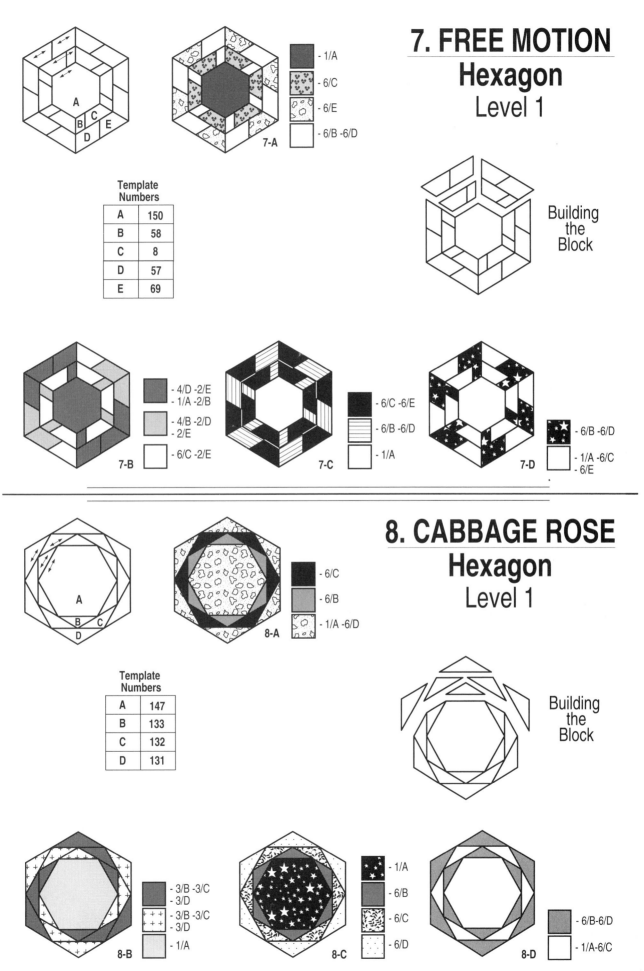

7. FREE MOTION
Hexagon
Level 1

7-A

- 1/A
- 6/C
- 6/E
- 6/B -6/D

Template Numbers

A	150
B	58
C	8
D	57
E	69

Building the Block

7-B
- 4/D -2/E 1/A -2/B
- 4/B -2/D -2/E
- 6/C -2/E

7-C
- 6/C -6/E
- 6/B -6/D
- 1/A

7-D
- 6/B -6/D
- 1/A -6/C -6/E

8. CABBAGE ROSE
Hexagon
Level 1

8-A
- 6/C
- 6/B
- 1/A -6/D

Template Numbers

A	147
B	133
C	132
D	131

Building the Block

8-B
- 3/B -3/C 3/D
- 3/B -3/C 3/D
- 1/A

8-C
- 1/A
- 6/B
- 6/C
- 6/D

8-D
- 6/B-6/D
- 1/A-6/C

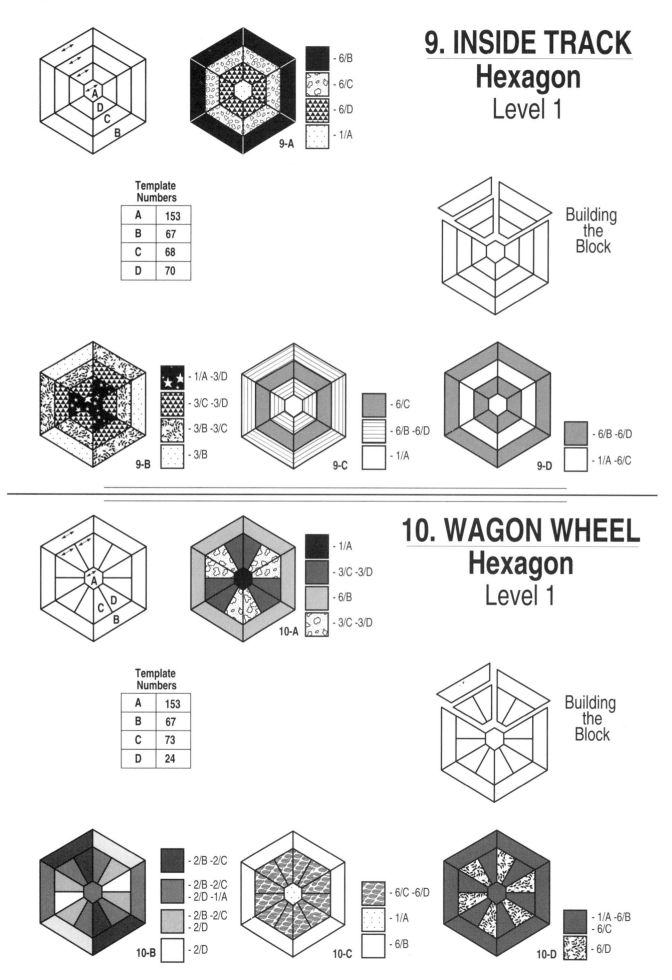

9. INSIDE TRACK
Hexagon
Level 1

9-A
- 6/B
- 6/C
- 6/D
- 1/A

Template Numbers

A	153
B	67
C	68
D	70

Building the Block

9-B
- 1/A -3/D
- 3/C -3/D
- 3/B -3/C
- 3/B

9-C
- 6/C
- 6/B -6/D
- 1/A

9-D
- 6/B -6/D
- 1/A -6/C

10. WAGON WHEEL
Hexagon
Level 1

10-A
- 1/A
- 3/C -3/D
- 6/B
- 3/C -3/D

Template Numbers

A	153
B	67
C	73
D	24

Building the Block

10-B
- 2/B -2/C
- 2/B -2/C
- 2/D -1/A
- 2/B -2/C
- 2/D
- 2/D

10-C
- 6/C -6/D
- 1/A
- 6/B

10-D
- 1/A -6/B
- 6/C
- 6/D

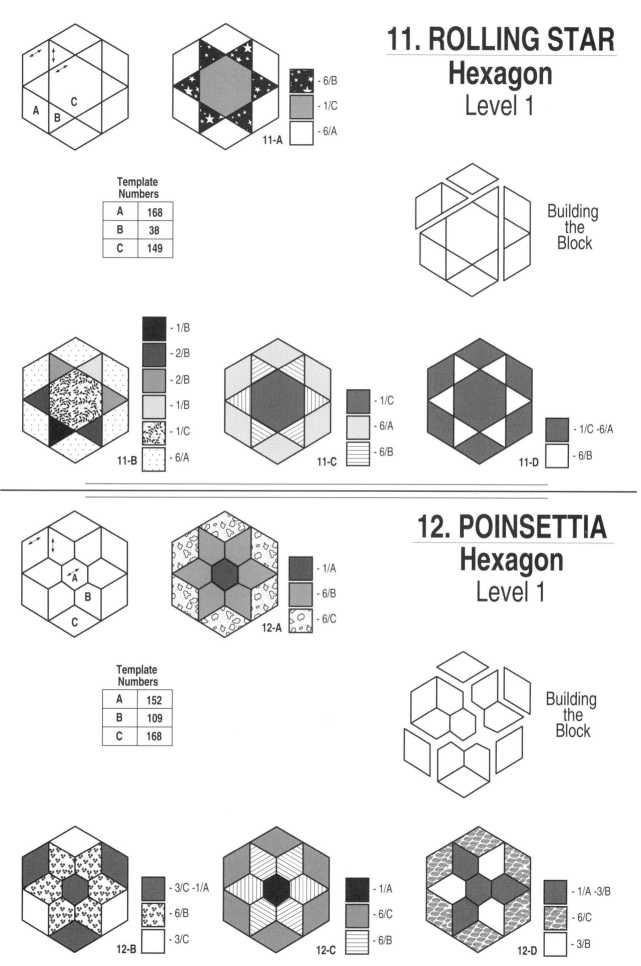

11. ROLLING STAR
Hexagon
Level 1

- 6/B
- 1/C
- 6/A

11-A

Building the Block

Template Numbers

A	168
B	38
C	149

- 1/B
- 2/B
- 2/B
- 1/B
- 1/C
- 6/A

11-B

- 1/C
- 6/A
- 6/B

11-C

- 1/C -6/A
- 6/B

11-D

12. POINSETTIA
Hexagon
Level 1

- 1/A
- 6/B
- 6/C

12-A

Building the Block

Template Numbers

A	152
B	109
C	168

- 3/C -1/A
- 6/B
- 3/C

12-B

- 1/A
- 6/C
- 6/B

12-C

- 1/A -3/B
- 6/C
- 3/B

12-D

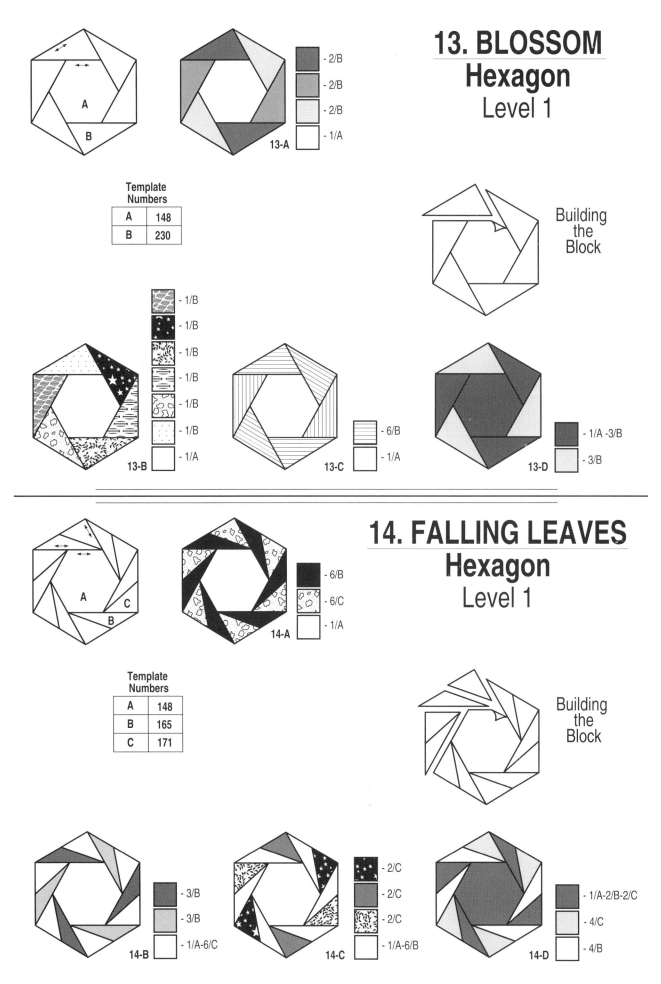

13. BLOSSOM
Hexagon
Level 1

13-A

- 2/B
- 2/B
- 2/B
- 1/A

Template Numbers

A	148
B	230

Building the Block

13-B

- 1/B
- 1/B
- 1/B
- 1/B
- 1/B
- 1/B
- 1/A

13-C

- 6/B
- 1/A

13-D

- 1/A -3/B
- 3/B

14. FALLING LEAVES
Hexagon
Level 1

14-A

- 6/B
- 6/C
- 1/A

Template Numbers

A	148
B	165
C	171

Building the Block

14-B

- 3/B
- 3/B
- 1/A-6/C

14-C

- 2/C
- 2/C
- 2/C
- 1/A-6/B

14-D

- 1/A-2/B-2/C
- 4/C
- 4/B

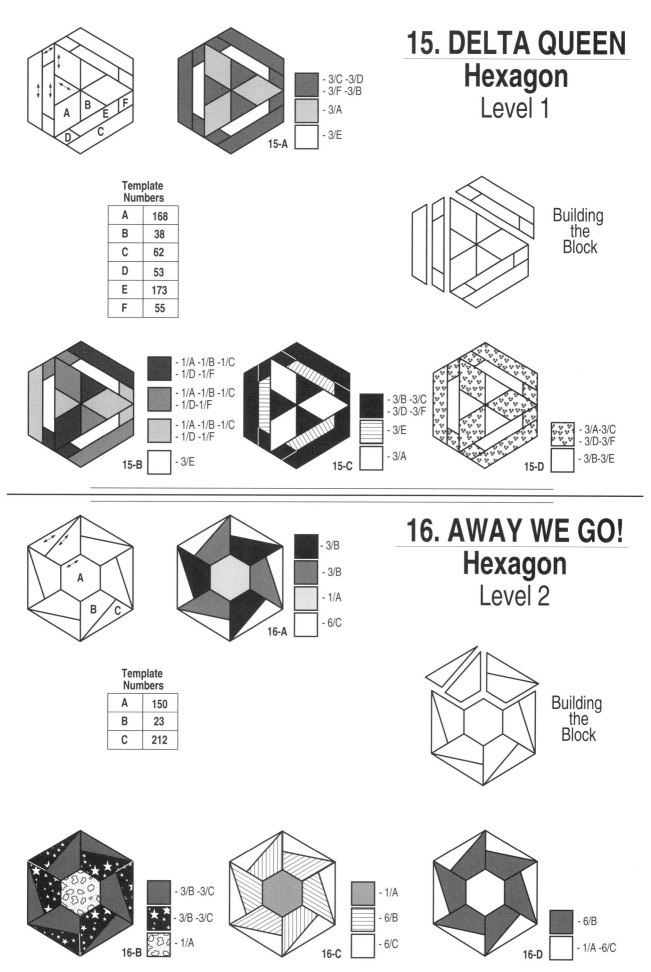

15. DELTA QUEEN
Hexagon
Level 1

15-A
- 3/C -3/D
- 3/F -3/B
- 3/A
- 3/E

Template Numbers

A	168
B	38
C	62
D	53
E	173
F	55

Building the Block

15-B
- 1/A -1/B -1/C -1/D -1/F
- 1/A -1/B -1/C -1/D-1/F
- 1/A -1/B -1/C -1/D -1/F
- 3/E

15-C
- 3/B -3/C -3/D -3/F
- 3/E
- 3/A

15-D
- 3/A-3/C -3/D-3/F
- 3/B-3/E

16. AWAY WE GO!
Hexagon
Level 2

16-A
- 3/B
- 3/B
- 1/A
- 6/C

Template Numbers

A	150
B	23
C	212

Building the Block

16-B
- 3/B -3/C
- 3/B -3/C
- 1/A

16-C
- 1/A
- 6/B
- 6/C

16-D
- 6/B
- 1/A -6/C

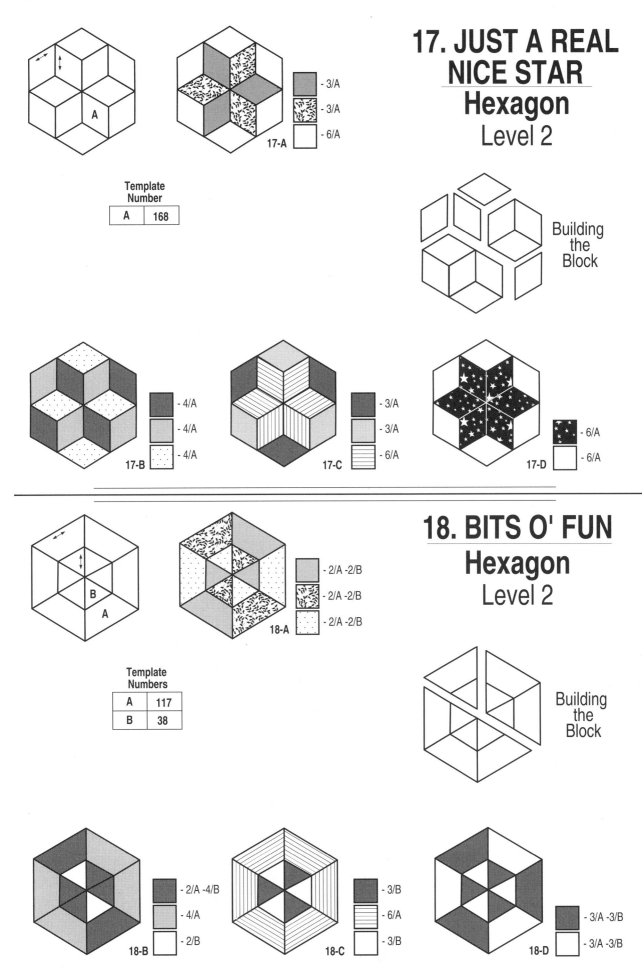

17. JUST A REAL NICE STAR
Hexagon
Level 2

17-A

- 3/A
- 3/A
- 6/A

Template Number

A	168

Building the Block

17-B

- 4/A
- 4/A
- 4/A

17-C

- 3/A
- 3/A
- 6/A

17-D

- 6/A
- 6/A

18. BITS O' FUN
Hexagon
Level 2

18-A

- 2/A -2/B
- 2/A -2/B
- 2/A -2/B

Template Numbers

A	117
B	38

Building the Block

18-B

- 2/A -4/B
- 4/A
- 2/B

18-C

- 3/B
- 6/A
- 3/B

18-D

- 3/A -3/B
- 3/A -3/B

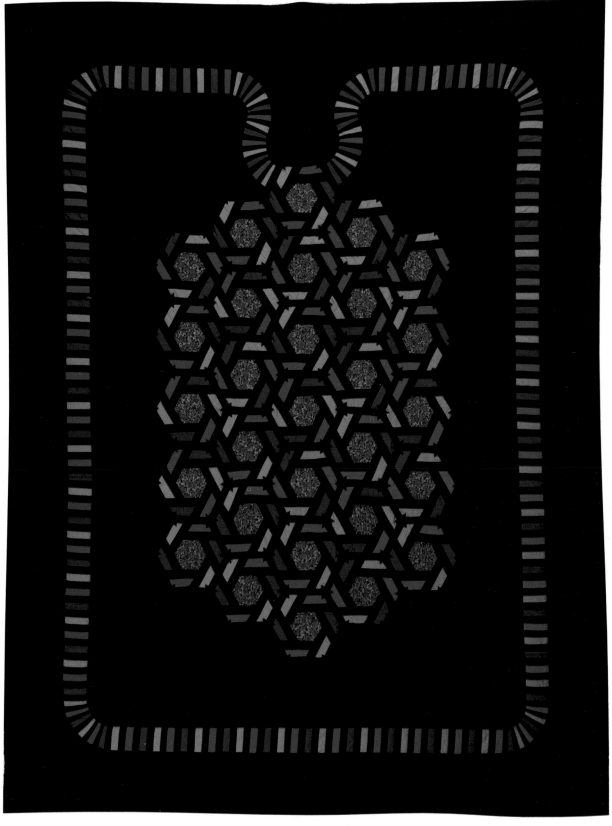

Hexagon Quilt Block 1, WHIRLYBIRD; Quilt Set 3; 108 x 83
Corner triangles machine-appliquéd
Border design and quilt by Joni Milstead

Octagon Quilt Block 9, PRIMROSE;
Quilt Set 1; 64 x 64
(Fabrics by Gutcheon Patchworks)
Quilt by Donna Poster

Hexagon Quilt Block 9, INSIDE TRACK; Quilt Set 1; 53 x 50
(Fabrics by Gutcheon Patchworks)
Quilt by Donna Poster

Hexagon Quilt Block 29, HIGH NOON; Quilt Set 1; 51 x 40
Tea-dyed after quilting
Quilt by Donna Poster

**Octagon Quilt Block 16,
HOLDING HANDS; Quilt Set 2;
Pieced Lattice Block 3; 63 x 49**
Quilt by Donna Poster

**Octagon Quilt Block 28,
FLIPPIN' STARS;
Quilt Set 1; 43 x 43**
Design by Susan Saiter
Quilt by Donna Poster

Hexagon Quilt Block 8, CABBAGE ROSE; Quilt Set 2; 60 x 54
(Fabrics by Gutcheon Patchworks)
Quilt by Donna Poster

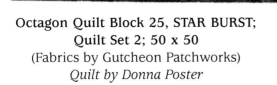

**Octagon Quilt Block 25, STAR BURST;
Quilt Set 2; 50 x 50**
(Fabrics by Gutcheon Patchworks)
Quilt by Donna Poster

Octagon Quilt Block 17, FLYING FLAGS; Quilt Set 3; 69 x 58
(Fabrics by Gutcheon Patchworks)
Quilt by Donna Poster

Octagon Quilt Block 31, FAIRY BLOSSOMS;
Quilt Set 1; 73 x 64
Quilt by Donna Poster

Sampler of Hexagon Quilt Blocks, Quilt Set 2, 55 x 52

TOP ROW, *left to right:* Quilt Block 7, FREE MOTION; *Joni Milstead;* Quilt Block 23, PILE OF POINTS; *Virginia Bobbitt;* Quilt Block 16, AWAY WE GO! *Elizabeth Z. Lewis;* Quilt Block 1, WHIRLYBIRD; *Leslie McFarlane.*

SECOND ROW, *left to right:* Quilt Block 15, DELTA QUEEN; *Trina Rehkemper;* Quilt Block 13, BLOSSOM; *Leslie McFarlane;* Quilt Block 25, STAR BRIGHT; *Nina Johnston.*

THIRD ROW, *left to right:* Quilt Block 25, STAR BRIGHT; *Joni Milstead;* Quilt Block 35, KALEIDOSCOPE; *Sue Miller;* Quilt Block 32, NORTHERN STAR; *Susan Saiter,* Quilt Block 27, STARS & STRIPES; *Iris Waal.*

FOURTH ROW, *left to right:* Quilt Block 5, ROUND CABIN; *Sherry Reid Carroll;* Quilt Block 6, TULIP; *Susan Saiter;* Quilt Block 22, ROLLING STAR; *Margaret Barncord.*

FIFTH ROW, *left to right:* Quilt Block 8, CABBAGE ROSE; *Donna Poster;* Quilt Block 26, STAR LIGHT; *Nina Johnston;* Quilt Block 2, SUNSHINE; *Susan Saiter;* Quilt Block 33, DOILY; *Nina Johnston.*

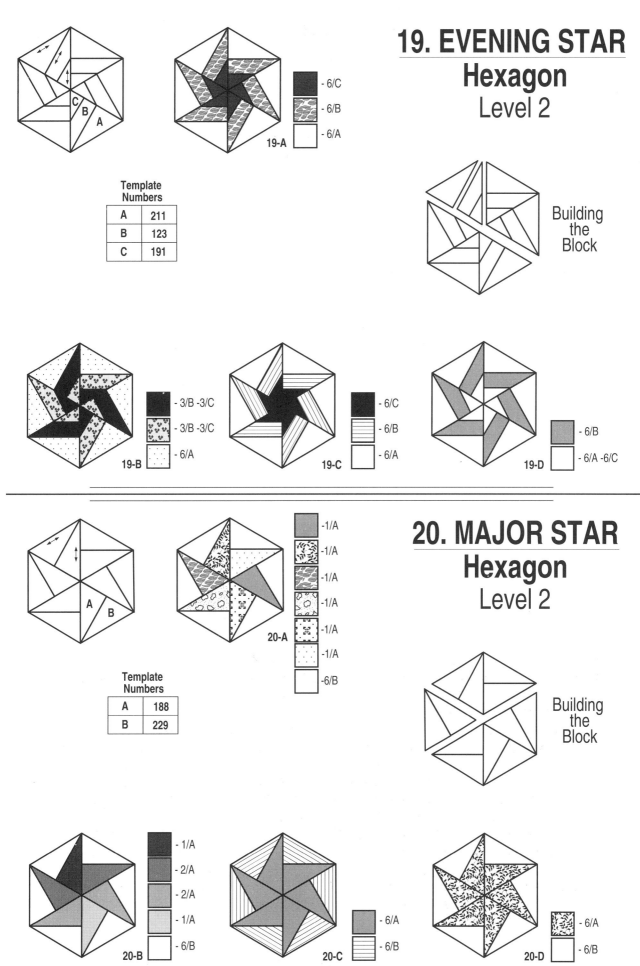

19. EVENING STAR
Hexagon
Level 2

6/C
6/B
6/A

19-A

Template Numbers

A	211
B	123
C	191

Building the Block

- 3/B -3/C
- 3/B -3/C
- 6/A

19-B

- 6/C
- 6/B
- 6/A

19-C

- 6/B
- 6/A -6/C

19-D

20. MAJOR STAR
Hexagon
Level 2

-1/A
-1/A
-1/A
-1/A
-1/A
-1/A
-6/B

20-A

Template Numbers

A	188
B	229

Building the Block

- 1/A
- 2/A
- 2/A
- 1/A
- 6/B

20-B

- 6/A
- 6/B

20-C

- 6/A
- 6/B

20-D

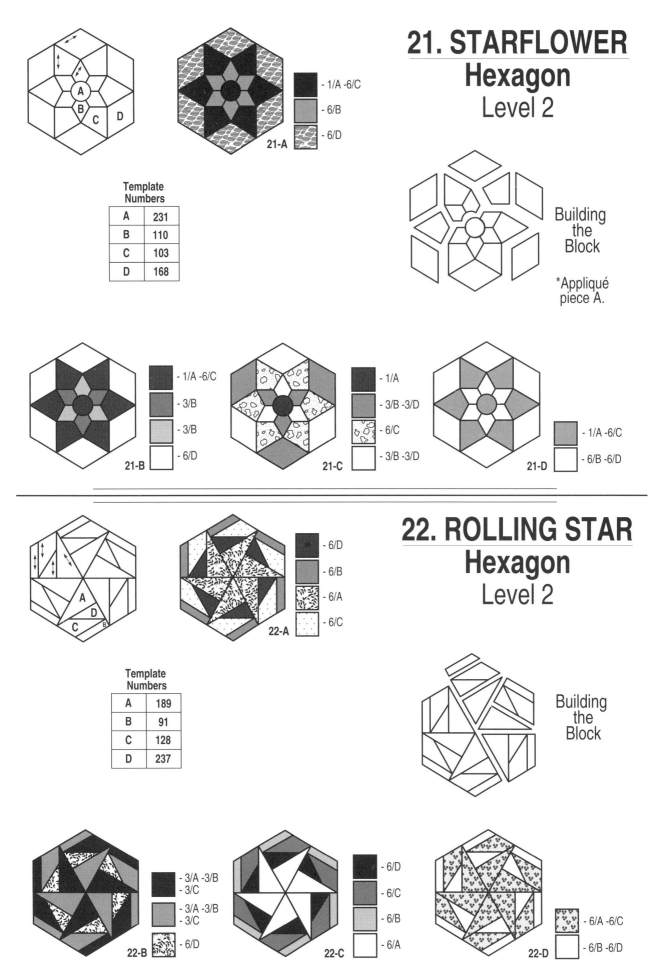

21. STARFLOWER
Hexagon
Level 2

- 1/A -6/C
- 6/B
- 6/D

21-A

Template Numbers	
A	231
B	110
C	103
D	168

Building the Block

*Appliqué piece A.

- 1/A -6/C
- 3/B
- 3/B
- 6/D

21-B

- 1/A
- 3/B -3/D
- 6/C
- 3/B -3/D

21-C

- 1/A -6/C
- 6/B -6/D

21-D

22. ROLLING STAR
Hexagon
Level 2

- 6/D
- 6/B
- 6/A
- 6/C

22-A

Template Numbers	
A	189
B	91
C	128
D	237

Building the Block

- 3/A -3/B 3/C
- 3/A -3/B 3/C
- 6/D

22-B

- 6/D
- 6/C
- 6/B
- 6/A

22-C

- 6/A -6/C
- 6/B -6/D

22-D

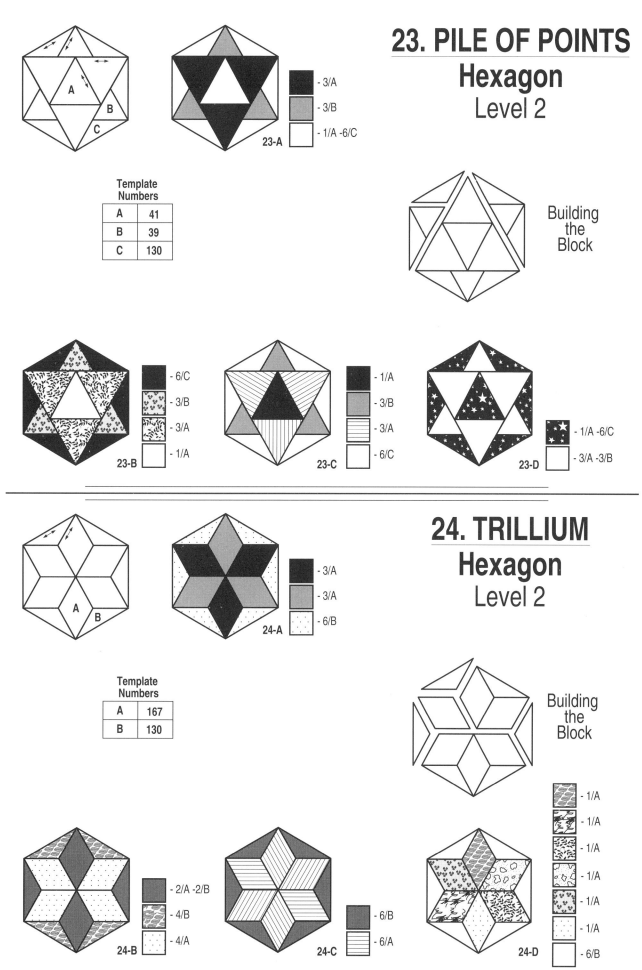

23. PILE OF POINTS
Hexagon
Level 2

23-A
- 3/A
- 3/B
- 1/A -6/C

Template Numbers

A	41
B	39
C	130

Building the Block

23-B
- 6/C
- 3/B
- 3/A
- 1/A

23-C
- 1/A
- 3/B
- 3/A
- 6/C

23-D
- 1/A -6/C
- 3/A -3/B

24. TRILLIUM
Hexagon
Level 2

24-A
- 3/A
- 3/A
- 6/B

Template Numbers

A	167
B	130

Building the Block

24-B
- 2/A -2/B
- 4/B
- 4/A

24-C
- 6/B
- 6/A

24-D
- 1/A
- 1/A
- 1/A
- 1/A
- 1/A
- 1/A
- 6/B

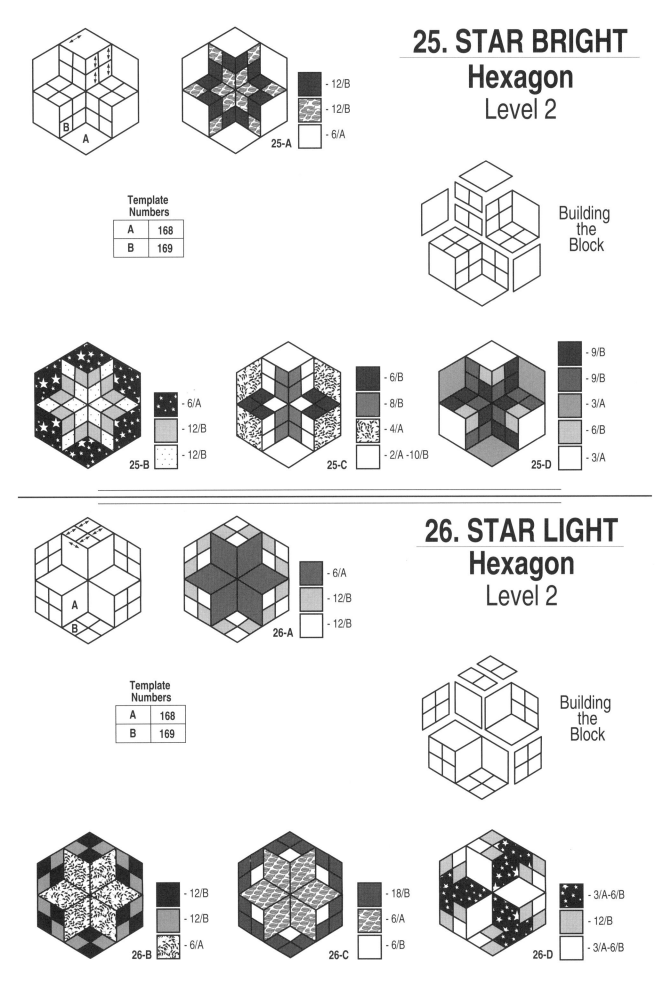

25. STAR BRIGHT
Hexagon
Level 2

25-A
- 12/B
- 12/B
- 6/A

Building
the
Block

Template Numbers	
A	168
B	169

25-B
- 6/A
- 12/B
- 12/B

25-C
- 6/B
- 8/B
- 4/A
- 2/A -10/B

25-D
- 9/B
- 9/B
- 3/A
- 6/B
- 3/A

26. STAR LIGHT
Hexagon
Level 2

26-A
- 6/A
- 12/B
- 12/B

Building
the
Block

Template Numbers	
A	168
B	169

26-B
- 12/B
- 12/B
- 6/A

26-C
- 18/B
- 6/A
- 6/B

26-D
- 3/A-6/B
- 12/B
- 3/A-6/B

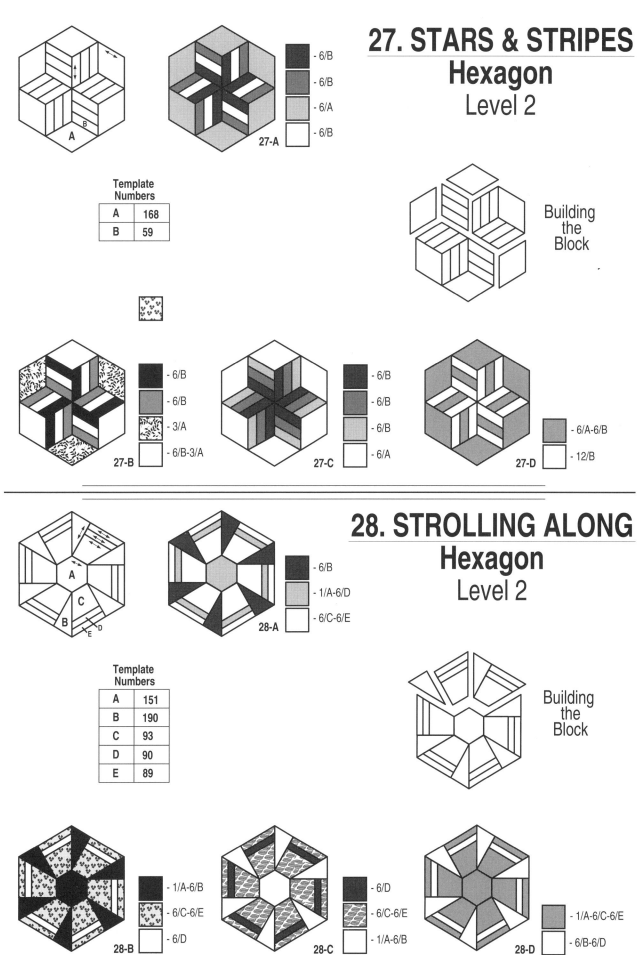

27. STARS & STRIPES
Hexagon
Level 2

27-A

- 6/B
- 6/B
- 6/A
- 6/B

Template
Numbers

A	168
B	59

Building
the
Block

27-B

- 6/B
- 6/B
- 3/A
- 6/B-3/A

27-C

- 6/B
- 6/B
- 6/B
- 6/A

27-D

- 6/A-6/B
- 12/B

28. STROLLING ALONG
Hexagon
Level 2

28-A

- 6/B
- 1/A-6/D
- 6/C-6/E

Template
Numbers

A	151
B	190
C	93
D	90
E	89

Building
the
Block

28-B

- 1/A-6/B
- 6/C-6/E
- 6/D

28-C

- 6/D
- 6/C-6/E
- 1/A-6/B

28-D

- 1/A-6/C-6/E
- 6/B-6/D

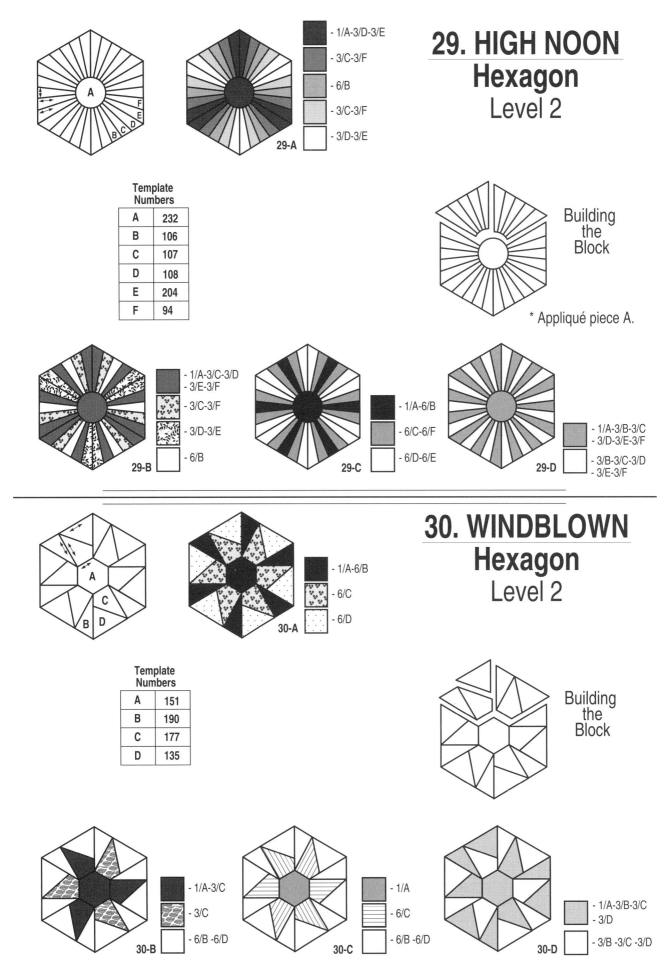

29. HIGH NOON
Hexagon
Level 2

29-A
- 1/A-3/D-3/E
- 3/C-3/F
- 6/B
- 3/C-3/F
- 3/D-3/E

Template Numbers

A	232
B	106
C	107
D	108
E	204
F	94

Building the Block

* Appliqué piece A.

29-B
- 1/A-3/C-3/D-3/E-3/F
- 3/C-3/F
- 3/D-3/E
- 6/B

29-C
- 1/A-6/B
- 6/C-6/F
- 6/D-6/E

29-D
- 1/A-3/B-3/C-3/D-3/E-3/F
- 3/B-3/C-3/D-3/E-3/F

30. WINDBLOWN
Hexagon
Level 2

30-A
- 1/A-6/B
- 6/C
- 6/D

Template Numbers

A	151
B	190
C	177
D	135

Building the Block

30-B
- 1/A-3/C
- 3/C
- 6/B -6/D

30-C
- 1/A
- 6/C
- 6/B -6/D

30-D
- 1/A-3/B-3/C
- 3/D
- 3/B -3/C -3/D

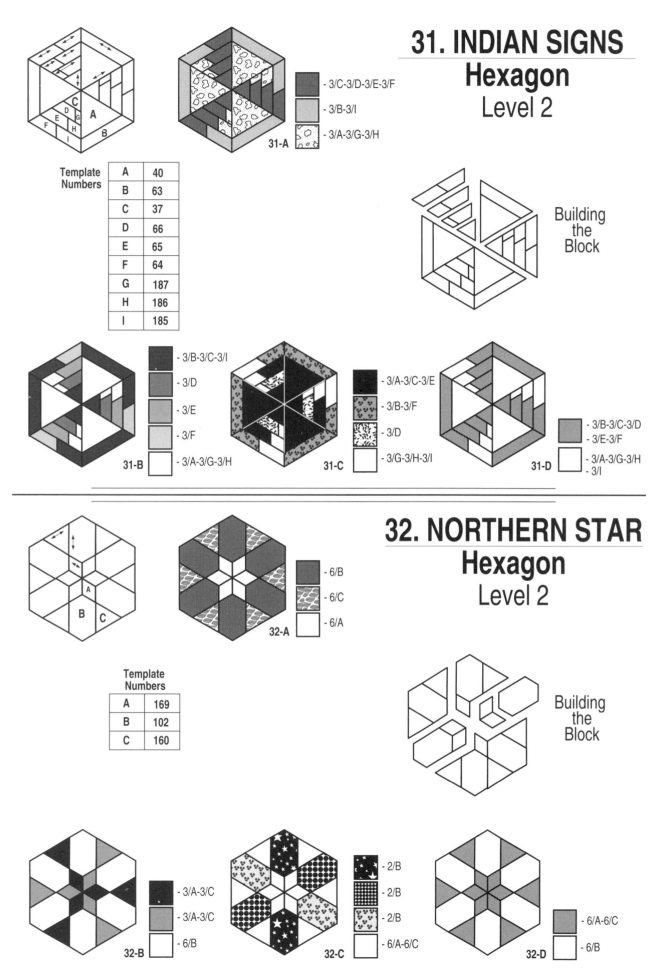

31. INDIAN SIGNS
Hexagon
Level 2

31-A
- 3/C-3/D-3/E-3/F
- 3/B-3/I
- 3/A-3/G-3/H

Template Numbers		
A	40
B	63
C	37
D	66
E	65
F	64
G	187
H	186
I	185

Building the Block

31-B
- 3/B-3/C-3/I
- 3/D
- 3/E
- 3/F
- 3/A-3/G-3/H

31-C
- 3/A-3/C-3/E
- 3/B-3/F
- 3/D
- 3/G-3/H-3/I

31-D
- 3/B-3/C-3/D
- 3/E-3/F
- 3/A-3/G-3/H
- 3/I

32. NORTHERN STAR
Hexagon
Level 2

32-A
- 6/B
- 6/C
- 6/A

Template Numbers	
A	169
B	102
C	160

Building the Block

32-B
- 3/A-3/C
- 3/A-3/C
- 6/B

32-C
- 2/B
- 2/B
- 2/B
- 6/A-6/C

32-D
- 6/A-6/C
- 6/B

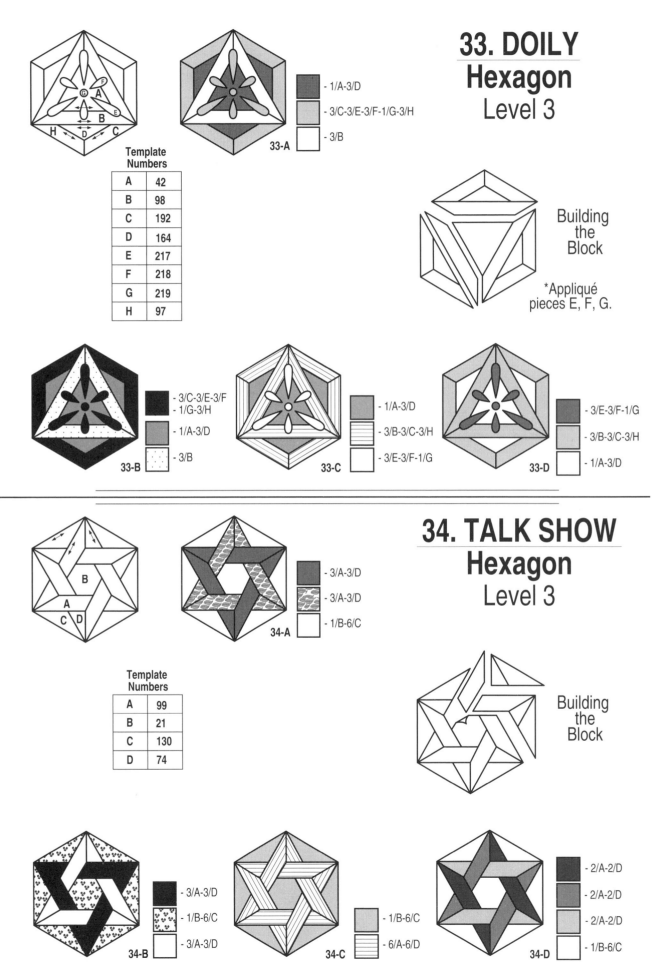

33. DOILY
Hexagon
Level 3

33-A
- 1/A-3/D
- 3/C-3/E-3/F-1/G-3/H
- 3/B

Template Numbers

A	42
B	98
C	192
D	164
E	217
F	218
G	219
H	97

Building the Block

*Appliqué pieces E, F, G.

33-B
- 3/C-3/E-3/F-1/G-3/H
- 1/A-3/D
- 3/B

33-C
- 1/A-3/D
- 3/B-3/C-3/H
- 3/E-3/F-1/G

33-D
- 3/E-3/F-1/G
- 3/B-3/C-3/H
- 1/A-3/D

34. TALK SHOW
Hexagon
Level 3

34-A
- 3/A-3/D
- 3/A-3/D
- 1/B-6/C

Template Numbers

A	99
B	21
C	130
D	74

Building the Block

34-B
- 3/A-3/D
- 1/B-6/C
- 3/A-3/D

34-C
- 1/B-6/C
- 6/A-6/D

34-D
- 2/A-2/D
- 2/A-2/D
- 2/A-2/D
- 1/B-6/C

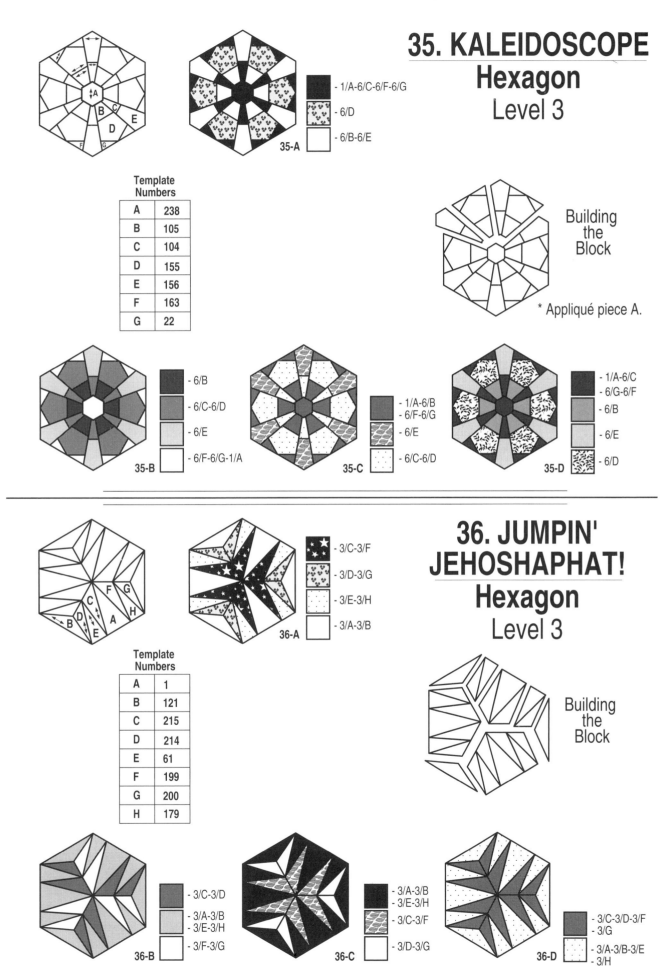

35. KALEIDOSCOPE
Hexagon
Level 3

35-A
- 1/A-6/C-6/F-6/G
- 6/D
- 6/B-6/E

Template Numbers

A	238
B	105
C	104
D	155
E	156
F	163
G	22

Building the Block

* Appliqué piece A.

35-B
- 6/B
- 6/C-6/D
- 6/E
- 6/F-6/G-1/A

35-C
- 1/A-6/B
- 6/F-6/G
- 6/E
- 6/C-6/D

35-D
- 1/A-6/C
- 6/G-6/F
- 6/B
- 6/E
- 6/D

36. JUMPIN' JEHOSHAPHAT!
Hexagon
Level 3

36-A
- 3/C-3/F
- 3/D-3/G
- 3/E-3/H
- 3/A-3/B

Template Numbers

A	1
B	121
C	215
D	214
E	61
F	199
G	200
H	179

Building the Block

36-B
- 3/C-3/D
- 3/A-3/B
- 3/E-3/H
- 3/F-3/G

36-C
- 3/A-3/B
- 3/E-3/H
- 3/C-3/F
- 3/D-3/G

36-D
- 3/C-3/D-3/F
- 3/G
- 3/A-3/B-3/E
- 3/H

144 OCTAGON QUILT BLOCKS

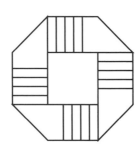

1. GOING UP

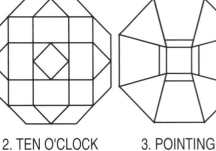

2. TEN O'CLOCK

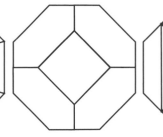

3. POINTING THE WAY

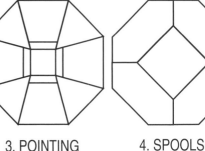

4. SPOOLS

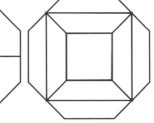

5. ON THE SQUARE

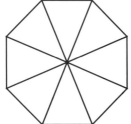

6. BIG WHEEL

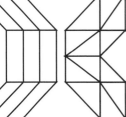

7. BOX O' FUN

8. LAZY SQUARE

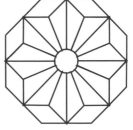

9. PRIMROSE

10. SUNFLOWER

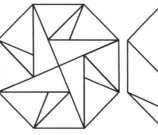

11. FOURTH OF JULY

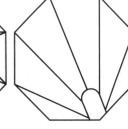

12. PEACOCK

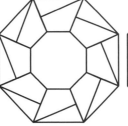

13. HOT DIGGITY!

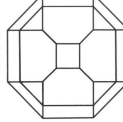

14. CROSSROADS

15. HURRICANE

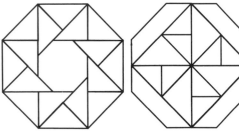

16. HOLDING HANDS

17. FLYING FLAGS

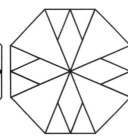

18. GOOD LUCK

19. HOLLYWOOD STAR

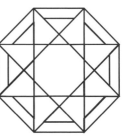

20. PRETTY STAR

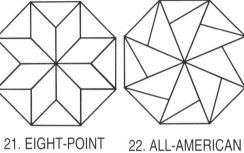

21. EIGHT-POINT
STAR

22. ALL-AMERICAN

23. HALLOWEEN

24. HAPPINESS

25. STAR BURST

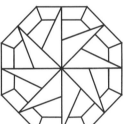

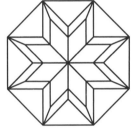

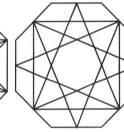

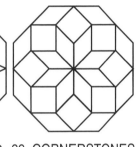

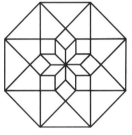

26. WHEELIES

27. CHRISTMAS STAR

28. FLIPPIN' STARS

29. CORNERSTONES

30. DOUBLE STAR

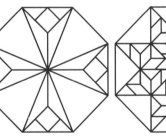

31. FAIRY BLOSSOMS

32. BIRDS IN FLIGHT

33. FAIRY WINGS

34. WINGS

35. FAIRY BOX

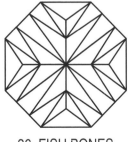

36. FISH BONES

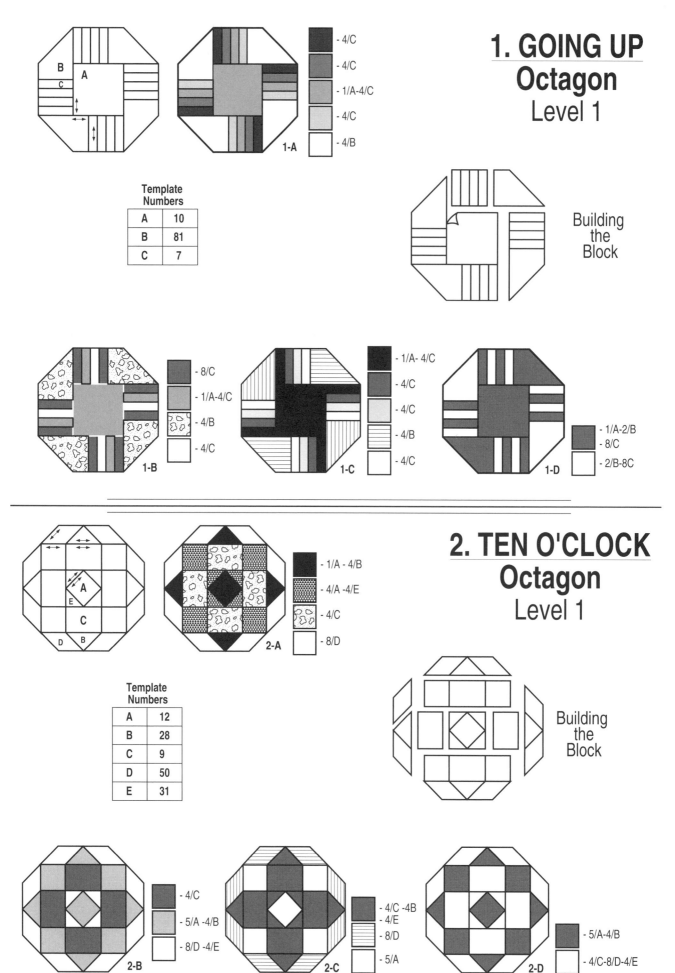

1. GOING UP
Octagon
Level 1

1-A

- 4/C
- 4/C
- 1/A-4/C
- 4/C
- 4/B

Template Numbers

A	10
B	81
C	7

Building the Block

1-B

- 8/C
- 1/A-4/C
- 4/B
- 4/C

1-C

- 1/A- 4/C
- 4/C
- 4/C
- 4/B
- 4/C

1-D

- 1/A-2/B
- 8/C
- 2/B-8C

2. TEN O'CLOCK
Octagon
Level 1

2-A

- 1/A - 4/B
- 4/A -4/E
- 4/C
- 8/D

Template Numbers

A	12
B	28
C	9
D	50
E	31

Building the Block

2-B

- 4/C
- 5/A -4/B
- 8/D -4/E

2-C

- 4/C -4B
- 4/E
- 8/D
- 5/A

2-D

- 5/A-4/B
- 4/C-8/D-4/E

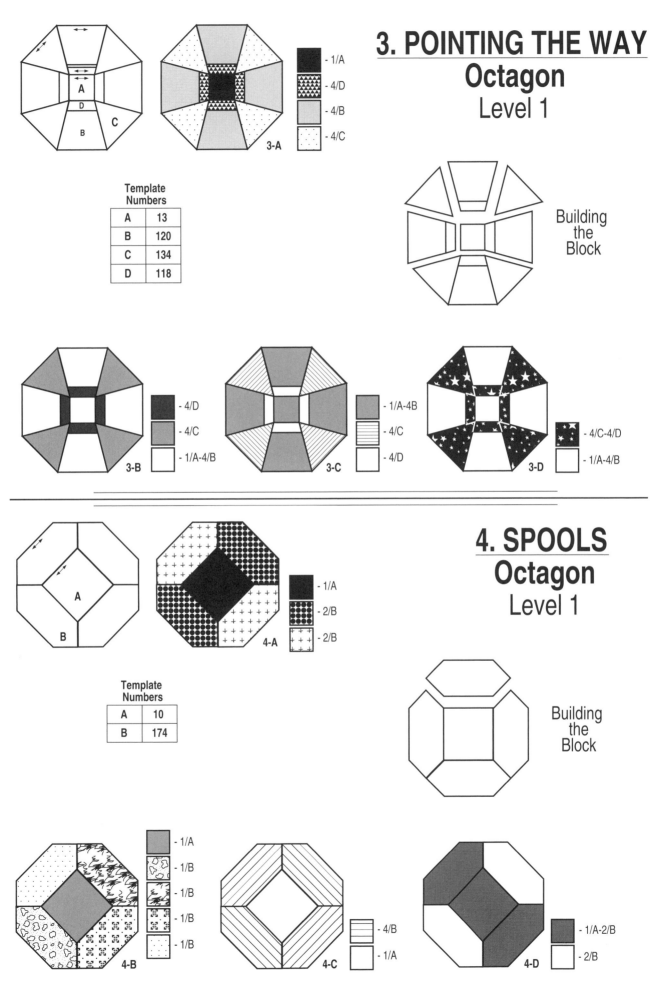

3. POINTING THE WAY
Octagon
Level 1

Building the Block

Template Numbers

A	13
B	120
C	134
D	118

3-A
- 1/A
- 4/D
- 4/B
- 4/C

3-B
- 4/D
- 4/C
- 1/A-4/B

3-C
- 1/A-4B
- 4/C
- 4/D

3-D
- 4/C-4/D
- 1/A-4/B

4. SPOOLS
Octagon
Level 1

Building the Block

Template Numbers

A	10
B	174

4-A
- 1/A
- 2/B
- 2/B

4-B
- 1/A
- 1/B
- 1/B
- 1/B
- 1/B

4-C
- 4/B
- 1/A

4-D
- 1/A-2/B
- 2/B

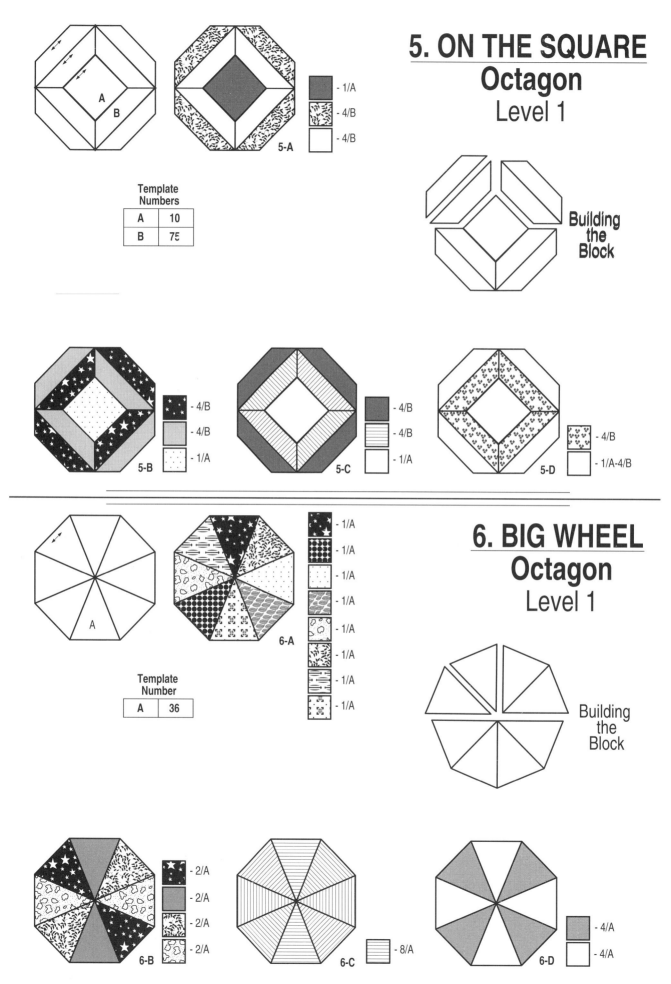

5. ON THE SQUARE
Octagon
Level 1

5-A

| - 1/A |
| - 4/B |
| - 4/B |

Template
Numbers

A	10
B	75

Building
the
Block

5-B

| - 4/B |
| - 4/B |
| - 1/A |

5-C

| - 4/B |
| - 4/B |
| - 1/A |

5-D

| - 4/B |
| - 1/A-4/B |

6. BIG WHEEL
Octagon
Level 1

6-A

| - 1/A |
| - 1/A |
| - 1/A |
| - 1/A |
| - 1/A |
| - 1/A |
| - 1/A |
| - 1/A |

Template
Number

A	36

Building
the
Block

6-B

| - 2/A |
| - 2/A |
| - 2/A |
| - 2/A |

6-C

| - 8/A |

6-D

| - 4/A |
| - 4/A |

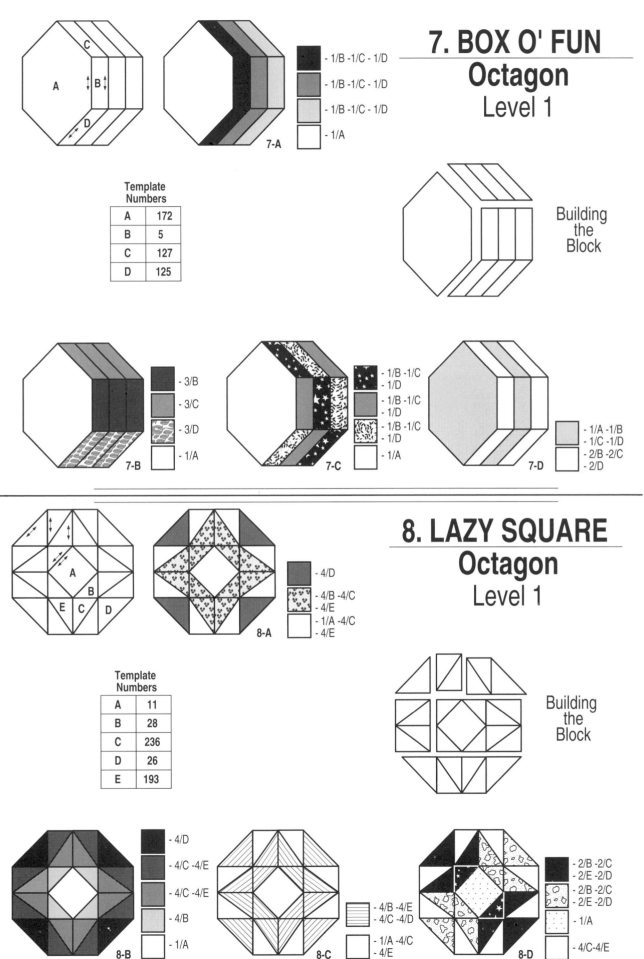

7. BOX O' FUN
Octagon
Level 1

- 1/B -1/C - 1/D
- 1/B -1/C - 1/D
- 1/B -1/C - 1/D
- 1/A

7-A

Template Numbers

A	172
B	5
C	127
D	125

Building the Block

- 3/B
- 3/C
- 3/D
- 1/A

7-B

- 1/B -1/C - 1/D
- 1/B -1/C - 1/D
- 1/B -1/C - 1/D
- 1/A

7-C

- 1/A -1/B - 1/C -1/D
- 2/B -2/C
- 2/D

7-D

8. LAZY SQUARE
Octagon
Level 1

- 4/D
- 4/B -4/C - 4/E
- 1/A -4/C - 4/E

8-A

Template Numbers

A	11
B	28
C	236
D	26
E	193

Building the Block

- 4/D
- 4/C -4/E
- 4/C -4/E
- 4/B
- 1/A

8-B

- 4/B -4/E
- 4/C -4/D
- 1/A -4/C - 4/E

8-C

- 2/B -2/C - 2/E -2/D
- 2/B -2/C - 2/E -2/D
- 1/A
- 4/C-4/E

8-D

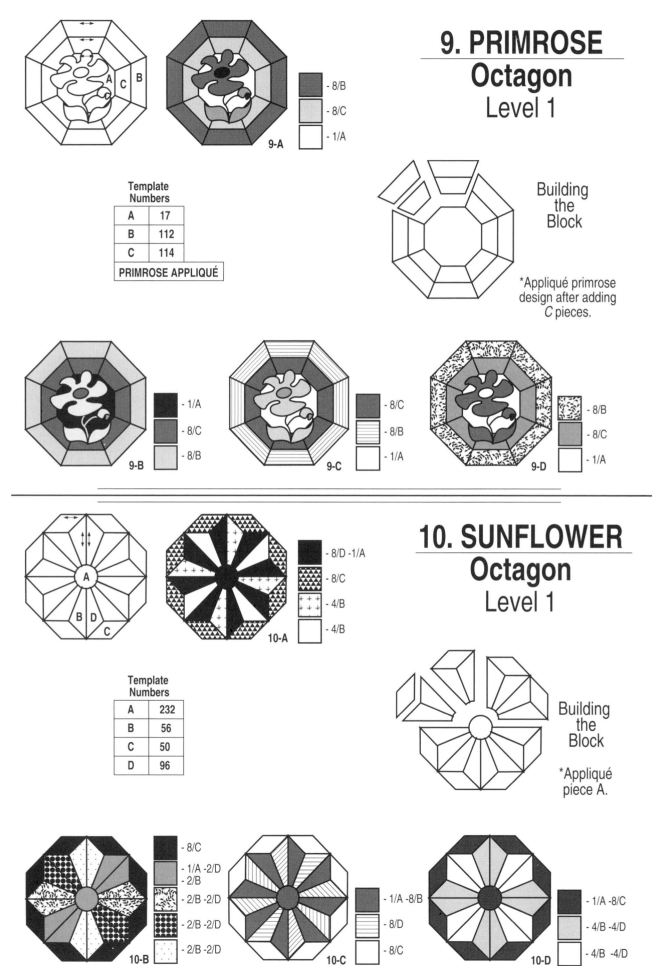

9. PRIMROSE
Octagon
Level 1

9-A

- 8/B
- 8/C
- 1/A

Template Numbers	
A	17
B	112
C	114
PRIMROSE APPLIQUÉ	

Building the Block

*Appliqué primrose design after adding *C* pieces.

9-B

- 1/A
- 8/C
- 8/B

9-C

- 8/C
- 8/B
- 1/A

9-D

- 8/B
- 8/C
- 1/A

10. SUNFLOWER
Octagon
Level 1

10-A

- 8/D -1/A
- 8/C
- 4/B
- 4/B

Template Numbers	
A	232
B	56
C	50
D	96

Building the Block

*Appliqué piece A.

10-B

- 8/C
- 1/A -2/D 2/B
- 2/B -2/D
- 2/B -2/D
- 2/B -2/D

10-C

- 1/A -8/B
- 8/D
- 8/C

10-D

- 1/A -8/C
- 4/B -4/D
- 4/B -4/D

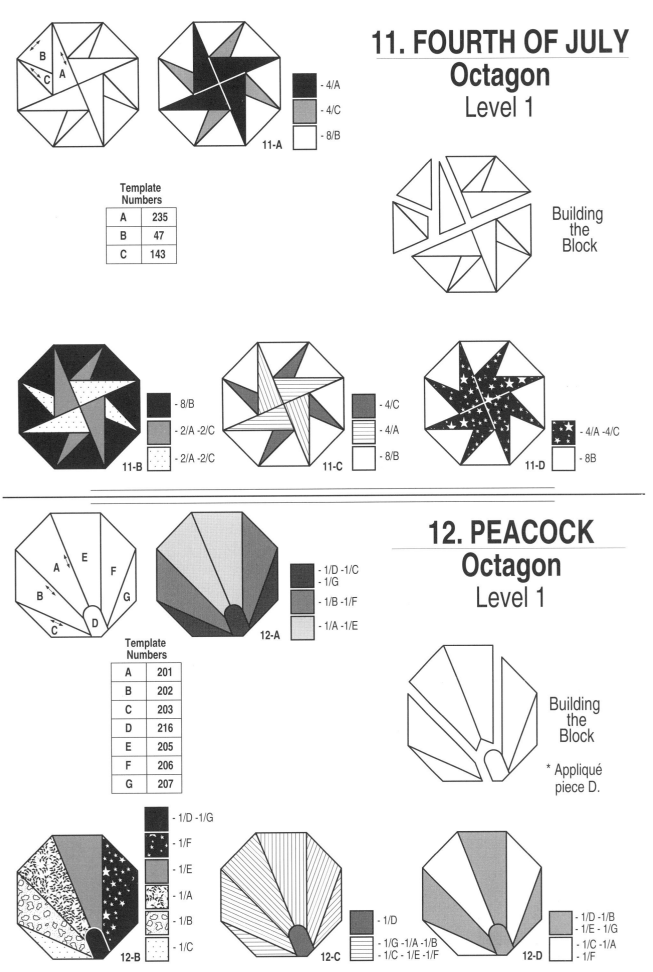

11. FOURTH OF JULY
Octagon
Level 1

- 4/A
- 4/C
- 8/B

11-A

Template Numbers

A	235
B	47
C	143

Building the Block

11-B
- 8/B
- 2/A -2/C
- 2/A -2/C

11-C
- 4/C
- 4/A
- 8/B

11-D
- 4/A -4/C
- 8B

12. PEACOCK
Octagon
Level 1

12-A
- 1/D -1/C
- 1/G
- 1/B -1/F
- 1/A -1/E

Template Numbers

A	201
B	202
C	203
D	216
E	205
F	206
G	207

Building the Block

* Appliqué piece D.

12-B
- 1/D -1/G
- 1/F
- 1/E
- 1/A
- 1/B
- 1/C

12-C
- 1/D
- 1/G -1/A -1/B
- 1/C - 1/E -1/F

12-D
- 1/D -1/B
- 1/E - 1/G
- 1/C -1/A
- 1/F

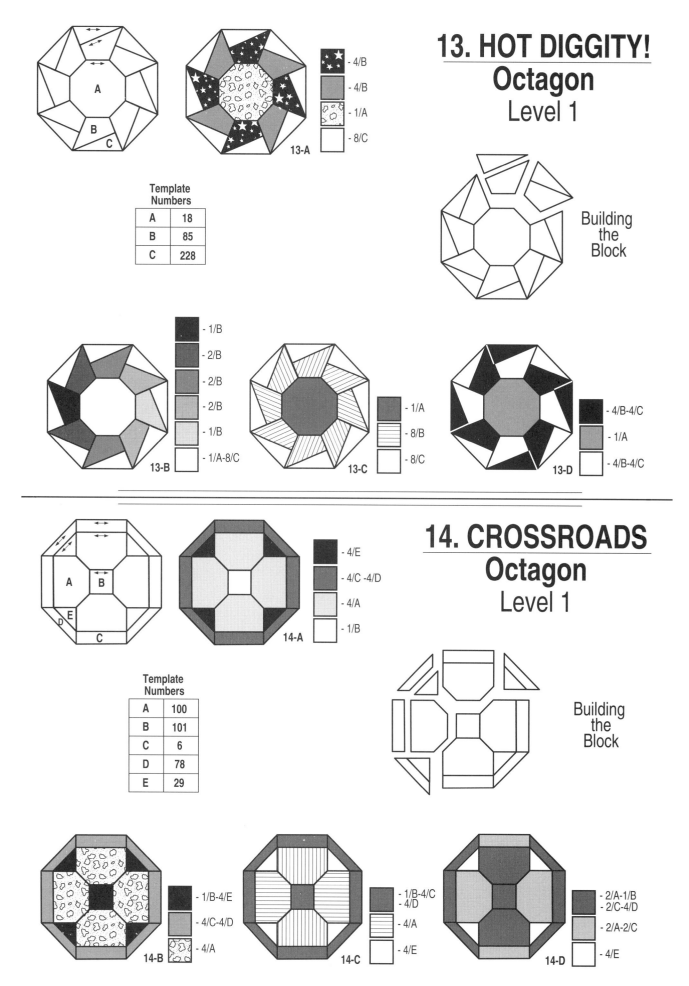

13. HOT DIGGITY!
Octagon
Level 1

- 4/B
- 4/B
- 1/A
- 8/C

13-A

Template Numbers

A	18
B	85
C	228

Building the Block

- 1/B
- 2/B
- 2/B
- 2/B
- 1/B
- 1/A-8/C

13-B

- 1/A
- 8/B
- 8/C

13-C

- 4/B-4/C
- 1/A
- 4/B-4/C

13-D

14. CROSSROADS
Octagon
Level 1

- 4/E
- 4/C -4/D
- 4/A
- 1/B

14-A

Template Numbers

A	100
B	101
C	6
D	78
E	29

Building the Block

- 1/B-4/E
- 4/C-4/D
- 4/A

14-B

- 1/B-4/C
- 4/D
- 4/A
- 4/E

14-C

- 2/A-1/B
- 2/C-4/D
- 2/A-2/C
- 4/E

14-D

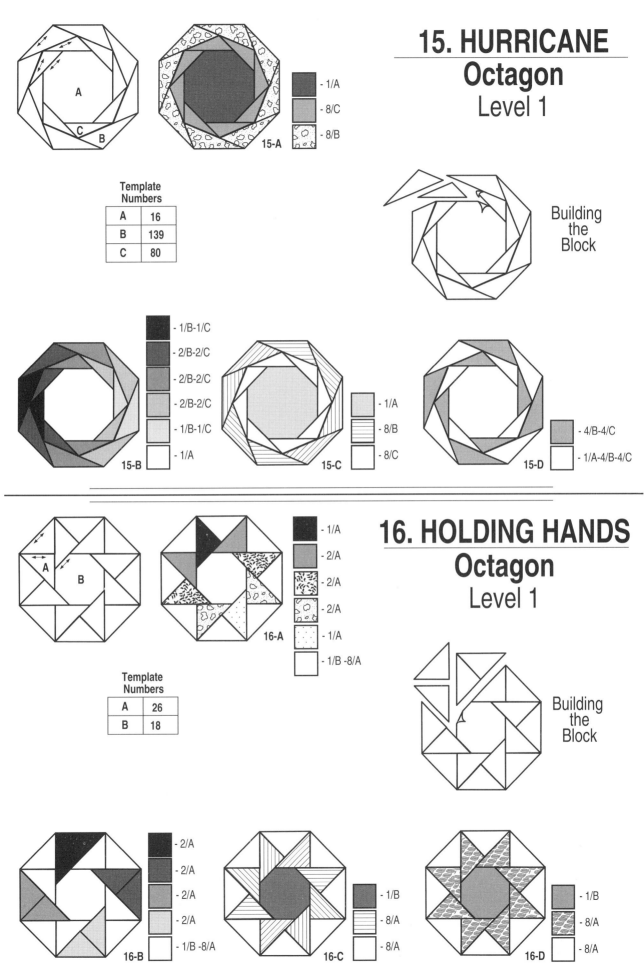

15. HURRICANE
Octagon
Level 1

15-A

- 1/A
- 8/C
- 8/B

Template Numbers

A	16
B	139
C	80

Building the Block

15-B

- 1/B-1/C
- 2/B-2/C
- 2/B-2/C
- 2/B-2/C
- 1/B-1/C
- 1/A

15-C

- 1/A
- 8/B
- 8/C

15-D

- 4/B-4/C
- 1/A-4/B-4/C

16. HOLDING HANDS
Octagon
Level 1

16-A

- 1/A
- 2/A
- 2/A
- 2/A
- 1/A
- 1/B -8/A

Template Numbers

A	26
B	18

Building the Block

16-B

- 2/A
- 2/A
- 2/A
- 2/A
- 1/B -8/A

16-C

- 1/B
- 8/A
- 8/A

16-D

- 1/B
- 8/A
- 8/A

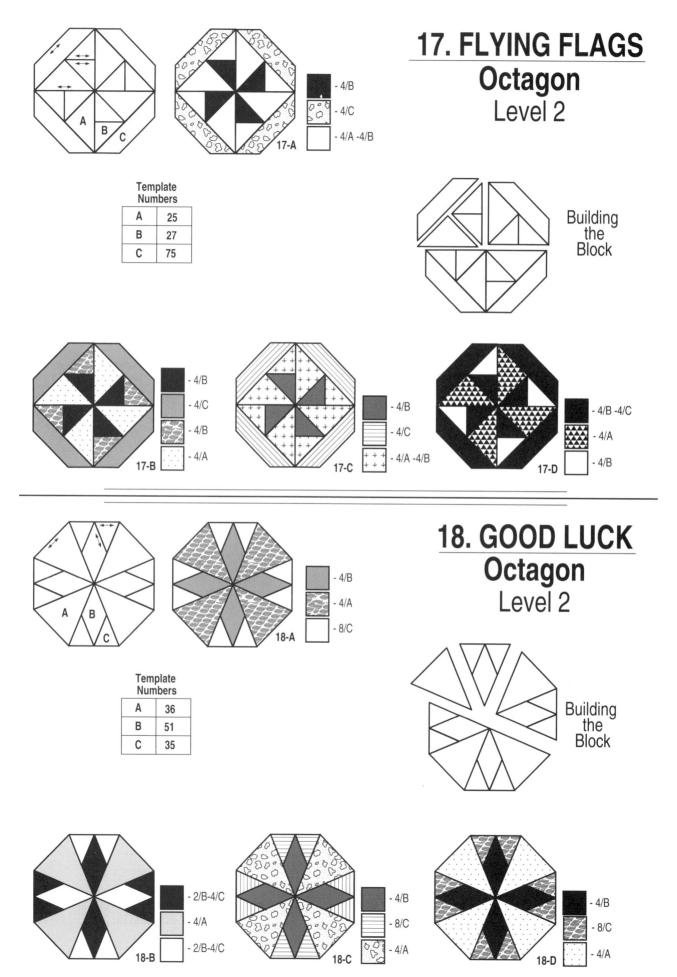

17. FLYING FLAGS
Octagon
Level 2

Template
Numbers

A	25
B	27
C	75

- 4/B
- 4/C
- 4/A -4/B

17-A

Building
the
Block

- 4/B
- 4/C
- 4/B
- 4/A

17-B

- 4/B
- 4/C
- 4/A -4/B

17-C

- 4/B -4/C
- 4/A
- 4/B

17-D

18. GOOD LUCK
Octagon
Level 2

Template
Numbers

A	36
B	51
C	35

- 4/B
- 4/A
- 8/C

18-A

Building
the
Block

- 2/B-4/C
- 4/A
- 2/B-4/C

18-B

- 4/B
- 8/C
- 4/A

18-C

- 4/B
- 8/C
- 4/A

18-D

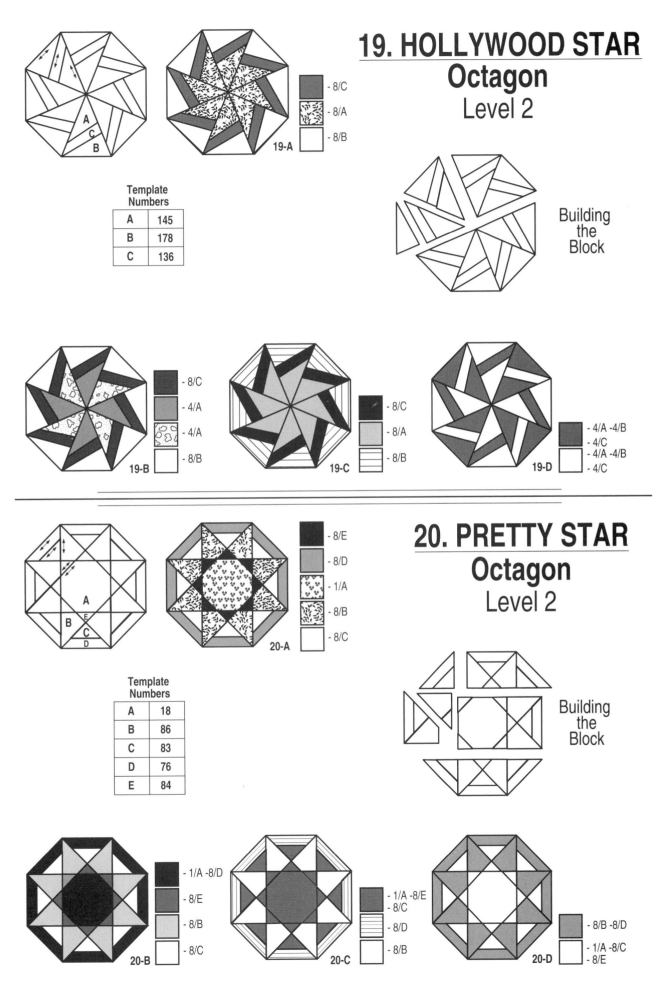

19. HOLLYWOOD STAR
Octagon
Level 2

- 8/C
- 8/A
- 8/B

19-A

Template Numbers

A	145
B	178
C	136

Building the Block

- 8/C
- 4/A
- 4/A
- 8/B

19-B

- 8/C
- 8/A
- 8/B

19-C

- 4/A -4/B
- 4/C
- 4/A -4/B
- 4/C

19-D

20. PRETTY STAR
Octagon
Level 2

- 8/E
- 8/D
- 1/A
- 8/B
- 8/C

20-A

Template Numbers

A	18
B	86
C	83
D	76
E	84

Building the Block

- 1/A -8/D
- 8/E
- 8/B
- 8/C

20-B

- 1/A -8/E
- 8/C
- 8/D
- 8/B

20-C

- 8/B -8/D
- 1/A -8/C
- 8/E

20-D

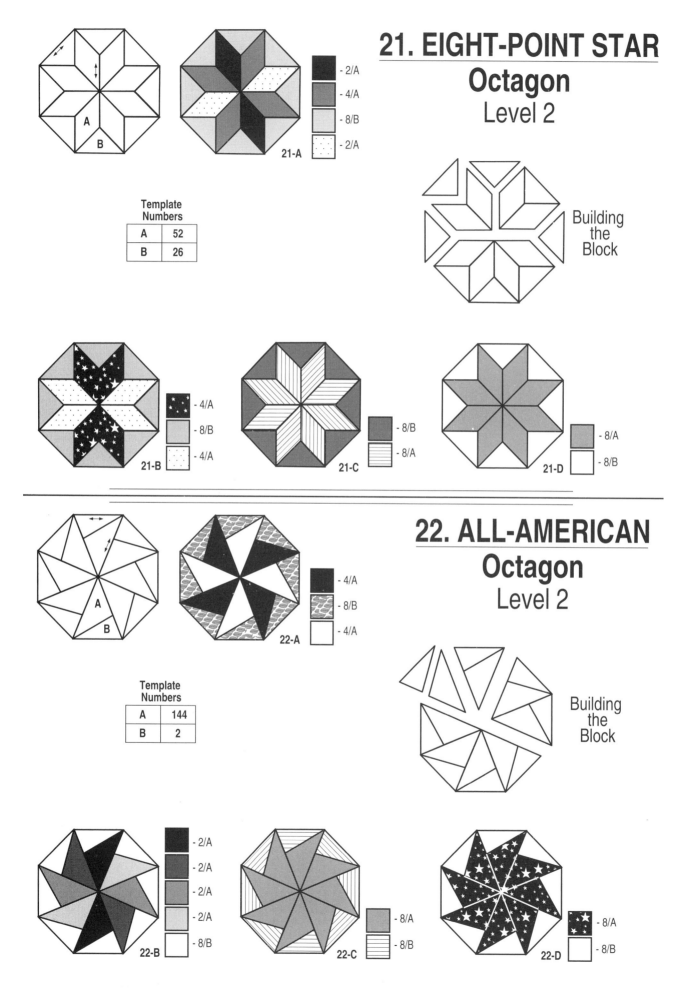

21. EIGHT-POINT STAR
Octagon
Level 2

- 2/A
- 4/A
- 8/B
- 2/A

Template Numbers

A	52
B	26

Building the Block

21-A

21-B
- 4/A
- 8/B
- 4/A

21-C
- 8/B
- 8/A

21-D
- 8/A
- 8/B

22. ALL-AMERICAN
Octagon
Level 2

22-A
- 4/A
- 8/B
- 4/A

Template Numbers

A	144
B	2

Building the Block

22-B
- 2/A
- 2/A
- 2/A
- 2/A
- 8/B

22-C
- 8/A
- 8/B

22-D
- 8/A
- 8/B

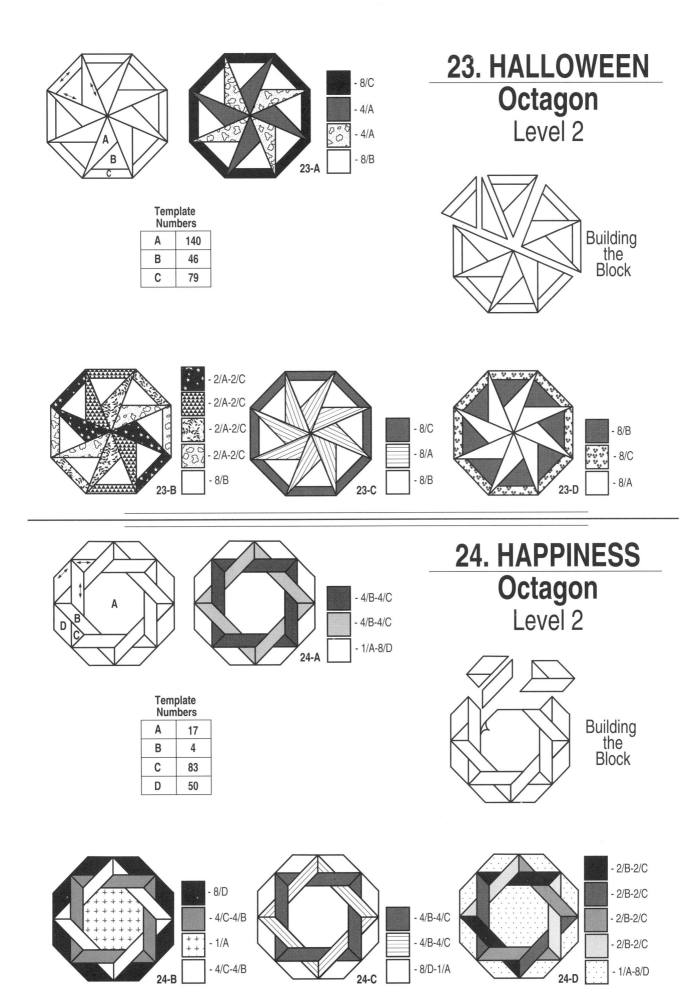

23. HALLOWEEN
Octagon
Level 2

- 8/C
- 4/A
- 4/A
- 8/B

23-A

Building the Block

Template Numbers

A	140
B	46
C	79

- 2/A-2/C
- 2/A-2/C
- 2/A-2/C
- 2/A-2/C
- 8/B

23-B

- 8/C
- 8/A
- 8/B

23-C

- 8/B
- 8/C
- 8/A

23-D

24. HAPPINESS
Octagon
Level 2

- 4/B-4/C
- 4/B-4/C
- 1/A-8/D

24-A

Building the Block

Template Numbers

A	17
B	4
C	83
D	50

- 8/D
- 4/C-4/B
- 1/A
- 4/C-4/B

24-B

- 4/B-4/C
- 4/B-4/C
- 8/D-1/A

24-C

- 2/B-2/C
- 2/B-2/C
- 2/B-2/C
- 2/B-2/C
- 1/A-8/D

24-D

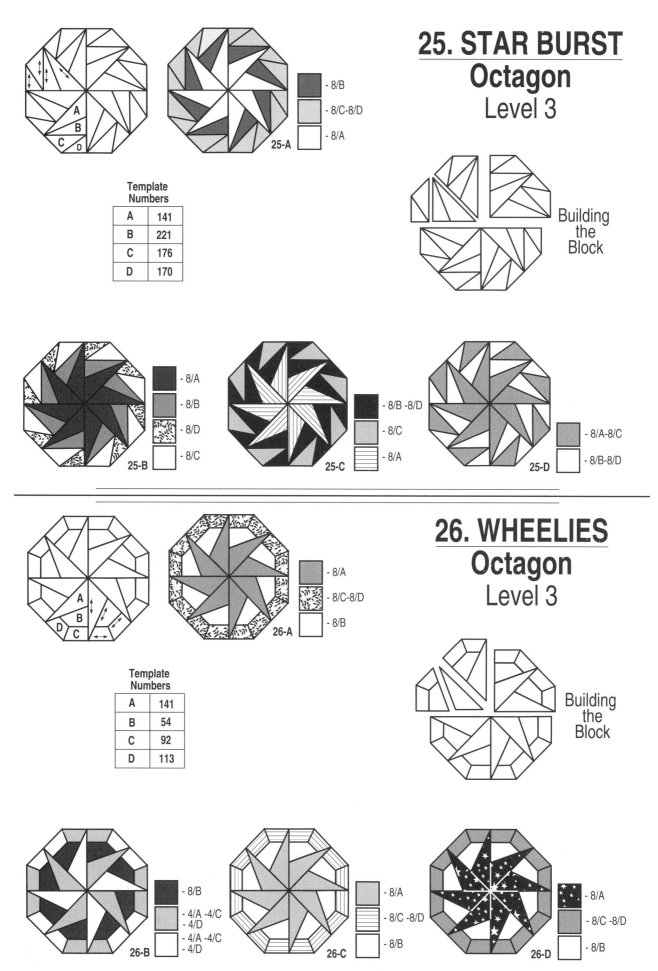

25. STAR BURST
Octagon
Level 3

- ■ - 8/B
- ▨ - 8/C-8/D
- □ - 8/A

25-A

Building the Block

Template Numbers

A	141
B	221
C	176
D	170

- ■ - 8/A
- ▨ - 8/B
- ▨ - 8/D
- □ - 8/C

25-B

- ■ - 8/B -8/D
- ▨ - 8/C
- ▤ - 8/A

25-C

- ▨ - 8/A-8/C
- □ - 8/B-8/D

25-D

26. WHEELIES
Octagon
Level 3

- ▨ - 8/A
- ▨ - 8/C-8/D
- □ - 8/B

26-A

Building the Block

Template Numbers

A	141
B	54
C	92
D	113

- ■ - 8/B
- ▨ - 4/A -4/C 4/D
- □ - 4/A -4/C 4/D

26-B

- ▨ - 8/A
- ▤ - 8/C -8/D
- □ - 8/B

26-C

- ■ - 8/A
- ▨ - 8/C -8/D
- □ - 8/B

26-D

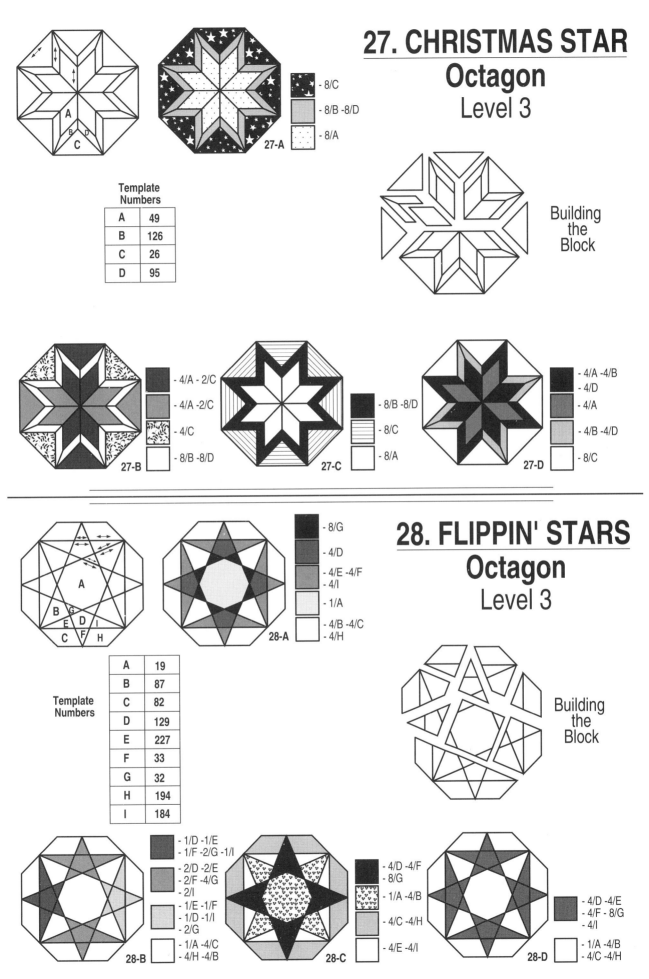

27. CHRISTMAS STAR
Octagon
Level 3

27-A

- 8/C
- 8/B -8/D
- 8/A

Building the Block

Template Numbers

A	49
B	126
C	26
D	95

27-B
- 4/A - 2/C
- 4/A -2/C
- 4/C
- 8/B -8/D

27-C
- 8/B -8/D
- 8/C
- 8/A

27-D
- 4/A -4/B
- 4/D
- 4/A
- 4/B -4/D
- 8/C

28. FLIPPIN' STARS
Octagon
Level 3

28-A
- 8/G
- 4/D
- 4/E -4/F
- 4/I
- 1/A
- 4/B -4/C
- 4/H

Building the Block

Template Numbers

A	19
B	87
C	82
D	129
E	227
F	33
G	32
H	194
I	184

28-B
- 1/D -1/E
- 1/F -2/G -1/I
- 2/D -2/E
- 2/F -4/G
- 2/I
- 1/E -1/F
- 1/D -1/I
- 2/G
- 1/A -4/C
- 4/H -4/B

28-C
- 4/D -4/F
- 8/G
- 1/A -4/B
- 4/C -4/H
- 4/E -4/I

28-D
- 4/D -4/E
- 4/F - 8/G
- 4/I
- 1/A -4/B
- 4/C -4/H

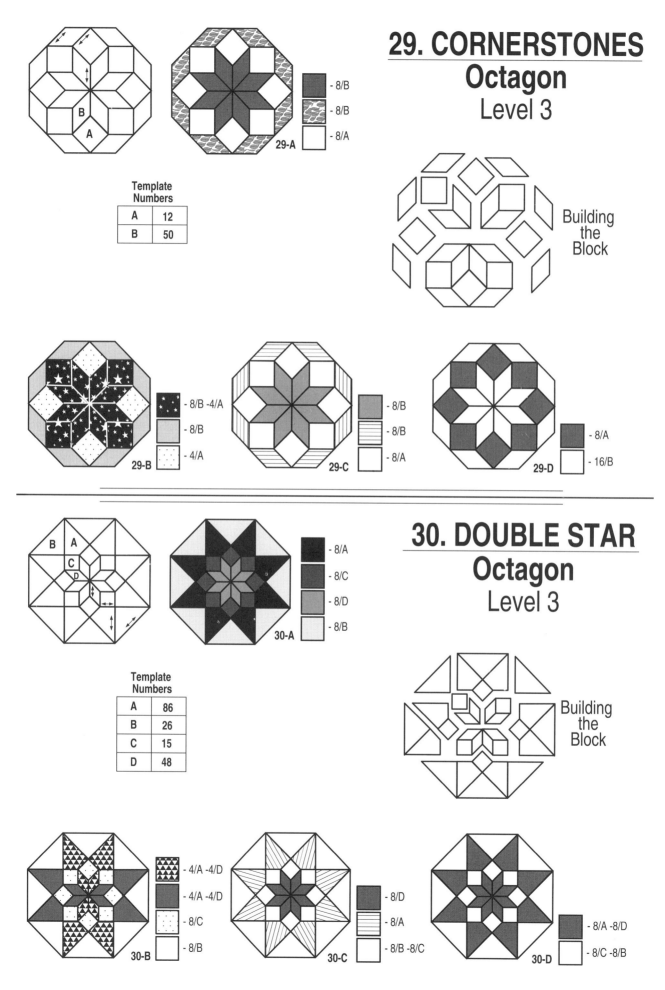

29. CORNERSTONES
Octagon
Level 3

Building the Block

29-A
- 8/B
- 8/B
- 8/A

Template Numbers

A	12
B	50

29-B
- 8/B -4/A
- 8/B
- 4/A

29-C
- 8/B
- 8/B
- 8/A

29-D
- 8/A
- 16/B

30. DOUBLE STAR
Octagon
Level 3

Building the Block

30-A
- 8/A
- 8/C
- 8/D
- 8/B

Template Numbers

A	86
B	26
C	15
D	48

30-B
- 4/A -4/D
- 4/A -4/D
- 8/C
- 8/B

30-C
- 8/D
- 8/A
- 8/B -8/C

30-D
- 8/A -8/D
- 8/C -8/B

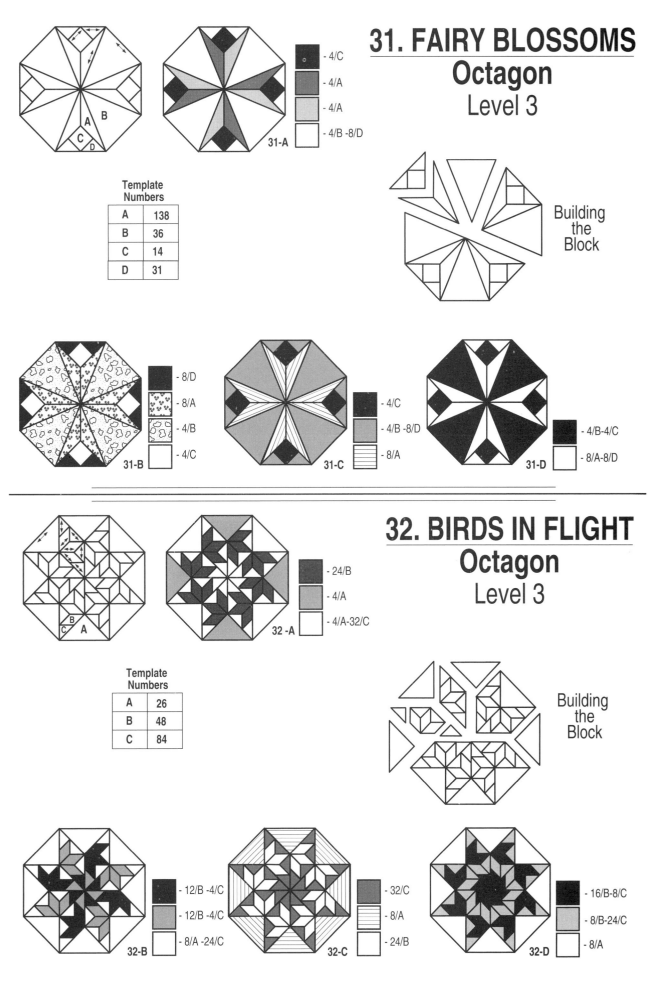

31. FAIRY BLOSSOMS
Octagon
Level 3

- 4/C
- 4/A
- 4/A
- 4/B -8/D

31-A

Template Numbers

A	138
B	36
C	14
D	31

Building the Block

- 8/D
- 8/A
- 4/B
- 4/C

31-B

- 4/C
- 4/B -8/D
- 8/A

31-C

- 4/B-4/C
- 8/A-8/D

31-D

32. BIRDS IN FLIGHT
Octagon
Level 3

- 24/B
- 4/A
- 4/A-32/C

32 -A

Template Numbers

A	26
B	48
C	84

Building the Block

- 12/B -4/C
- 12/B -4/C
- 8/A -24/C

32-B

- 32/C
- 8/A
- 24/B

32-C

- 16/B-8/C
- 8/B-24/C
- 8/A

32-D

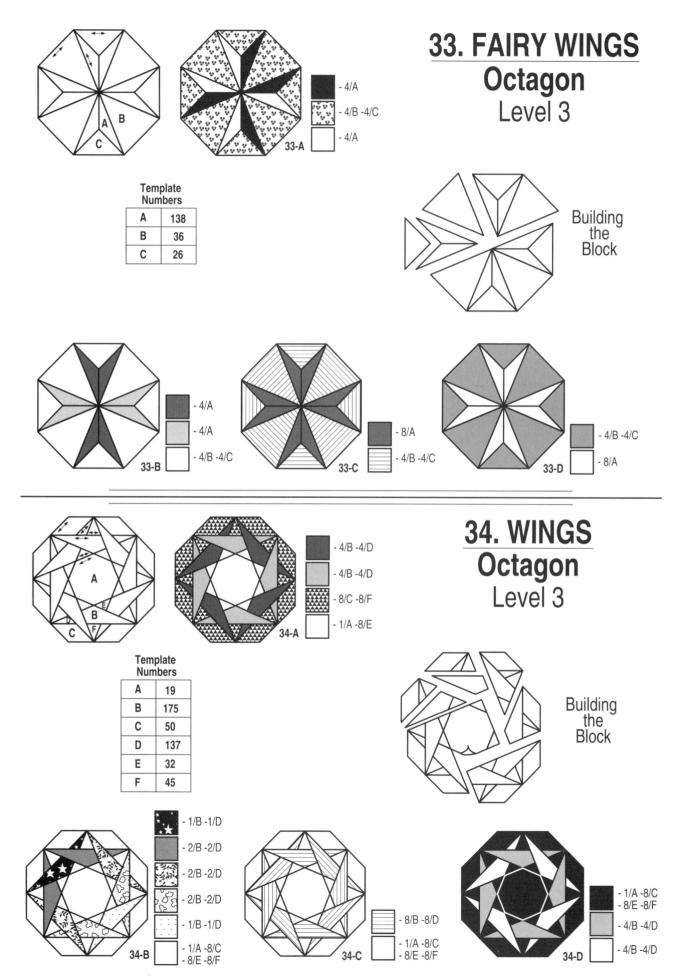

33. FAIRY WINGS
Octagon
Level 3

- 4/A
- 4/B -4/C
- 4/A

33-A

Template Numbers

A	138
B	36
C	26

Building the Block

- 4/A
- 4/A
- 4/B -4/C

33-B

- 8/A
- 4/B -4/C

33-C

- 4/B -4/C
- 8/A

33-D

34. WINGS
Octagon
Level 3

- 4/B -4/D
- 4/B -4/D
- 8/C -8/F
- 1/A -8/E

34-A

Template Numbers

A	19
B	175
C	50
D	137
E	32
F	45

Building the Block

- 1/B -1/D
- 2/B -2/D
- 2/B -2/D
- 2/B -2/D
- 1/B -1/D
- 1/A -8/C
- 8/E -8/F

34-B

- 8/B -8/D
- 1/A -8/C
- 8/E -8/F

34-C

- 1/A -8/C
- 8/E -8/F
- 4/B -4/D
- 4/B -4/D

34-D

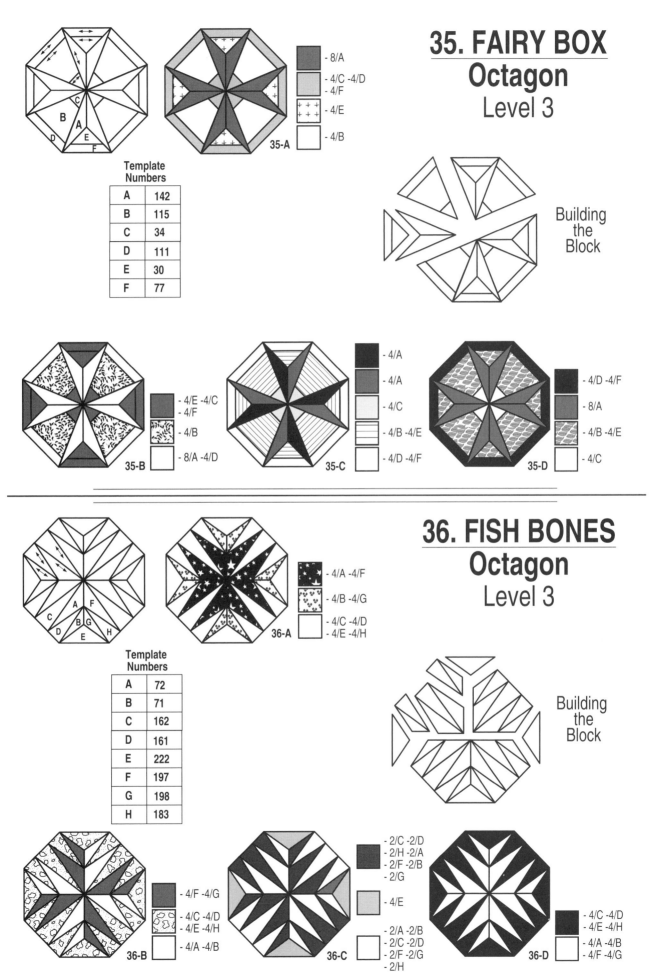

35. FAIRY BOX
Octagon
Level 3

35-A

- 8/A
- 4/C -4/D
- 4/F
- 4/E
- 4/B

Building
the
Block

Template Numbers	
A	142
B	115
C	34
D	111
E	30
F	77

35-B

- 4/E -4/C
- 4/F
- 4/B
- 8/A -4/D

35-C

- 4/A
- 4/A
- 4/C
- 4/B -4/E
- 4/D -4/F

35-D

- 4/D -4/F
- 8/A
- 4/B -4/E
- 4/C

36. FISH BONES
Octagon
Level 3

36-A

- 4/A -4/F
- 4/B -4/G
- 4/C -4/D
- 4/E -4/H

Building
the
Block

Template Numbers	
A	72
B	71
C	162
D	161
E	222
F	197
G	198
H	183

36-B

- 4/F -4/G
- 4/C -4/D
- 4/E -4/H
- 4/A -4/B

36-C

- 2/C -2/D
- 2/H -2/A
- 2/F -2/B
- 2/G
- 4/E
- 2/A -2/B
- 2/C -2/D
- 2/F -2/G
- 2/H

36-D

- 4/C -4/D
- 4/E -4/H
- 4/A -4/B
- 4/F -4/G

QUILT SETS AND OTHER BASICS

HEXAGON QUILT SET 1

	W	CR	T	D	Q	K	SQ	OB
Finished Size	39x39	50x53	75x98	83x106	90x106	107x108	65x62	54x66
NUMBER NEEDED								
Total Quilt Blocks	8	23	60	60	86	105	39	28
Across	3	5	7	7	9	11	7	5
Down	3	5	9	9	10	10	6	6
A—Half-Hexagons	2	4	6	6	8	10	6	4
B—Edge Pieces	4	8	16	16	18	18	10	10
C—Corner Pieces	2	2	2	2	2	2	2	2
D—Corner Pieces	2	2	2	2	2	2	2	2
CUT WIDTHS								
Width of Borders	7"	5"	10"	14"	10"	11"	5"	7"
Border—1	2½"	2"	2"	2½"	2"	2"	2"	2½"
Border—2	7"	5½"	3½"	4½"	3½"	3½"	5½"	7"
Border—3	—	—	7½"	2½"	7½"	2"	—	—
Border—4	—	—	—	8"	—	7"	—	—
YARDAGES								
A—Half-Hexagons	¼	¼	½	½	½	½	½	¼
B—Edge Pieces	⅛	¼	⅜	⅜	⅜	⅜	¼	¼
C & D—Corner Pieces	⅛	⅛	⅛	⅛	⅛	⅛	⅛	⅛
Border—1	½	½	¾	1	¾	¾	¾	¾
Border—2	1	1¼	1	1½	1¼	1½	1½	1¾
Border—3	—	—	2	1	2¼	¾	—	—
Border—4	—	—	—	2½	—	2¾	—	—
Backing	1⅜	3¼	6	8¼	8¼	10	4	3½

CUTTING BORDERS

• To determine outer border lengths, add 6 inches to the finished measurement of each side of quilt.
• Cut all other borders to finished measurement of each side of quilt.
• After sewing border in place, trim as needed.
• All outer borders include 1½ inches extra to turn back for finished edge.

YARDAGE NOTES

• All yardages include a small amount for shrinkage and waste.
• Yardages are for pieced borders, to conserve fabric. You may prefer an unpieced border, especially on wider borders. Use the longest side of your finished quilt to determine how many yards to buy.

PLANNING PAGE—HEXAGON SET 1

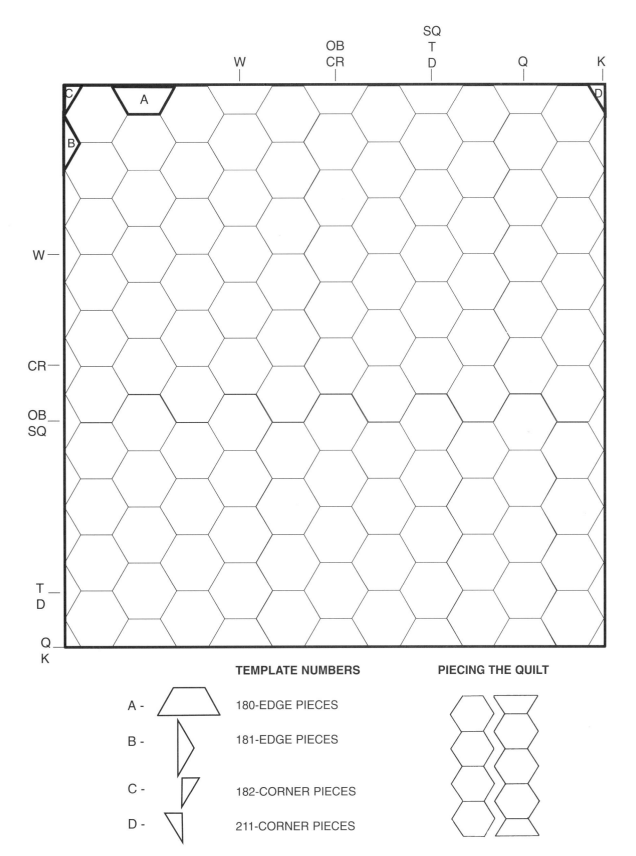

TEMPLATE NUMBERS

A - 180-EDGE PIECES

B - 181-EDGE PIECES

C - 182-CORNER PIECES

D - 211-CORNER PIECES

PIECING THE QUILT

HEXAGON QUILT SET 2

		W	CR	T	D	Q	K	SQ	OB
	Finished Size	44x40	50x53	72x100	84x102	88x106	108x106	68x68	64x74
NUMBER NEEDED	**Total Quilt Blocks**	8	18	41	50	50	68	39	32
	Across	3	4	5	6	6	8	6	5
	Down	3	5	9	9	9	9	7	7
	A—Half-Hexagons	2	4	8	8	8	8	6	6
	B—Lattice Blocks	14	34	80	98	98	134	76	62
	C—Edge Pieces	4	6	10	10	10	10	8	8
	D—Edge Pieces	4	6	10	10	10	10	8	8
CUT WIDTHS	**Width of Borders**	7"	5"	11"	12"	14"	14"	4"	7"
	Border—1	2½"	2"	2"	2"	2½"	2½"	1½"	2½"
	Border—2	7"	5½"	3½"	3½"	4½"	4½"	5"	7"
	Border—3	–	–	2"	2"	2½"	2½"	–	–
	Border—4	–	–	7"	8"	8"	8"	–	–
YARDAGES	A—Half-Hexagons	¼	¼	½	½	½	½	½	½
	B—Lattice Blocks	⅜	½	1¼	1½	1½	2	1	1
	C & D—Edge Pieces	⅛	⅛	¼	¼	¼	¼	¼	¼
	Border—1	½	½	¾	¾	1	1	½	¾
	Border—2	1	1¼	1	1¼	1½	1¾	1¼	1¾
	Border—3	–	–	¾	¾	1	1	–	–
	Border—4	–	–	2	2½	2½	3	–	–
	Backing	1½	3¼	6	8	8¼	10	4¼	4

CUTTING BORDERS

• To determine outer border lengths, add 6 inches to the finished measurement of each side of quilt.
• Cut all other borders to finished measurement of each side of quilt.
• After sewing border in place, trim as needed.
• All outer borders include 1½ inches extra to turn back for finished edge.

OPTIONS

See OPTIONAL PIECED LATTICE BLOCKS on page 128.

YARDAGE NOTES

• All yardages include a small amount for shrinkage and waste.
• Yardages are for pieced borders, to conserve fabric. You may prefer an unpieced border, especially on wider borders. Use the longest side of your finished quilt to determine how many yards to buy.

PLANNING PAGE—HEXAGON SET 2

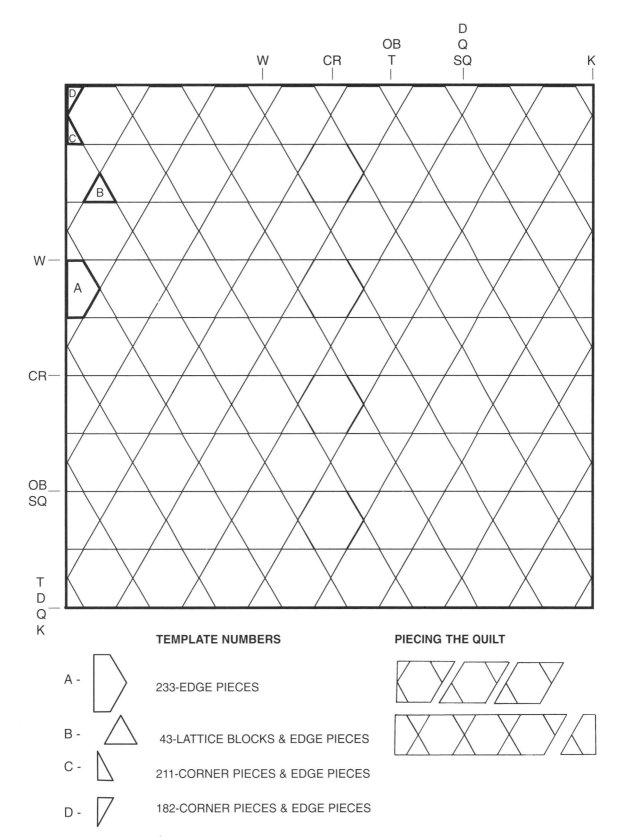

TEMPLATE NUMBERS

A - 233—EDGE PIECES

B - 43—LATTICE BLOCKS & EDGE PIECES

C - 211—CORNER PIECES & EDGE PIECES

D - 182—CORNER PIECES & EDGE PIECES

PIECING THE QUILT

HEXAGON QUILT SET 3

		W	CR	T	D	Q	K	SQ	OB
	Finished Size	42x38	57x53	71x104	88x102	94x108	106x111	62x63	58x67
NUMBER NEEDED	**Total Quilt Blocks**	8	23	43	60	60	77	23	28
	Across	3	5	5	7	7	9	5	5
	Down	3	5	9	9	9	9	5	6
	A–Half-Hexagons	2	4	4	6	6	8	4	4
	B–Lattice Corners	20	54	102	136	136	170	54	66
	C–Lattice Strips	31	82	150	203	203	256	82	99
	D–Edge Pieces	4	8	16	16	16	16	8	10
	E–Corner Pieces	2	2	2	2	2	2	2	2
	F–Corner Pieces	2	2	2	2	2	2	2	2
CUT WIDTHS	**Width of Borders**	5"	3"	10"	9"	12"	11"	8"	6"
	Border–1	1½"	5"	1½"	1½"	1½"	1½"	1½"	1½"
	Border–2	6"	–	3½"	3"	3½"	3½"	2½"	7"
	Border–3	–	–	1½"	1½"	1½"	1½"	1½"	–
	Border–4	–	–	6½"	6"	8½"	7½"	5½"	–
YARDAGES	A–Half-Hexagons	¼	¼	¼	½	½	½	¼	¼
	B–Lattice Corners	⅛	⅛	¼	¼	¼	⅜	⅛	⅛
	C–Lattice Strips	¼	⅝	1	1½	1½	1¾	¾	1
	D–Edge Pieces	⅛	¼	⅜	⅜	⅜	⅜	¼	¼
	E & F–Corner Pieces	⅛	⅛	⅛	⅛	⅛	⅛	⅛	⅛
	Border–1	½	1¼	½	¾	¾	¾	½	½
	Border–2	¾	–	1¼	1	1¼	1½	¾	1¾
	Border–3	–	–	½	¾	¾	¾	½	–
	Border–4	–	–	2¼	2¼	2¾	2¾	1¼	–
	Backing	1½	3½	6¼	8	8¼	10	4	3¾

CUTTING BORDERS

• To determine outer border lengths, add 6 inches to the finished measurement of each side of quilt.
• Cut all other borders to finished measurement of each side of quilt.
• After sewing border in place, trim as needed.
• All outer borders include 1½ inches extra to turn back for finished edge.

YARDAGE NOTES

• All yardages include a small amount for shrinkage and waste.
• Yardages are for pieced borders, to conserve fabric. You may prefer an unpieced border, especially on wider borders. Use the longest side of your finished quilt to determine how many yards to buy.

PLANNING PAGE – HEXAGON SET 3

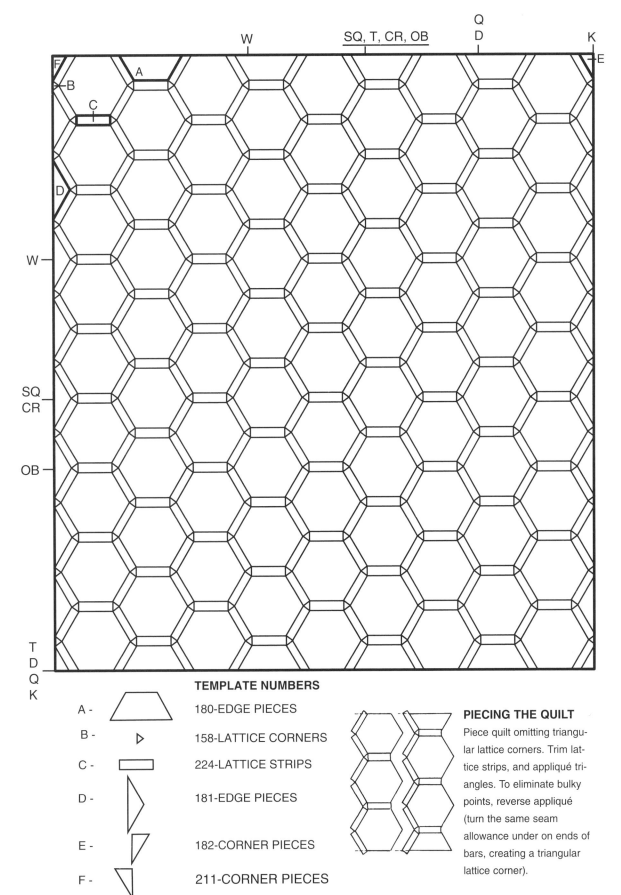

TEMPLATE NUMBERS

A - 180-EDGE PIECES

B - 158-LATTICE CORNERS

C - 224-LATTICE STRIPS

D - 181-EDGE PIECES

E - 182-CORNER PIECES

F - 211-CORNER PIECES

PIECING THE QUILT

Piece quilt omitting triangular lattice corners. Trim lattice strips, and appliqué triangles. To eliminate bulky points, reverse appliqué (turn the same seam allowance under on ends of bars, creating a triangular lattice corner).

OCTAGON QUILT SET 1

		W	CR	T	D	Q	K	SQ	OB
	Finished Size	40x40	50x60	72x102	84x104	88x108	108x108	64x64	64x74
NUMBER NEEDED	**Total Quilt Blocks**	9	20	40	48	48	64	25	30
	Across	3	4	5	6	6	8	5	5
	Down	3	5	8	8	8	8	5	6
	A—Lattice Blocks	4	12	28	35	35	49	16	20
	B—Edge Pieces	8	14	22	24	24	28	16	18
	C—Corner Pieces	4	4	4	4	4	4	4	4
CUT WIDTHS	**Width of Borders**	5"	5"	11"	12"	14"	14"	7"	7"
	Border—1	2"	2"	2"	2"	2½"	2½"	2½"	2½"
	Border—2	5½"	5½"	3½"	3½"	4½"	4½"	7"	7"
	Border—3	–	–	2"	2"	2½"	2½"	–	–
	Border—4	–	–	7"	8"	8"	8"	–	–
YARDAGES	A—Lattice Blocks	¼	⅜	⅝	¾	¾	1	½	½
	B—Edge Pieces	¼	¼	½	½	½	½	¼	⅜
	C—Corner Pieces	⅛	⅛	⅛	⅛	⅛	⅛	⅛	⅛
	Border—1	½	½	¾	¾	1	1	¾	¾
	Border—2	¾	1¼	1	1¼	1½	1¾	1¾	1¾
	Border—3	–	–	¾	¾	1	1	–	–
	Border—4	–	–	2	2½	2½	3	–	–
	Backing	1¼	3	6	8	8¼	10	4	4

CUTTING BORDERS

• To determine outer border lengths, add 6 inches to the finished measurement of each side of quilt.

• Cut all other borders to finished measurement of each side of quilt.

• After sewing border in place, trim as needed.

• All outer borders include 1½ inches extra to turn back for finished edge.

YARDAGE NOTES

• All yardages include a small amount for shrinkage and waste.

• Yardages are for pieced borders, to conserve fabric. You may prefer an unpieced border, especially on wider borders. Use the longest side of your finished quilt to determine how many yards to buy.

OPTIONS

See OPTIONAL PIECED LATTICE BLOCKS on page 128.

PLANNING PAGE—OCTAGON SET 1

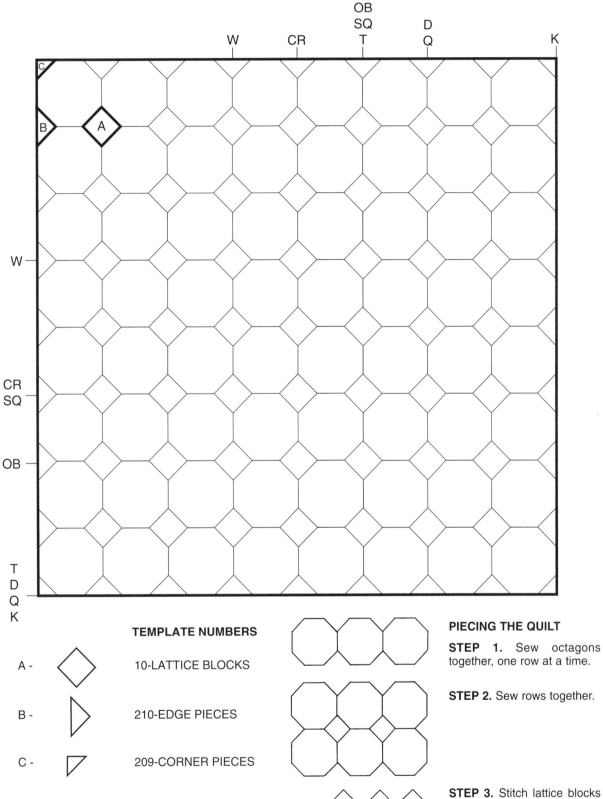

TEMPLATE NUMBERS

A - 10-LATTICE BLOCKS

B - 210-EDGE PIECES

C - 209-CORNER PIECES

PIECING THE QUILT

STEP 1. Sew octagons together, one row at a time.

STEP 2. Sew rows together.

STEP 3. Stitch lattice blocks in place and then add corner and edge pieces.

OCTAGON QUILT SET 2

		W	CR	T	D	Q	K	SQ	OB
	Finished Size	40x40	49x63	72x100	88x1042	92x106	108x108	64x64	58x72
NUMBER NEEDED	**Total Quilt Blocks**	5	18	39	50	50	61	25	18
	Across	2	3	4	5	5	6	4	3
	Down	2	4	6	6	6	6	4	4
	A—Lattice Blocks	4	17	38	49	49	60	24	17
	B—Edge Pieces	4	10	16	18	18	20	12	10
	C—Corner Pieces	4	4	4	4	4	4	4	4
CUT WIDTHS	**Width of Borders**	4"	5½"	10"	11"	13"	14"	6"	10"
	Border—1	1½"	1½"	2"	2"	2"	2½"	2½"	2"
	Border—2	5"	2"	3½"	3½"	4½"	4½"	6"	3½"
	Border—3	–	4½"	7½"	2"	2"	2½"	–	7½"
	Border—4	–	–	–	7"	8"	8"	–	–
YARDAGES	A—Lattice Blocks	¼	½	¾	1	1	1¼	½	½
	B—Edge Pieces	¼	¼	½	½	½	½	½	¼
	C—Corner Pieces	⅛	⅛	⅛	⅛	⅛	⅛	⅛	⅛
	Border—1	¼	½	¾	¾	¾	1	¾	½
	Border—2	¾	½	1	1¼	1½	1¾	1½	1
	Border—3	–	1	2	¾	¾	1	–	1¾
	Border—4	–	–	–	2¼	2½	3	–	–
	Backing	1⅜	3¼	6	8	8¼	10	4	3¾

CUTTING BORDERS

• To determine outer border lengths, add 6 inches to the finished measurement of each side of quilt.
• Cut all other borders to finished measurement of each side of quilt.
• After sewing border in place, trim as needed.
• All outer borders include 1½ inches extra to turn back for finished edge.

YARDAGE NOTES

• All yardages include a small amount for shrinkage and waste.
• Yardages are for pieced borders, to conserve fabric. You may prefer an unpieced border, especially on wider borders. Use the longest side of your finished quilt to determine how many yards to buy.

OPTIONS

See OPTIONAL PIECED LATTICE BLOCKS on page 128.

PLANNING PAGE — OCTAGON SET 2

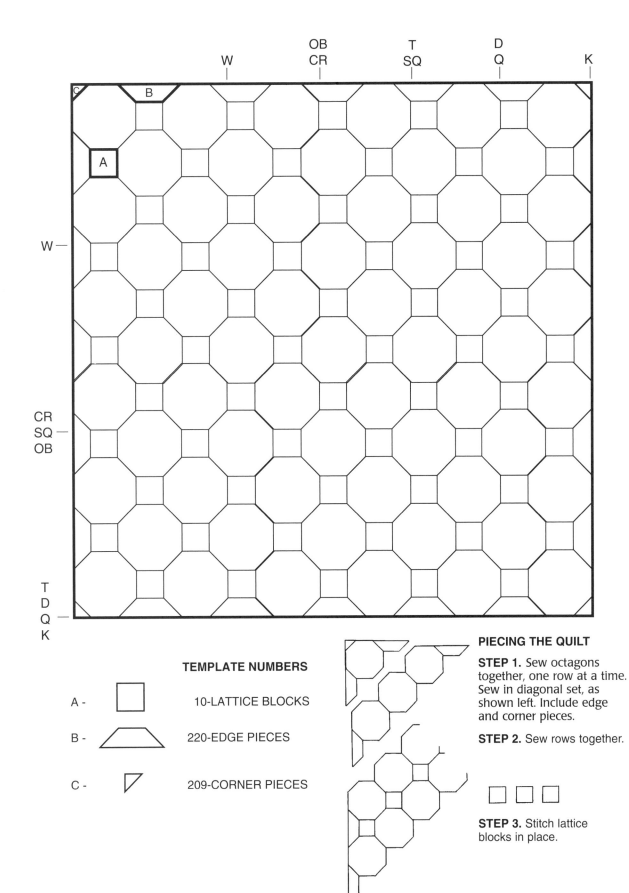

TEMPLATE NUMBERS

A - ⬜ 10-LATTICE BLOCKS

B - ⬭ 220-EDGE PIECES

C - ◺ 209-CORNER PIECES

PIECING THE QUILT

STEP 1. Sew octagons together, one row at a time. Sew in diagonal set, as shown left. Include edge and corner pieces.

STEP 2. Sew rows together.

STEP 3. Stitch lattice blocks in place.

OCTAGON QUILT SET 3

	W	CR	T	D	Q	K	SQ	OB
Finished Size	36x36	48x60	70x106	84x108	86x110	108x108	64x64	60x72
NUMBER NEEDED								
Total Quilt Blocks	4	12	28	35	35	49	16	20
Across	2	3	4	5	5	7	4	4
Down	2	4	7	7	7	7	4	5
A–Lattice Blocks	1	6	18	24	24	36	9	12
B–Lattice Pieces	12	36	76	92	92	124	46	56
C–Lattice Pieces	2	12	36	48	48	72	18	24
D–Edge Pieces	4	10	18	20	20	24	12	14
E–Corner Pieces	4	4	4	4	4	4	4	4
F–Lattice Strips	16	48	112	140	140	196	64	80
CUT WIDTHS								
Width of Borders	6"	6"	11"	12"	13"	12"	8"	6"
Border–1	2½"	2½"	2"	2"	2"	2"	2"	2½"
Border–2	6"	6"	3½"	3½"	4½"	3½"	3"	6"
Border–3	–	–	2"	2"	2"	2"	6"	–
Border–4	–	–	7"	8"	8"	8"	–	–
YARDAGES								
A–Lattice Blocks	¼	¼	½	½	½	¾	⅜	⅜
B–Lattice Pieces	⅛	⅜	⅝	¾	¾	1	½	½
C–Lattice Pieces	⅛	⅛	¼	⅜	⅜	½	⅛	¼
D–Edge Pieces	⅛	⅛	⅜	⅜	⅜	⅜	⅛	¼
E–Corner Pieces	⅛	⅛	⅛	⅛	⅛	⅛	⅛	⅛
F–Lattice Strips	⅛	¼	½	¾	¾	1	⅜	⅜
Border–1	½	¾	¾	¾	¾	¾	¾	¾
Border–2	¾	1½	1	1¼	1½	1½	1	1½
Border–3	–	–	¾	¾	¾	¾	1½	–
Border–4	–	–	2	2½	2½	3	–	–
Backing	1¼	3¼	6½	8¼	8½	10	4	3¾

CUTTING BORDERS
• To determine outer border lengths, add 6 inches to the finished measurement of each side of quilt.
• Cut all other borders to finished measurement of each side of quilt.
• After sewing border in place, trim as needed.
• All outer borders include 1½ inches extra to turn back for finished edge.

YARDAGE NOTES
• All yardages include a small amount for shrinkage and waste.
• Yardages are for pieced borders, to conserve fabric. You may prefer an unpieced border, especially on wider borders. Use the longest side of your finished quilt to determine how many yards to buy.

OPTIONS
See OPTIONAL PIECED LATTICE BLOCKS on page 128.

PLANNING PAGE — OCTAGON SET 3

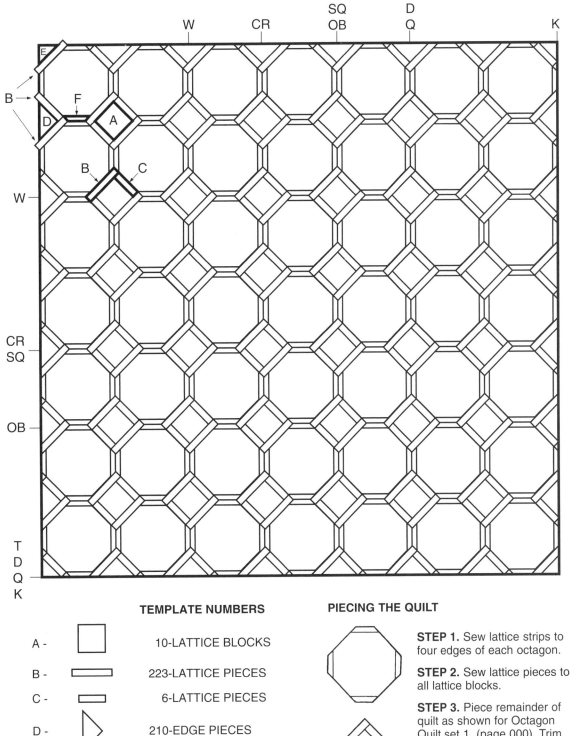

TEMPLATE NUMBERS

A - ☐ 10-LATTICE BLOCKS

B - ▭ 223-LATTICE PIECES

C - ▭ 6-LATTICE PIECES

D - ◁ 210-EDGE PIECES

E - ◹ 209-CORNER PIECES

F - ▱ 78-LATTICE STRIPS

PIECING THE QUILT

STEP 1. Sew lattice strips to four edges of each octagon.

STEP 2. Sew lattice pieces to all lattice blocks.

STEP 3. Piece remainder of quilt as shown for Octagon Quilt set 1. (page 000). Trim extending lattice strips.

OPTIONAL PIECED LATTICE BLOCKS

OPTIONAL LATTICE BLOCKS FOR HEXAGON QUILT SET 2

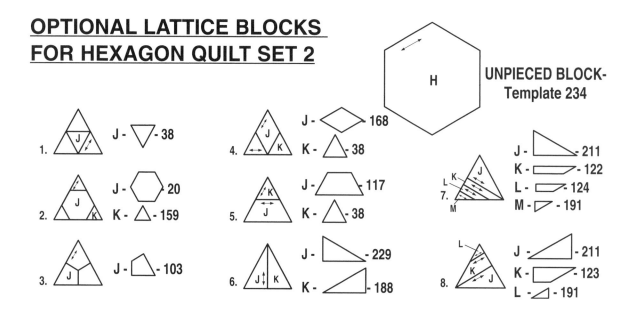

UNPIECED BLOCK-
Template 234

1. J - ▽ - 38
2. J - ⬡ - 20
   K - △ - 159
3. J - ⬠ - 103
4. J - ◇ - 168
   K - △ - 38
5. J - ⬭ - 117
   K - △ - 38
6. J - ◺ - 229
   K - ◹ - 188
7. J - ◹ - 211
   K - ▱ - 122
   L - ▱ - 124
   M - ◺ - 191
8. J - ◹ - 211
   K - ▱ - 123
   L - ◿ - 191

OPTIONAL LATTICE BLOCKS FOR OCTAGON QUILT SETS 1, 2 and 3

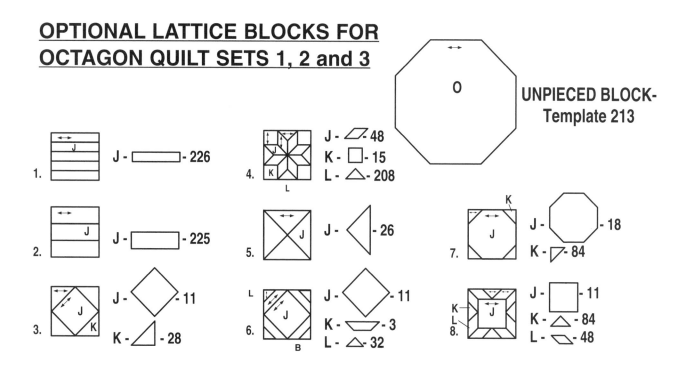

UNPIECED BLOCK-
Template 213

1. J - ▭ - 226
2. J - ▭ - 225
3. J - ◇ - 11
   K - ◺ - 28
4. J - ⬦ - 48
   K - ▢ - 15
   L - △ - 208
5. J - ◁ - 26
6. J - ◇ - 11
   K - ▱ - 3
   L - △ - 32
7. J - ⬡ - 18
   K - ◹ - 84
8. J - ▢ - 11
   K - △ - 84
   L - ⬦ - 48

BORDERS AND BACKING

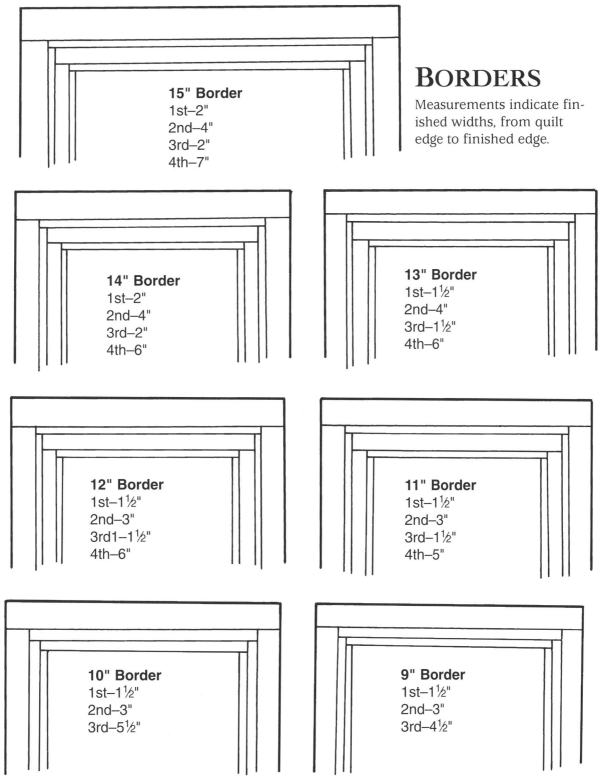

BORDERS

Measurements indicate finished widths, from quilt edge to finished edge.

15" Border
1st–2"
2nd–4"
3rd–2"
4th–7"

14" Border
1st–2"
2nd–4"
3rd–2"
4th–6"

13" Border
1st–1½"
2nd–4"
3rd–1½"
4th–6"

12" Border
1st–1½"
2nd–3"
3rd1–1½"
4th–6"

11" Border
1st–1½"
2nd–3"
3rd–1½"
4th–5"

10" Border
1st–1½"
2nd–3"
3rd–5½"

9" Border
1st–1½"
2nd–3"
3rd–4½"

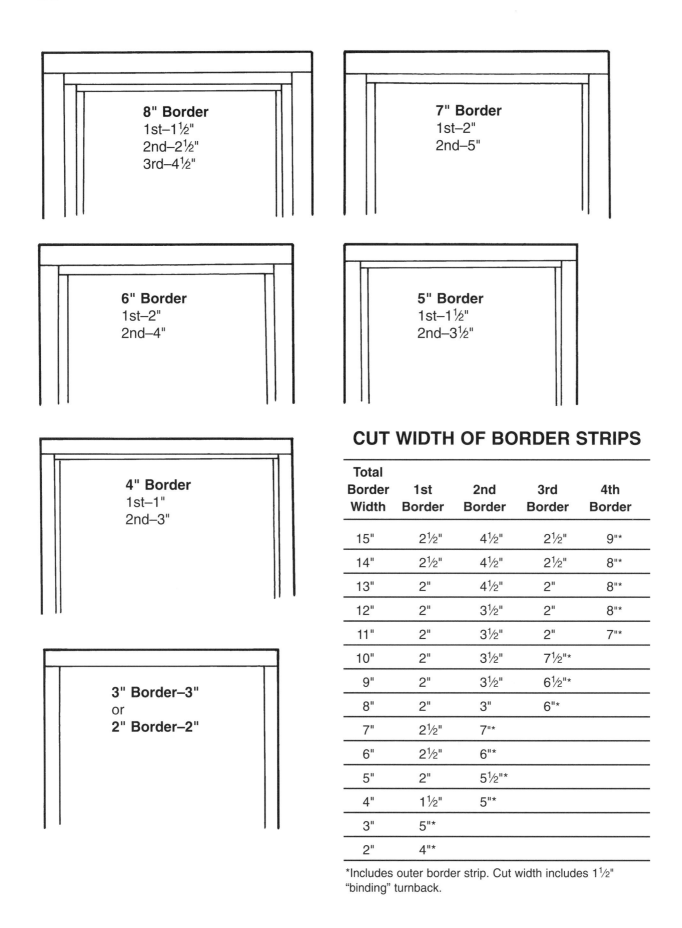

8" Border
1st–1½"
2nd–2½"
3rd–4½"

7" Border
1st–2"
2nd–5"

6" Border
1st–2"
2nd–4"

5" Border
1st–1½"
2nd–3½"

4" Border
1st–1"
2nd–3"

3" Border–3"
or
2" Border–2"

CUT WIDTH OF BORDER STRIPS

Total Border Width	1st Border	2nd Border	3rd Border	4th Border
15"	2½"	4½"	2½"	9"*
14"	2½"	4½"	2½"	8"*
13"	2"	4½"	2"	8"*
12"	2"	3½"	2"	8"*
11"	2"	3½"	2"	7"*
10"	2"	3½"	7½"*	
9"	2"	3½"	6½"*	
8"	2"	3"	6"*	
7"	2½"	7"*		
6"	2½"	6"*		
5"	2"	5½"*		
4"	1½"	5"*		
3"	5"*			
2"	4"*			

*Includes outer border strip. Cut width includes 1½" "binding" turnback.

YARDAGE AND PIECING GUIDES FOR BACKING

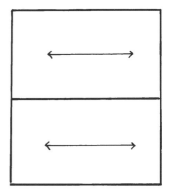

Crib: 3¼ yards.
Oblong tablecloth: 3¾ yards

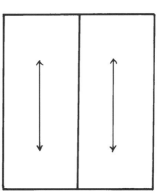

Twin: 6¾ yards.
Square tablecloth: 4 yards

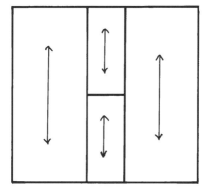

Double: 8½ yards.
Queen: 8½ yards

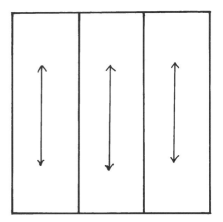

King: 10¼ yards.

Wall Hanging: No piecing needed.

Yardage includes small amounts for shrinkage and waste.

⟵————⟶ indicates lengthwise grain of fabric.

COPY, CUT AND PASTE FUN

All the pieces here as well as those in APPENDIX A: 144 HEXAGON QUILT BLOCKS and APPENDIX B: 144 OCTAGON QUILT BLOCKS have been designed to fit together. You may photocopy the pages, cut out the various pieces and use them to design your quilt.

Ready to copy, cut and paste? These are the tools that you'll need:

Scissors. Get a good comfy pair and reserve them for paper.

#2 Lead pencils. These are the only pencils that I use (I "see" better in grays than in color).

Colored pencils. Try a small set first to determine whether you enjoy playing in color. If you do, invest in a jumbo set. They're fun!

Pencil sharpener. You needn't get an electric one; a manual one works fine.

Egg carton bottoms. These are ideal for organizing small pieces of paper and can be stacked.

Pointed tweezers. These are great for picking up tiny pieces of paper.

Tack a Note. This is the same "nonglue" used on Post-it Notes. A glue stick works too, but a tacky stick allows you to use the pieces repeatedly.

Plastic pouch. Use this for stowing pencils, scissors and tweezers. Be sure to get one with holes so that you can put it in your three-ring binder.

Clear plastic pages with pockets. Get the type with holes to fit your three-ring binder and with pockets sized for slides. Use the pages for storing the quilt block cutouts.

Letraset. Letraset is a peel-off paper that you can use to fill areas with an allover design, such as flowers or dots. Ask for it at an art supply store. It's expensive, so you might want to use it only for making a final copy of your favorite design.

Donna's Hint

When you photocopy, keep these tips in mind:
• Photocopying a copy will result in distorted images, so always photocopy directly from the book. If this isn't possible, preserve your original copy for reuse. To protect the originals, you may want to use clear laminating paper or plastic page protectors.
• Some photocopy machines produce better copies than others do. Check your copies for distortion.
• If you reduce or enlarge anything, you must do the same for all the other pages that you use.

Donna's Hint

When designing your quilt, be careful not to put too many points together. What looks simple on paper may be a nightmare at the sewing machine. Try the following if needed:
• Stagger the heavily seamed areas. For example:
• Use quilt sets with unpieced lattice blocks or alternate pieced quilt blocks and some unpieced quilt blocks. For example:

COPY, CUT AND PASTE FUN INSTRUCTIONS

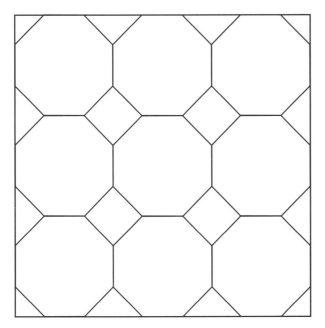

STEP 1. Photocopy the Play Pages (see following pages) of your favorite quilt sets.

STEP 3. Paste your favorite combinations of quilt blocks and quilt sets together. (*Hint:* Use the glue stick lightly so the photocopies can be used several times.)

Copy several times.

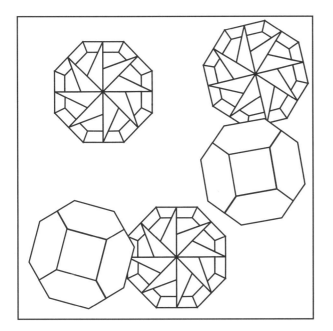

STEP 2. Photocopy your favorite hexagon or octagon quilt block design(s) from APPENDIX A or B several times.

Cut out the quilt blocks and arrange them on the copies of the quilt sets.

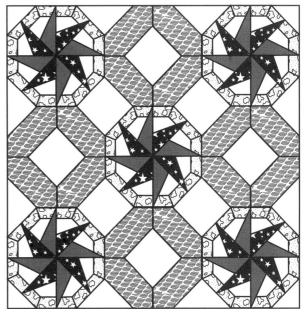

STEP 4. Use #2 lead pencils or colored pencils to color your design.

To design the entire quilt, refer to PART II: GETTING READY TO MAKE YOUR QUILT and APPENDIX C: QUILT SETS AND OTHER BASICS .

PLAY PAGE
HEXAGON QUILT SET 1

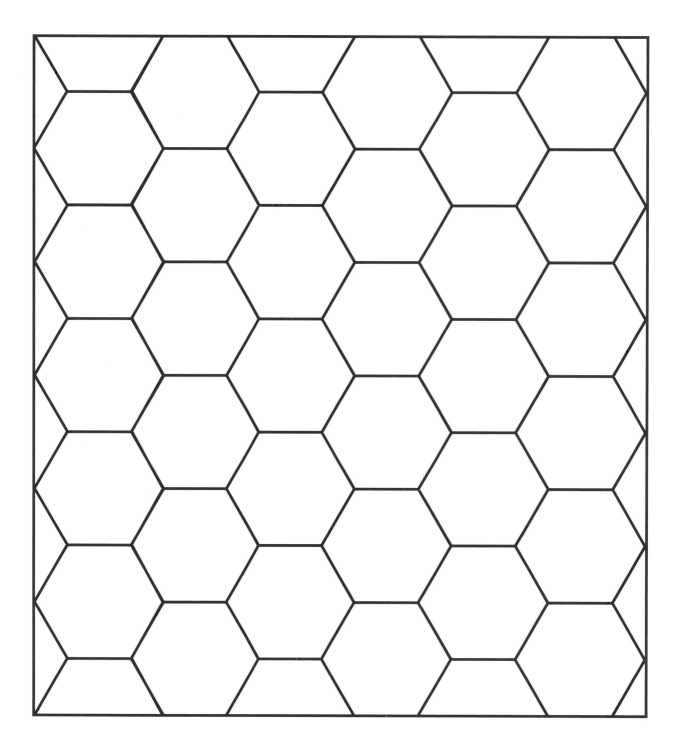

PLAY PAGE
HEXAGON QUILT SET 2

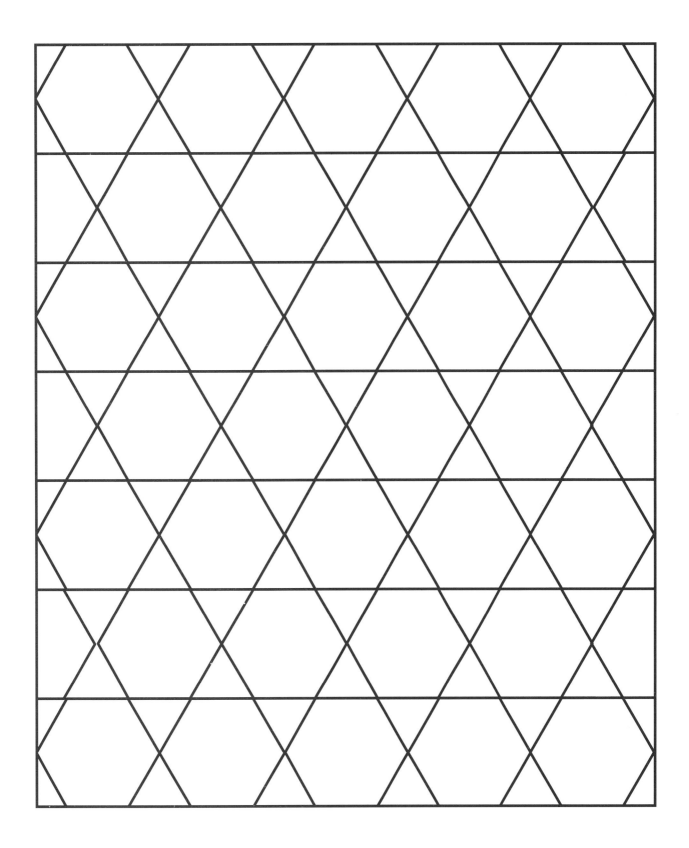

PLAY PAGE
HEXAGON QUILT SET 3

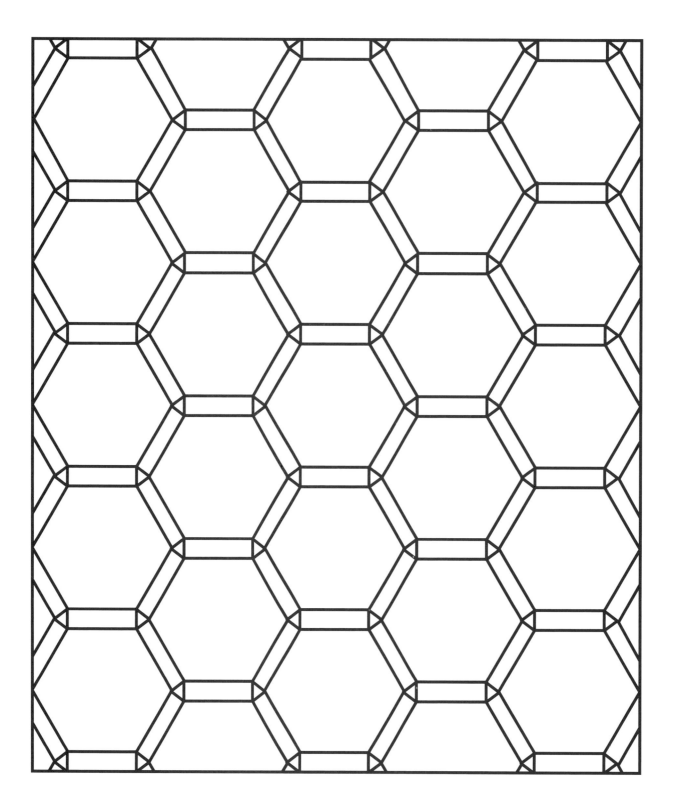

PLAY PAGE
OCTAGON QUILT SET 1

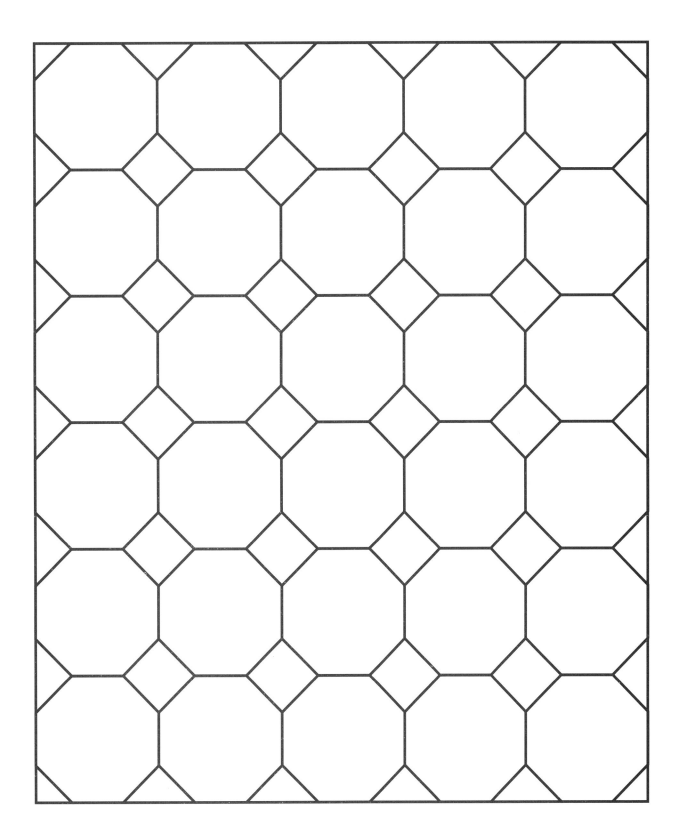

PLAY PAGE
OCTAGON QUILT SET 2

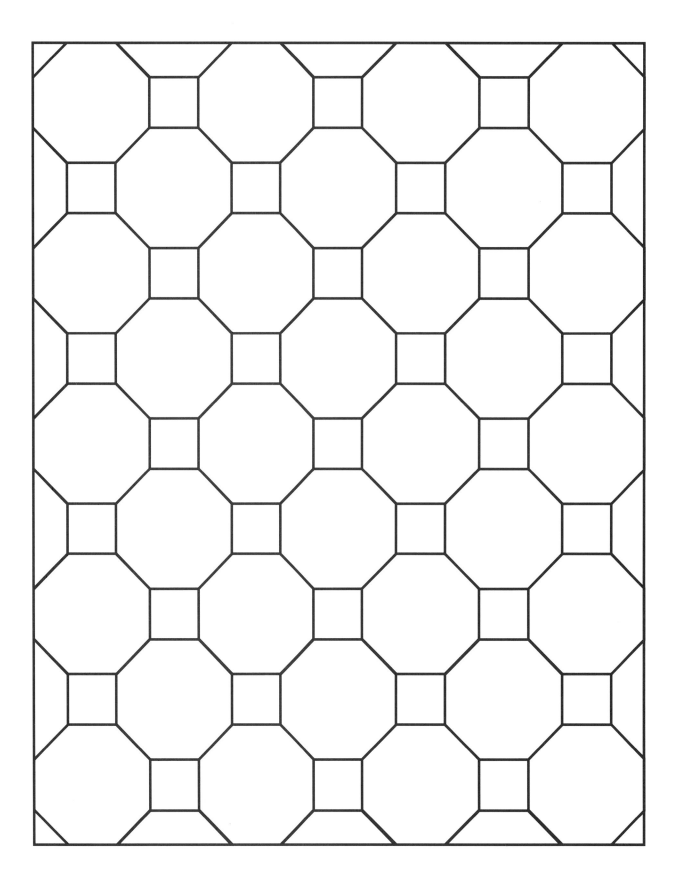

PLAY PAGE
OCTAGON QUILT SET 3

56 SAMPLE COMBINATIONS

SAMPLE COMBINATIONS: HEXAGONS

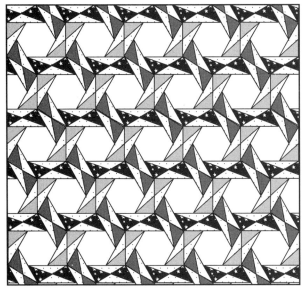

HEXAGON QUILT SET 1
QUILT BLOCK 14, Falling Leaves
Designed by Launa Hall

HEXAGON QUILT SET 1
QUILT BLOCK 29, High Noon
Designed by Donna Poster

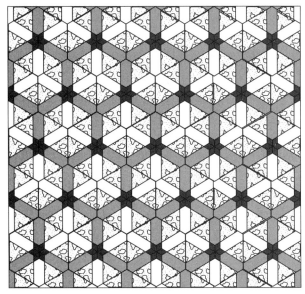

HEXAGON QUILT SET 1
QUILT BLOCK 32, Northern Star
Designed by Donna Poster

HEXAGON QUILT SET 1
QUILT BLOCK 18, Bits O' Fun
Designed by Donna Poster

HEXAGON QUILT SET 1
QUILT BLOCKS 25, Star Bright
26, Star Light
Designed by Launa Hall

HEXAGON QUILT SET 1
QUILT BLOCK 13, Blossom
Designed by Leslie McFarlane

HEXAGON QUILT SET 1
QUILT BLOCKS 3, Camping Out
21, Starflower
Designed by Donna Poster

HEXAGON QUILT SET 1
QUILT BLOCK 30, Windblown
Designed by Donna Poster

HEXAGON QUILT SET 1
QUILT BLOCK 31, Indian Signs
Designed by Donna Poster

HEXAGON QUILT SET 1
QUILT BLOCK 3, Camping Out
Designed by Donna Poster

HEXAGON QUILT SET 2
QUILT BLOCK 5, Round Cabin
Designed by Donna Poster

HEXAGON QUILT SET 2
QUILT BLOCKS 1, Whirlybird
Unpieced Hexagon
Designed by Iris Waal

HEXAGON QUILT SET 2
QUILT BLOCK 12, Poinsettia
PIECED LATTICE BLOCK 1
Designed by Donna Poster

HEXAGON QUILT SET 2
QUILT BLOCK 11, Rolling Star
Designed by Elizabeth Z. Lewis

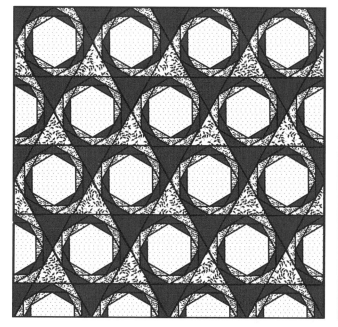

HEXAGON QUILT SET 2
QUILT BLOCK 8, Cabbage Rose
Designed by Donna Poster

HEXAGON QUILT SET 2
QUILT BLOCKS 2, Sunshine
6, Tulip
Designed by Susan Saiter

HEXAGON QUILT SET 2
QUILT BLOCKS 10, Wagon Wheel
33, Doily
Designed by Nina Johnston

HEXAGON QUILT SET 2
QUILT BLOCK 32, Northern Star
Designed by Donna Poster

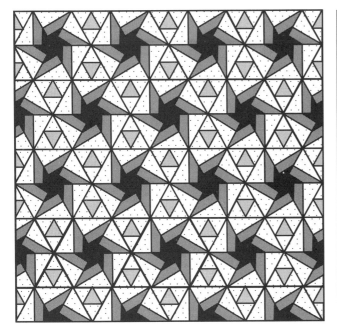

HEXAGON QUILT SET 2
QUILT BLOCK 19, Evening Star
PIECED LATTICE BLOCK 1
Designed by Donna Poster

HEXAGON QUILT SET 2
QUILT BLOCK 15, Delta Queen
Designed by Nina Johnston

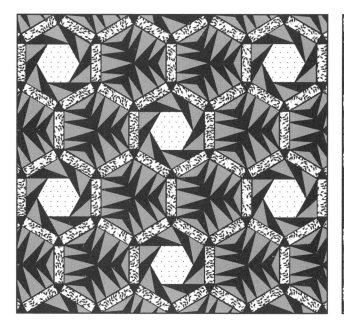

HEXAGON QUILT SET 3
QUILT BLOCKS 14, Falling Leaves
36, Jumpin' Jehoshaphat!
Designed by Joni Milstead

HEXAGON QUILT SET 3
QUILT BLOCK 35, Kaleidoscope
Designed by Donna Poster

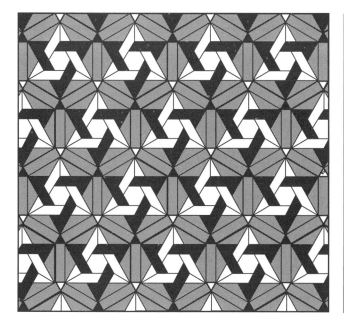

HEXAGON QUILT SET 3
QUILT BLOCK 34, Talk Show
Designed by Susan Saiter

HEXAGON QUILT SET 3
QUILT BLOCK 28, Strolling Along
Designed by Margaret Barncord

HEXAGON QUILT SET 3
QUILT BLOCK 22, Rolling Star
Designed by Donna Poster

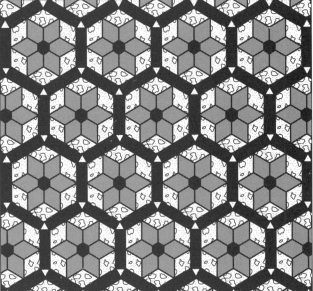

HEXAGON QUILT SET 3
QUILT BLOCK 12, Poinsettia
Designed by Elizabeth Z. Lewis

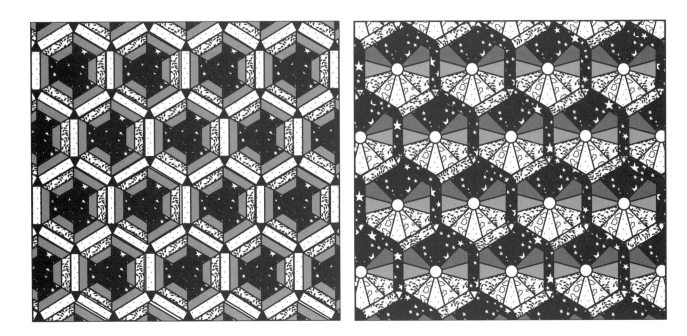

HEXAGON QUILT SET 3
QUILT BLOCK 9, Inside Track
Designed by Donna Poster

HEXAGON QUILT SET 3
QUILT BLOCK 2, Sunshine
Designed by Donna Poster

SAMPLE COMBINATIONS: OCTAGONS

OCTAGON QUILT SET 1
QUILT BLOCKS 3, Pointing the Way
26, Wheelies
Designed by Susan Saiter

OCTAGON QUILT SET 1
QUILT BLOCK 21, Eight-Point Star
PIECED LATTICE BLOCK 4
Designed by Susan Saiter

OCTAGON QUILT SET 1
QUILT BLOCKS 3, Pointing The Way
18, Good Luck
Designed by Donna Poster

OCTAGON QUILT SET 1
QUILT BLOCK 10, Sunflower
Designed by Elizabeth Z. Lewis

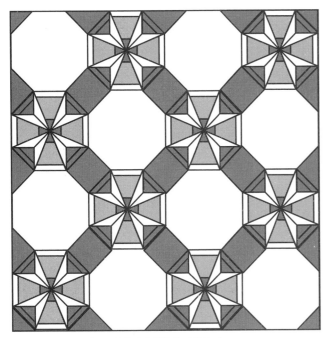

OCTAGON QUILT SET 1
QUILT BLOCKS 35, Fairy Box
Unpieced Octagon
Designed by Donna Poster

OCTAGON QUILT SET 1
QUILT BLOCKS 30, Double Star
Unpieced Octagon
Designed by Donna Poster

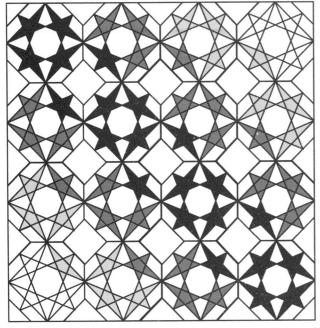

OCTAGON QUILT SET 1
QUILT BLOCK 28, Flippin' Stars
Designed by Susan Saiter

OCTAGON QUILT SET - 1
QUILT BLOCKS 4, Spools
27, Christmas Star
Designed by Elizabeth Z. Lewis

OCTAGON QUILT SET 1
QUILT BLOCK 4, Spools
PEICED LATTICE BLOCK 4
Designed by Iris Waal

OCTAGON QUILT SET 1
QUILT BLOCK 8, Lazy Square
Designed by Donna Poster

OCTAGON QUILT SET 2
QUILT BLOCK 2, Ten O'Clock
PIECED LATTICE BLOCK 5
Designed by Donna Poster

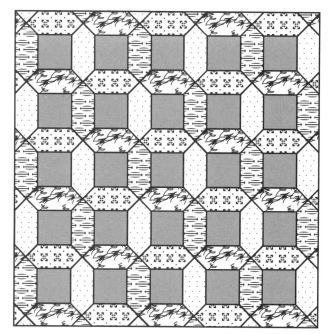

OCTAGON QUILT SET 2
QUILT BLOCK 4, Spools
Designed by Jarod Rehkemper, Age 6

OCTAGON QUILT SET 2
QUILT BLOCK 6, Big Wheel
Designed by Sherry Reid Carroll

OCTAGON QUILT SET 2
QUILT BLOCKS 5, On the Square
9, Primrose
Designed by Iris Waal

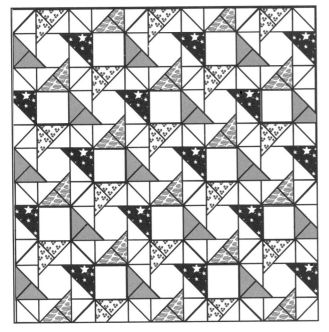

OCTAGON QUILT SET 2
QUILT BLOCK 16, Holding Hands
Designed by Susan Saiter

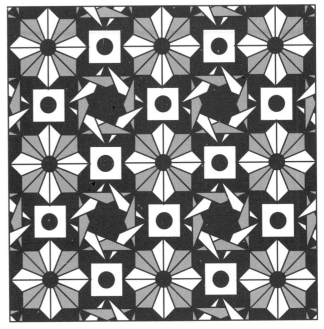

OCTAGON QUILT SET 2
QUILT BLOCKS 10, Sunflower
34, Wings
Appliqué Piece A from #10
Designed by Susan Saiter

OCTAGON QUILT SET 2
QUILT BLOCKS 32, Birds In Flight
Unpieced Octagon
PIECED LATTICE BLOCK 3
Designed by Donna Poster

OCTAGON QUILT SET 2
QUILT BLOCK 25, Star Burst
Designed by Susan Saiter

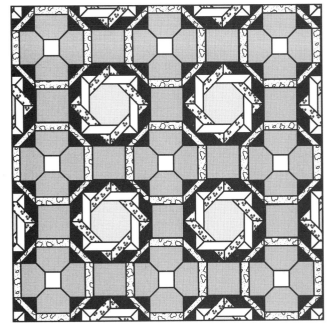

OCTAGON QUILT SET 2
QUILT BLOCKS 14, Crossroads
24, Happiness
Designed by Iris Waal

OCTAGON QUILT SET 2
QUILT BLOCK 18, Good Luck
Designed by Jarod Rehkemper, Age 6

OCTAGON QUILT SET 3
QUILT BLOCK 16, Holding Hands
PIECED LATTICE BLOCK 8
Designed by Donna Poster

OCTAGON QUILT SET 3
QUILT BLOCK 17, Flying Flags
Designed by Donna Poster

OCTAGON QUILT SET 3
QUILT BLOCK 20, Pretty Star
PIECED LATTICE BLOCK 7
Designed by Donna Poster

OCTAGON QUILLT SET 3
QUILT BLOCK 24, Happiness
Designed by Donna Poster

OCTAGON QUILT SET 3
QUILT BLOCK 25, Star Burst
Designed by Donna Poster

OCTAGON QUILT SET 3
QUILT BLOCK 32, Birds in Flight
Designed by Donna Poster

OCTAGON QUILT SET 3
QUILT BLOCK 34, Wings
Designed by Donna Poster

OCTAGON QUILT SET 3
QUILT BLOCK 36, Fish Bones
Designed by Donna Poster

YARDAGE TABLE FOR TEMPLATES

Template Number	¼ Yd.	½ Yd.	1 Yd.	Template Number	¼ Yd.	½ Yd.	1 Yd.	Template Number	¼ Yd.	½ Yd.	1 Yd.
	NUMBER OF PIECES FROM:				**NUMBER OF PIECES FROM:**				**NUMBER OF PIECES FROM:**		
1	24	60	132	40	15	60	120	79	48	104	208
2	26	65	156	41	14	42	91	80	44	99	209
3	78	156	351	42	13	39	78	81	24	48	108
4	36	81	171	43	12	36	72	82	36	96	192
5	27	72	144	44	8	16	32	83	96	192	416
6	40	80	110	45	117	234	507	84	125	250	500
7	66	143	286	46	38	95	209	85	20	50	120
8	64	144	304	47	19	57	133	86	32	80	192
9	33	66	143	48	100	200	440	87	48	96	192
10	8	24	56	49	48	128	256	88	120	320	680
11	22	44	99	50	42	112	224	89	66	143	286
12	30	90	180	51	33	66	143	90	72	156	312
13	51	119	238	52	20	50	120	91	55	110	242
14	60	160	320	53	80	180	380	92	80	160	352
15	88	198	418	54	30	60	130	93	48	112	224
16	6	12	30	55	80	180	380	94	40	80	176
17	7	21	42	56	24	64	128	95	60	130	260
18	8	24	56	57	64	144	304	96	24	64	128
19	9	27	63	58	80	180	380	97	32	72	160
20	20	50	100	59	78	169	338	98	20	45	100
21	22	55	121	60	18	36	78	99	36	81	171
22	186	372	744	61	48	128	256	100	16	32	72
23	18	45	99	62	30	60	132	101	30	90	180
24	44	110	264	63	40	80	176	102	16	40	96
25	22	55	110	64	60	120	264	103	32	80	192
26	26	65	156	65	70	140	308	104	78	156	338
27	45	90	195	66	100	200	440	105	90	210	420
28	57	133	285	67	32	72	152	106	50	100	220
29	57	152	304	68	40	90	190	107	40	80	176
30	60	120	240	69	52	117	247	108	40	80	176
31	92	207	437	70	64	144	304	109	26	78	156
32	120	320	640	71	65	130	286	110	80	180	380
33	120	240	480	72	30	80	160	111	45	90	198
34	62	155	341	73	44	110	264	112	36	81	171
35	50	100	225	74	51	136	272	113	85	170	374
36	15	30	75	75	15	40	80	114	48	108	228
37	93	248	496	76	50	100	220	115	24	72	144
38	42	105	231	77	40	80	176	116	22	66	132
39	38	95	190	78	60	130	260	117	16	40	96

YARDAGE TABLE FOR TEMPLATES — *continued*

Template Number	NUMBER OF PIECES FROM: ¼ Yd.	½ Yd.	1 Yd.	Template Number	NUMBER OF PIECES FROM: ¼ Yd.	½ Yd.	1 Yd.	Template Number	NUMBER OF PIECES FROM: ¼ Yd.	½ Yd.	1 Yd.
118	75	150	330	158	156	312	624	198	65	130	286
119	20	80	160	159	93	217	465	199	42	84	182
120	20	40	90	160	46	115	253	200	48	112	240
121	36	81	171	161	48	128	256	201	4	12	28
122	48	112	256	162	30	80	160	202	10	20	45
123	40	90	190	163	186	372	744	203	21	49	98
124	60	140	300	164	52	104	234	204	40	80	176
125	40	80	176	165	36	81	171	205	4	12	28
126	60	130	260	166	7	21	42	206	10	20	45
127	40	80	176	167	22	55	121	207	21	49	98
128	44	99	209	168	36	72	144	208	108	252	540
129	51	136	272	169	80	180	380	209	40	80	160
130	27	72	144	170	57	152	304	210	16	48	108
131	44	99	209	171	48	96	216	211	28	70	140
132	52	117	247	172	5	10	20	212	27	72	144
133	75	150	330	173	32	72	152	213	0	3	9
134	15	45	105	174	10	20	45	214	48	112	240
135	36	90	198	175	33	88	176	215	42	84	182
136	50	100	220	176	45	120	240	216	36	96	192
137	120	240	528	177	42	84	182	217	126	252	504
138	36	81	171	178	26	65	156	218	189	378	756
139	22	55	121	179	48	128	256	219	145	290	580
140	27	63	126	180	4	12	28	220	10	20	45
141	27	72	144	181	14	35	70	221	48	112	240
142	36	81	171	182	28	70	140	222	44	99	209
143	44	99	209	183	48	128	256	223	30	66	132
144	18	45	99	184	68	153	340	224	35	70	154
145	39	91	182	185	80	160	352	225	40	80	176
146	5	10	20	186	110	220	484	226	40	88	192
147	5	10	25	187	160	320	640	227	68	153	340
148	6	18	36	188	28	70	140	228	33	88	176
149	7	21	42	189	32	80	176	229	28	70	140
150	7	21	49	190	54	108	234	230	24	48	108
151	22	55	121	191	66	176	352	231	88	198	418
152	26	78	156	192	32	72	160	232	51	119	238
153	42	84	182	193	40	100	220	233	4	12	24
154	51	136	289	194	36	96	192	234	0	3	9
155	34	85	204	195	18	36	78	235	20	50	110
156	32	80	176	196	48	96	208	236	40	100	220
157	17	51	119	197	30	80	160	237	96	216	432
								238	48	128	256

Yardage figures are based on 42 inches of usable fabric width (after shrinkage and removal of selvages). A small amount has been allowed in the length for shrinkage and waste.

FULL-SIZE TEMPLATES

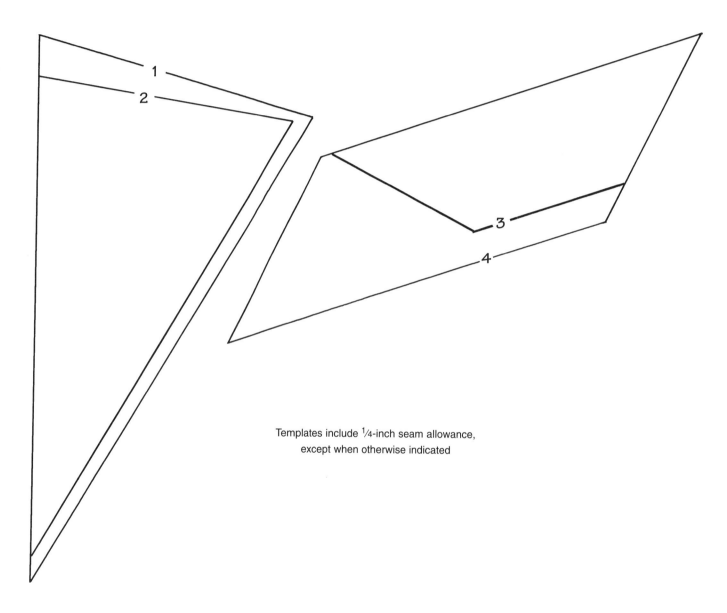

Templates include ¼-inch seam allowance,
except when otherwise indicated

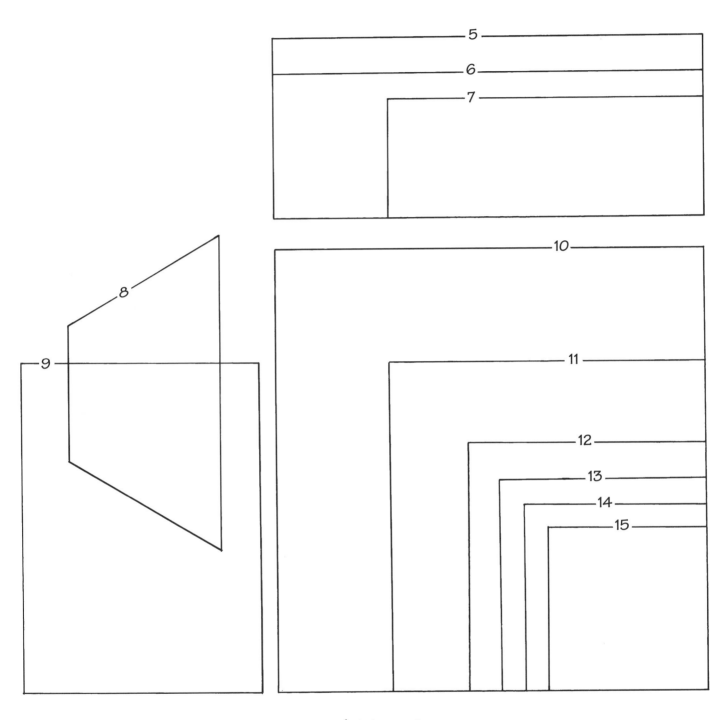

Templates include ¼-inch seam allowance,
except when otherwise indicated

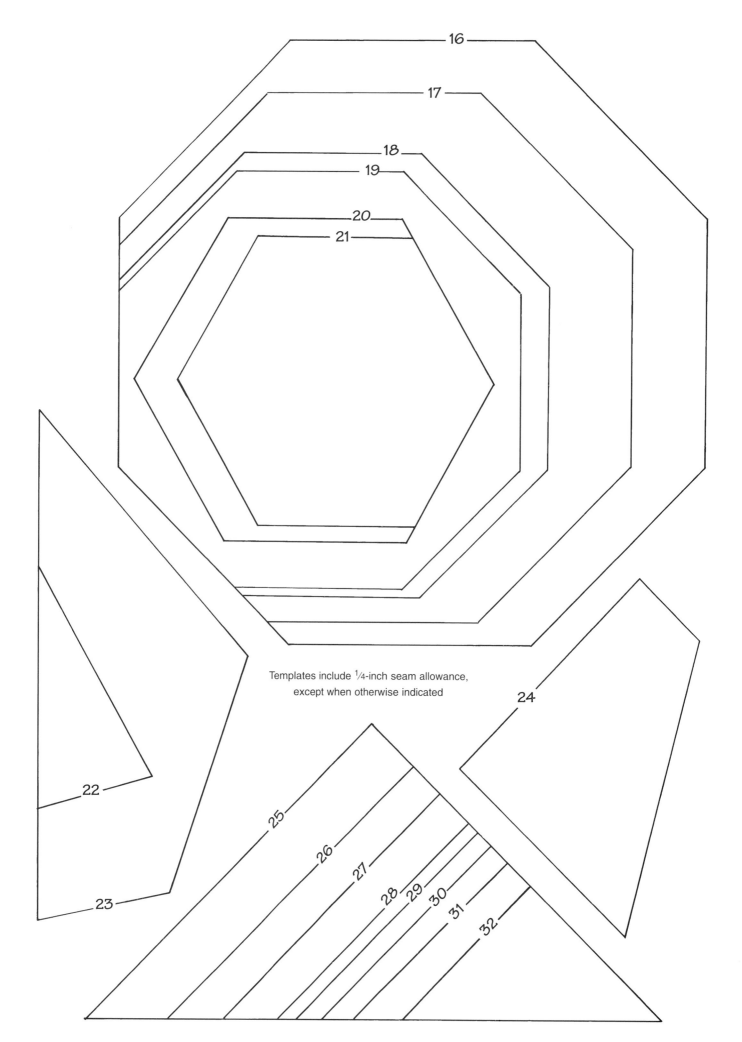

Templates include ¹/₄-inch seam allowance,
except when otherwise indicated

Templates include ¼-inch seam allowance, except when otherwise indicated

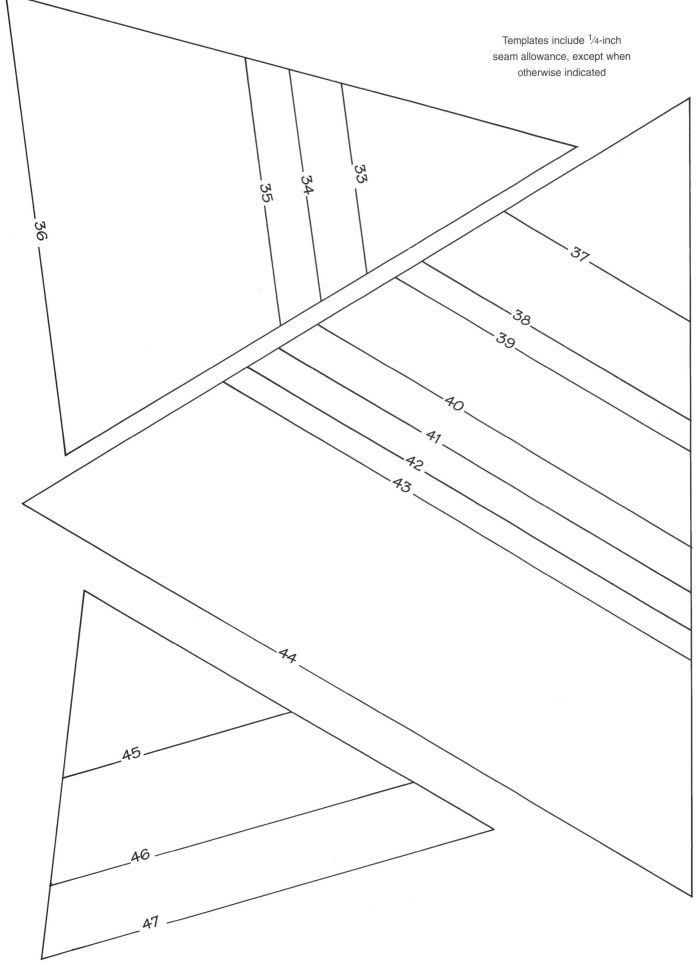

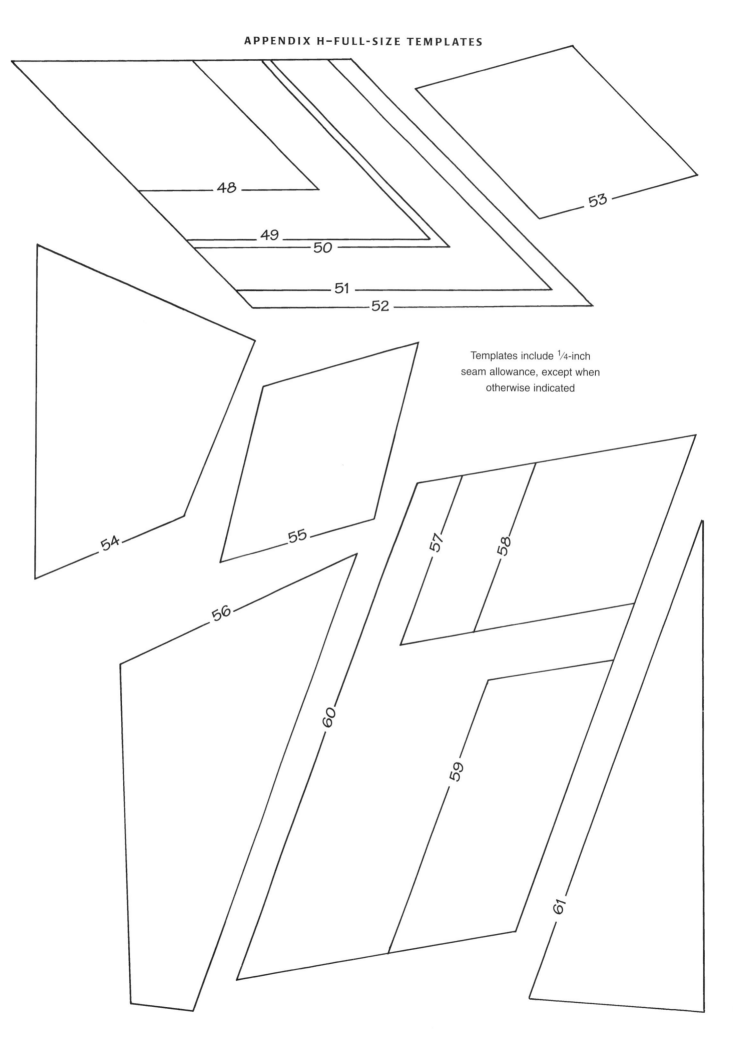

Templates include ¼-inch
seam allowance, except when
otherwise indicated

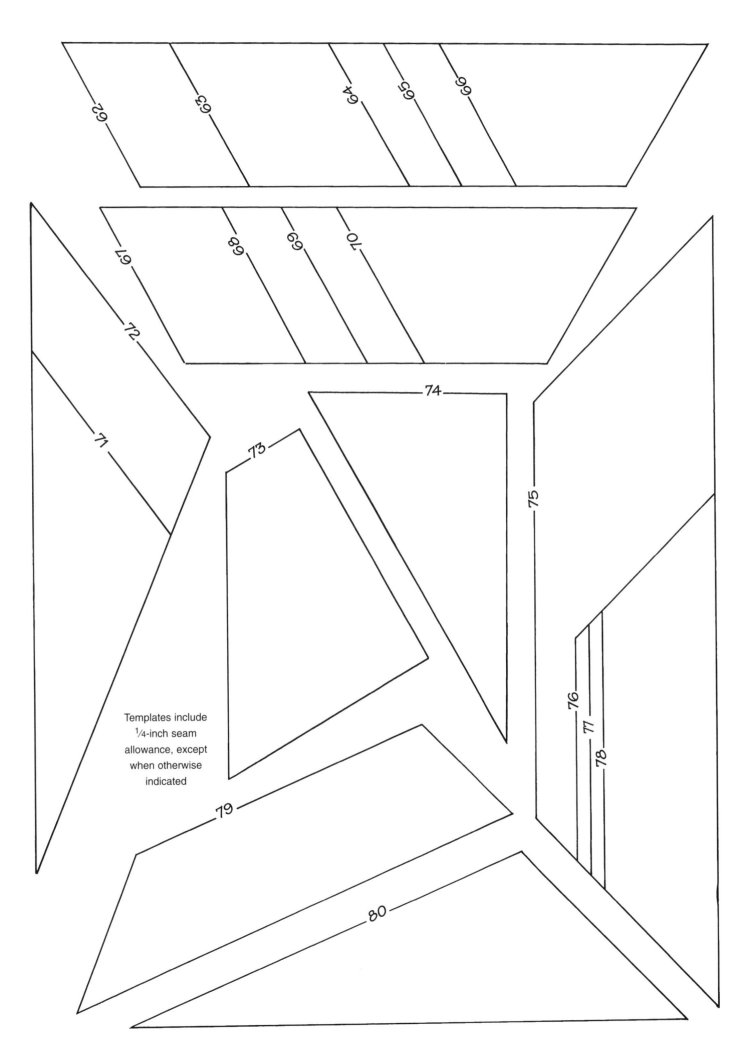

Templates include
¼-inch seam
allowance, except
when otherwise
indicated

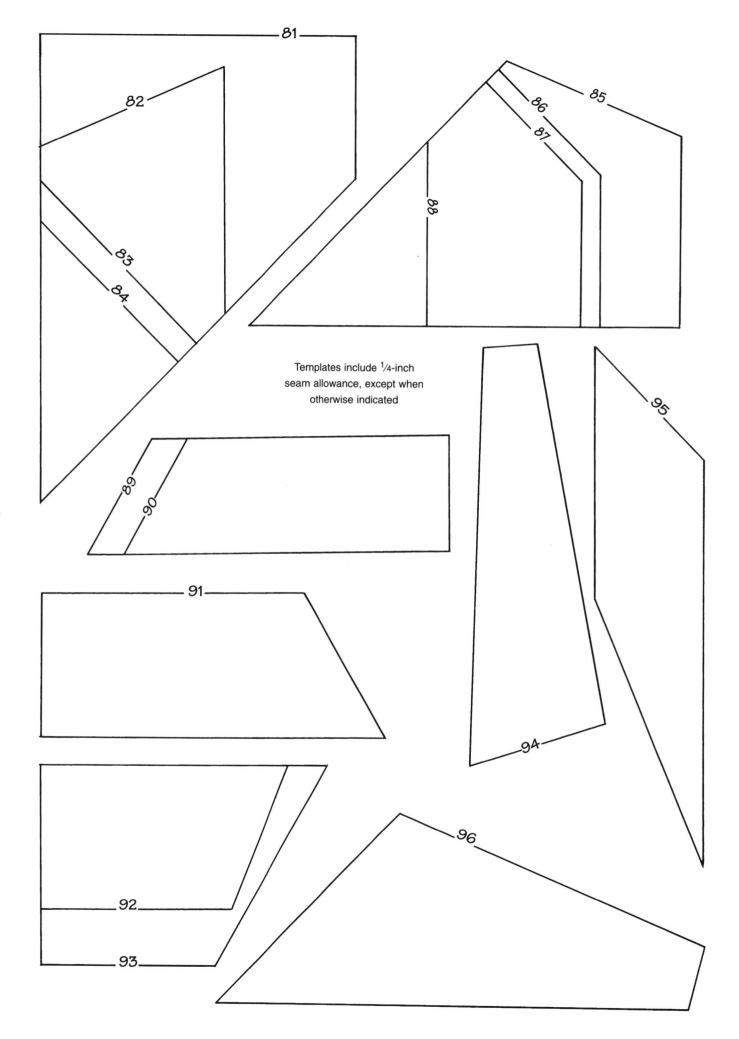

Templates include ¼-inch
seam allowance, except when
otherwise indicated

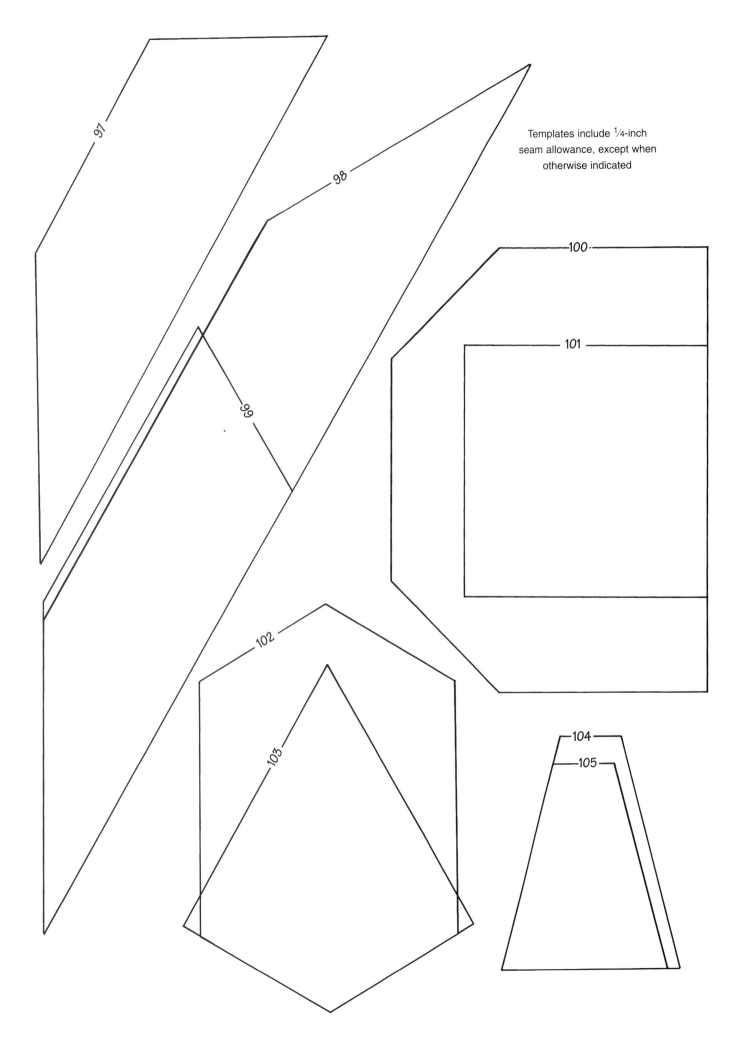

97

98

99

Templates include ¼-inch
seam allowance, except when
otherwise indicated

100

101

102

103

104

105

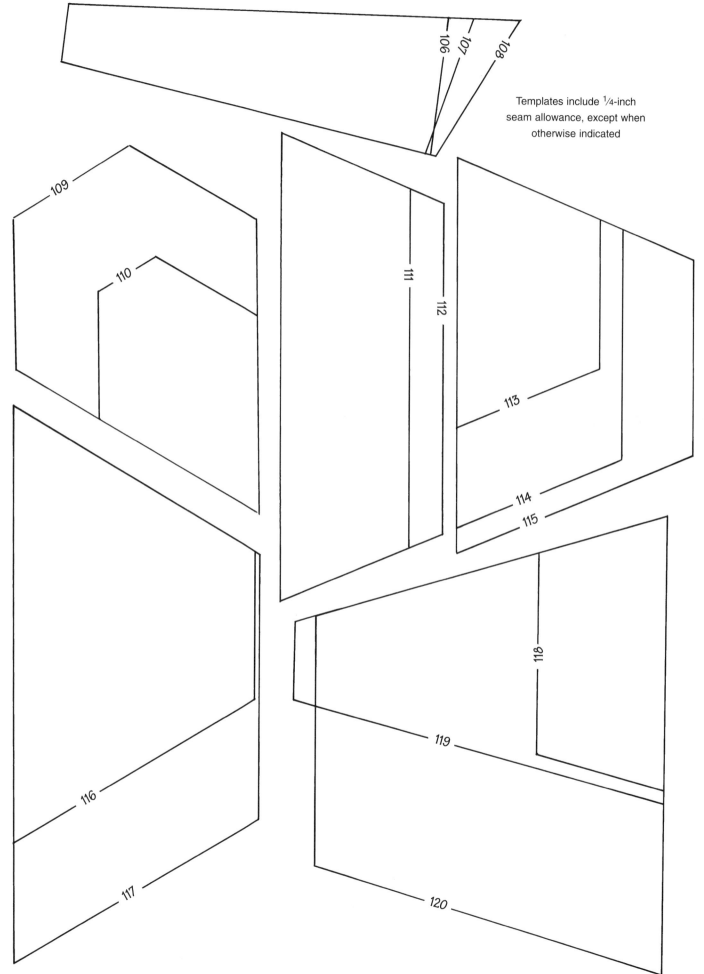

Templates include ¼-inch seam allowance, except when otherwise indicated

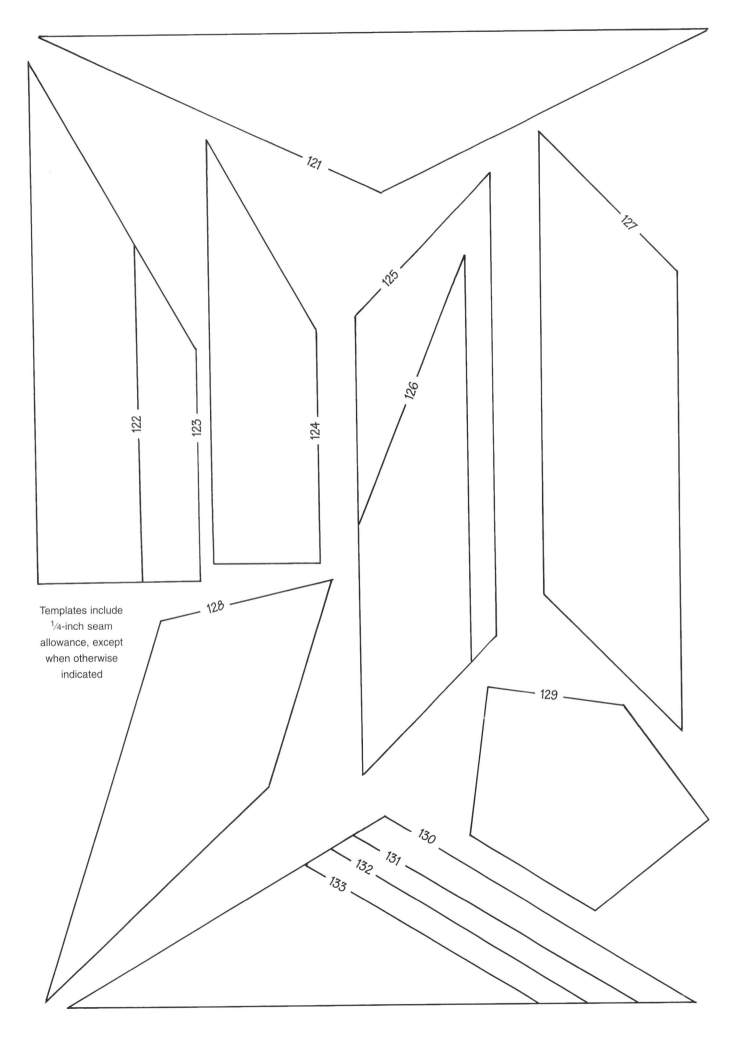

121

127

122 123

125

126

124

Templates include
¹/₄-inch seam
allowance, except
when otherwise
indicated

128

129

130
131
132
133

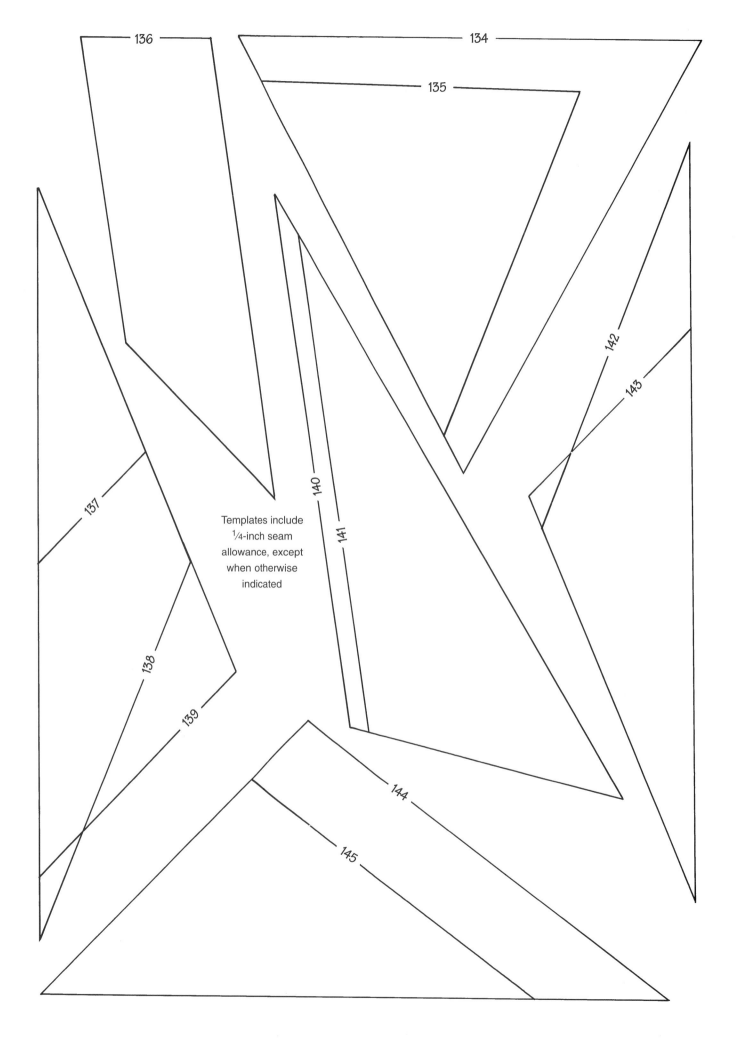

136

134

135

142

143

137

140

141

Templates include
¼-inch seam
allowance, except
when otherwise
indicated

138

139

144

145

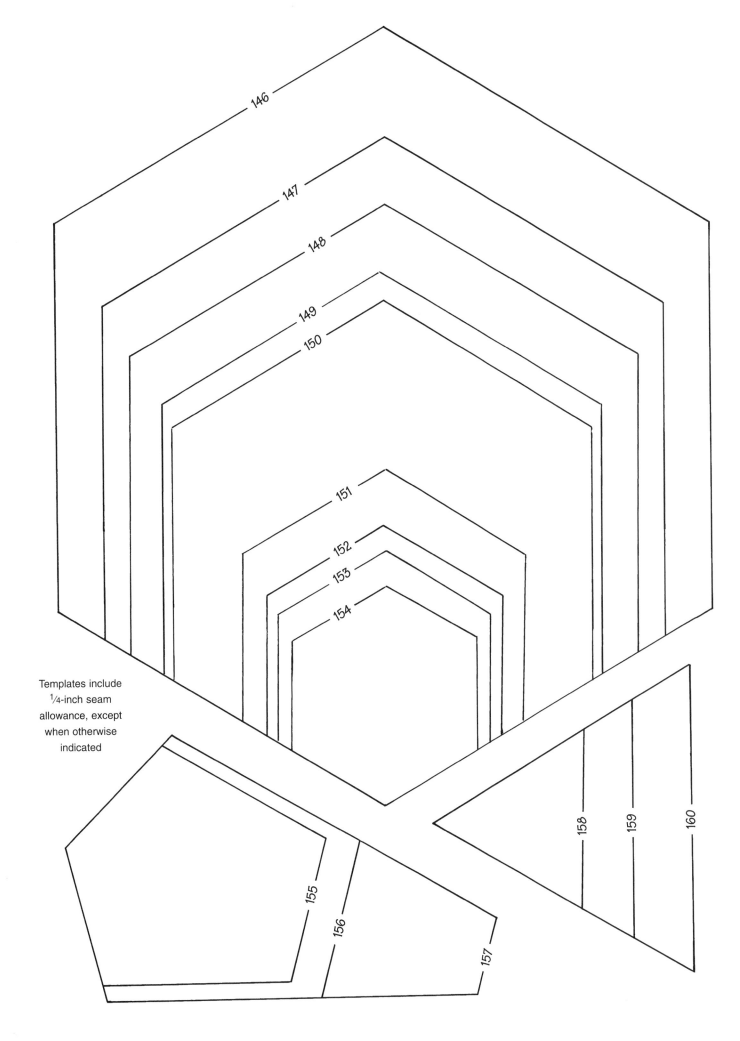

146

147

148

149

150

151

152

153

154

Templates include
¼-inch seam
allowance, except
when otherwise
indicated

155

156

157

158

159

160

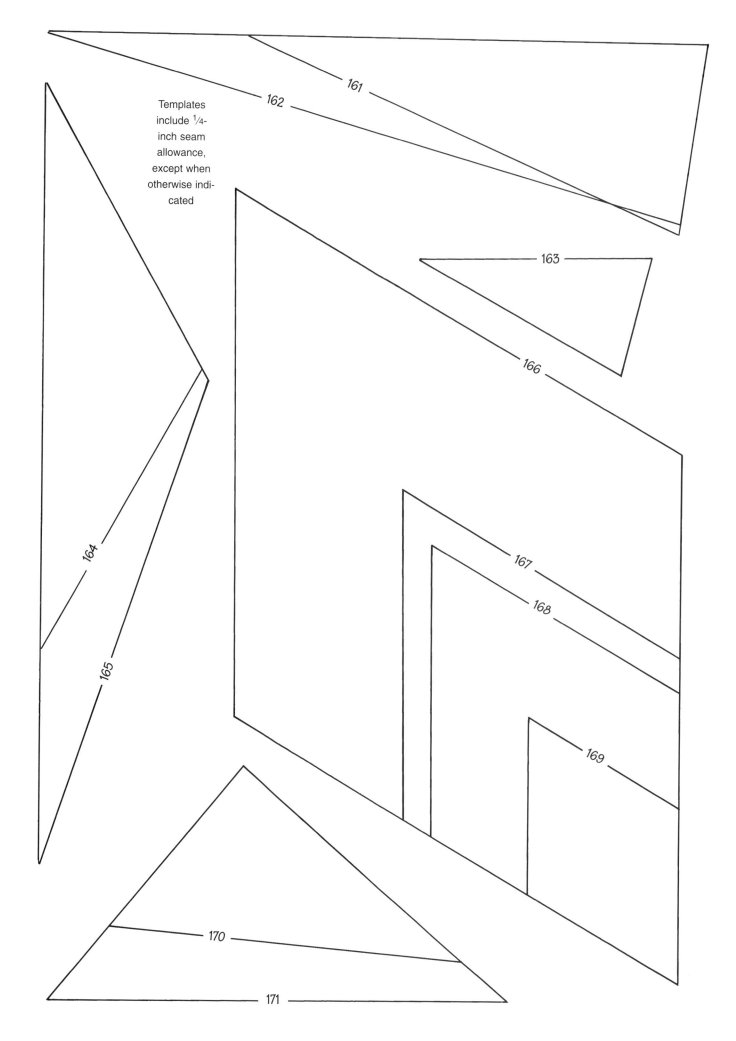

Templates include ¼-inch seam allowance, except when otherwise indicated

161

162

163

164

165

166

167

168

169

170

171

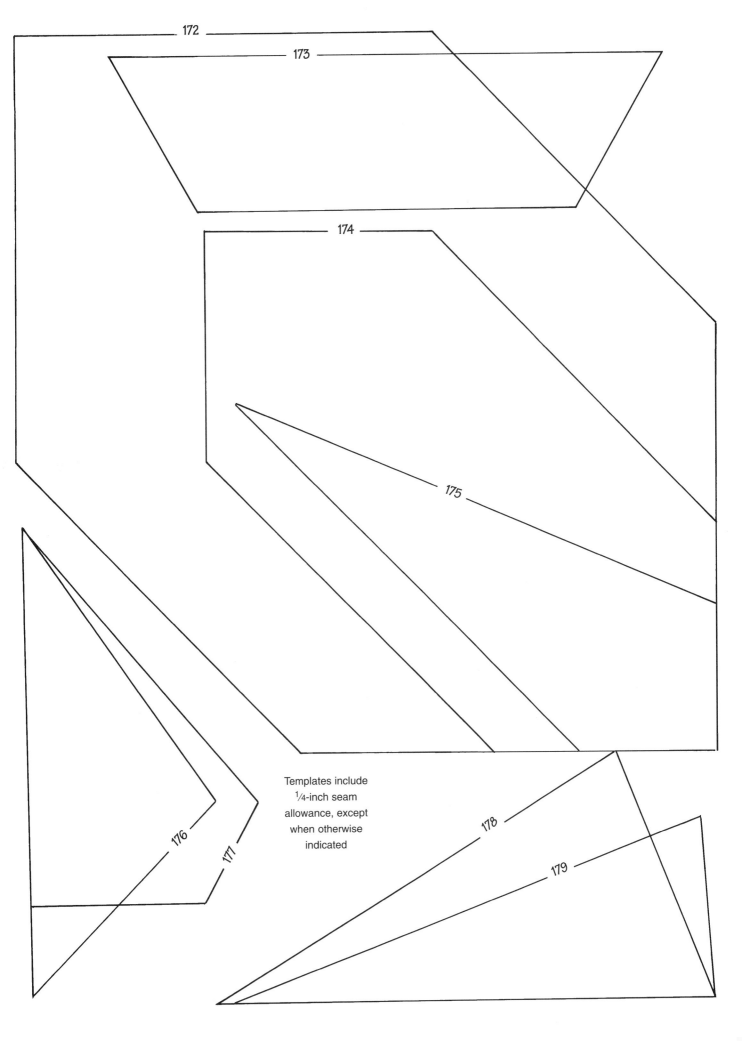

172

173

174

175

176

177

Templates include
$\frac{1}{4}$-inch seam
allowance, except
when otherwise
indicated

178

179

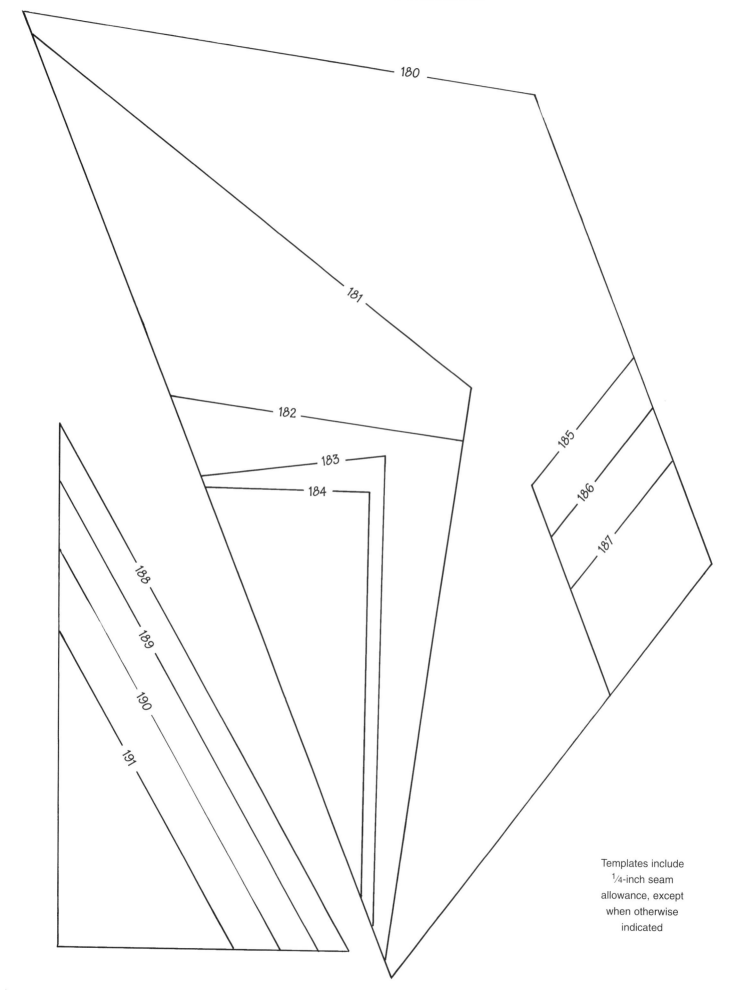

180

181

182

183

184

185

186

187

188

189

190

191

Templates include
¼-inch seam
allowance, except
when otherwise
indicated

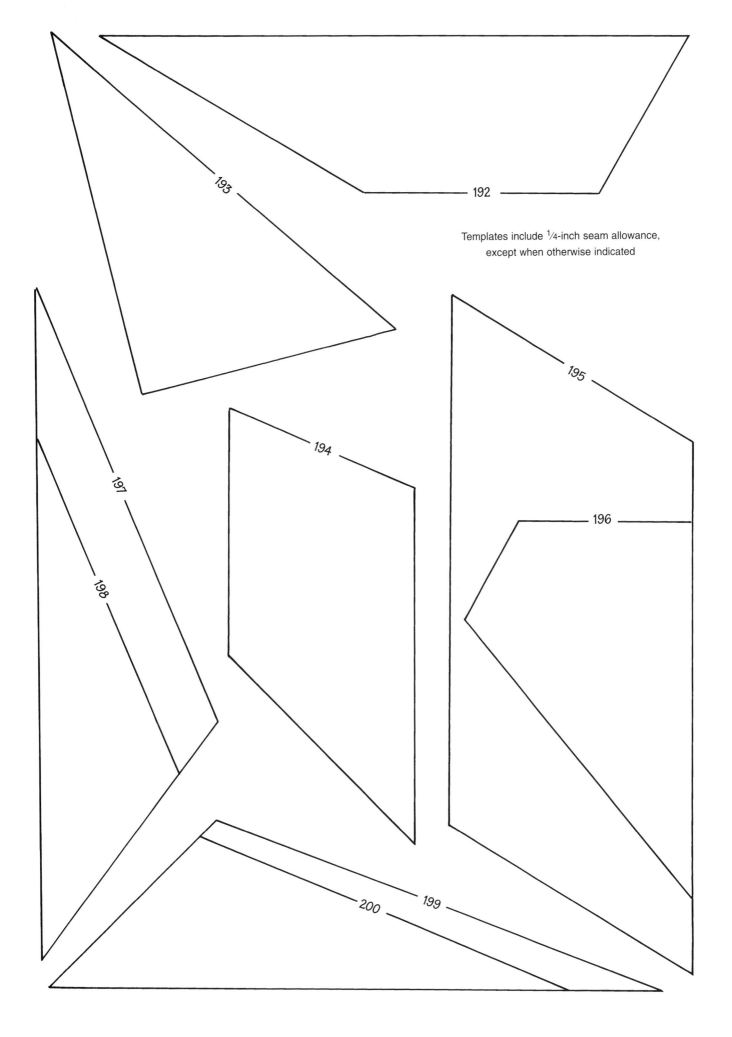

193

192

Templates include ¼-inch seam allowance,
except when otherwise indicated

195

197

194

196

198

200   199

Templates include ¼-inch seam allowance,
except when otherwise indicated

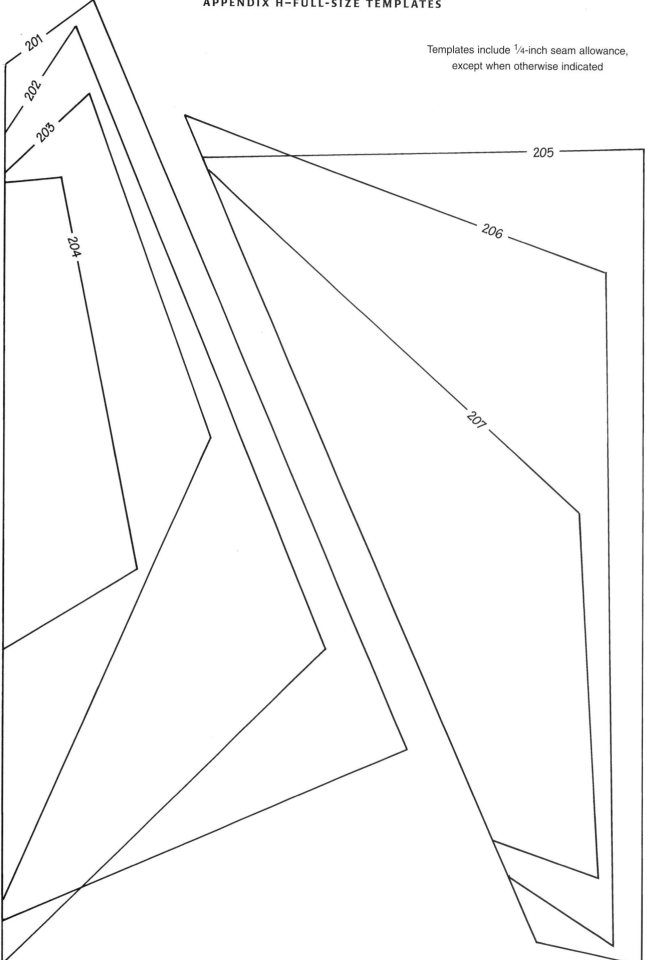

201

202

203

204

205

206

207

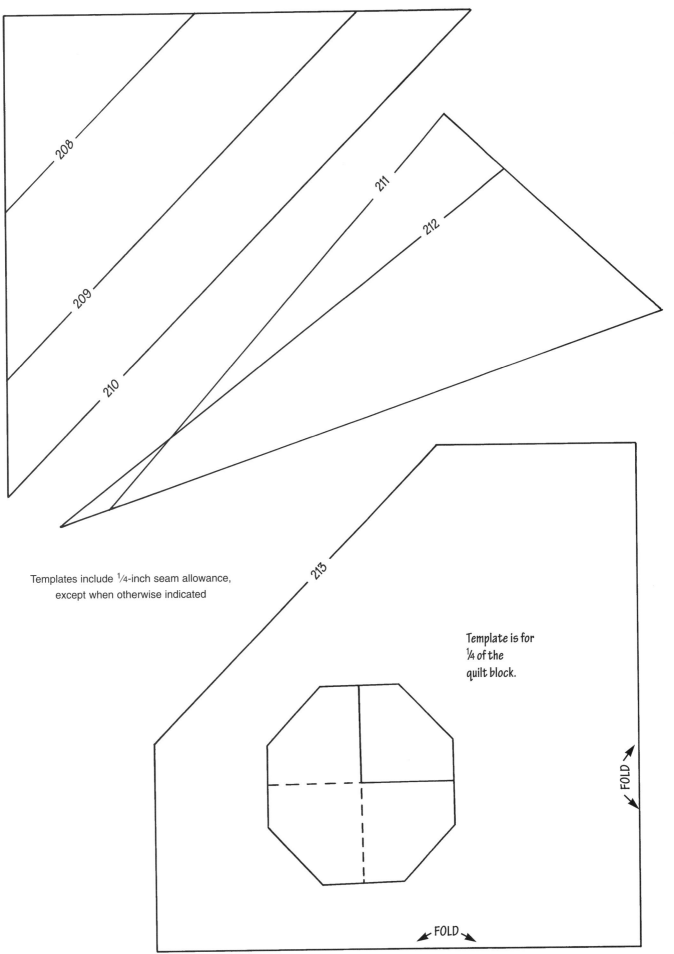

208

209

210

211

212

213

Templates include ¼-inch seam allowance,
except when otherwise indicated

Template is for
¼ of the
quilt block.

FOLD

FOLD

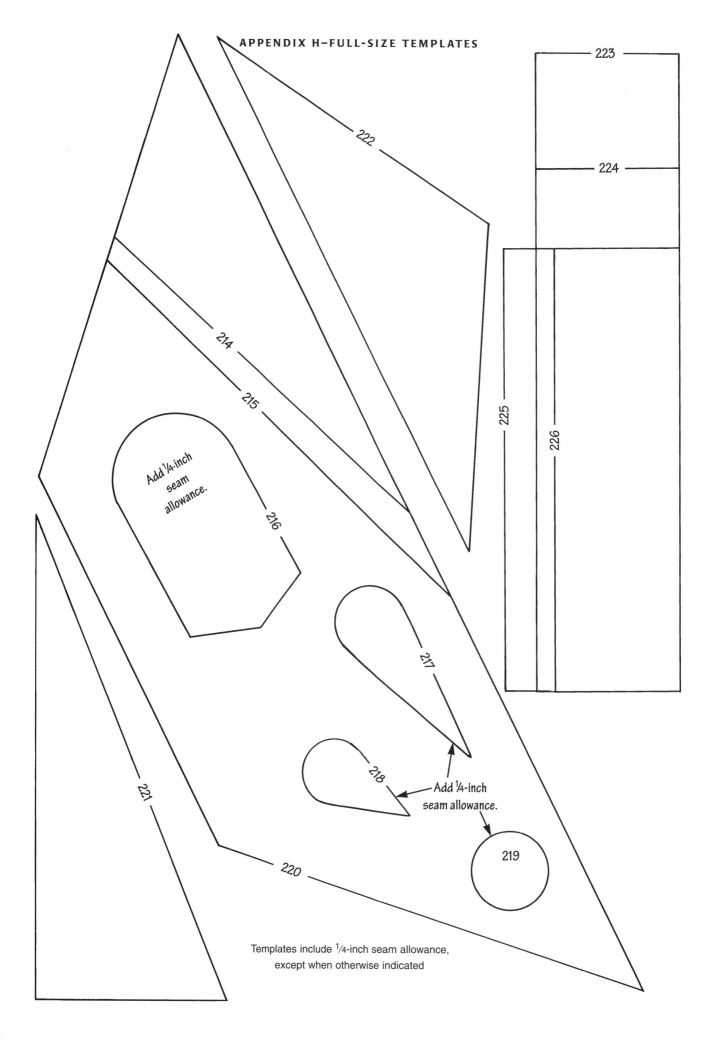

APPENDIX H–FULL-SIZE TEMPLATES

223

224

222

225

226

214

215

Add ¼-inch seam allowance.

216

217

218

Add ¼-inch seam allowance.

219

221

220

Templates include ¼-inch seam allowance,
except when otherwise indicated

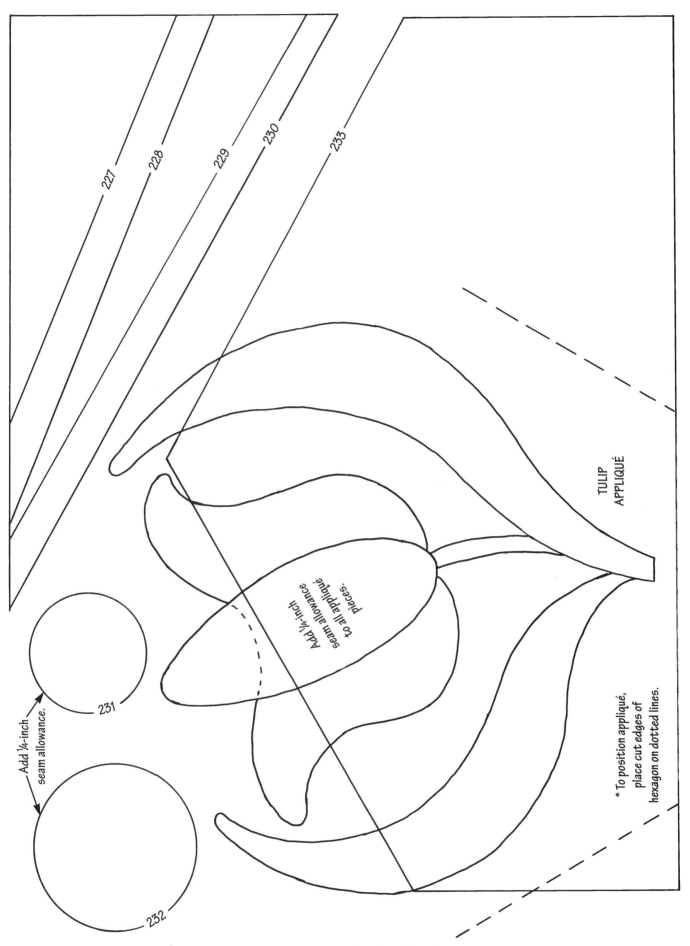

227

228

229

230

233

TULIP
APPLIQUÉ

231

Add ¼-inch
seam allowance.

232

Add ¼-inch
seam allowance
to all appliqué
pieces.

* To position appliqué,
place cut edges of
hexagon on dotted lines.

Templates include ¼-inch seam allowance, except when otherwise indicated

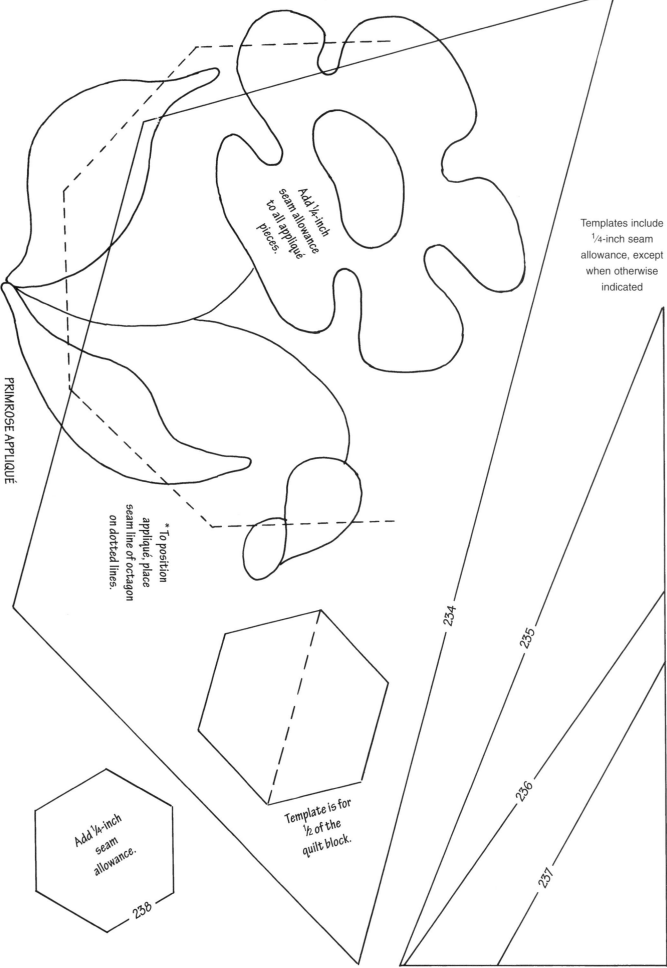

Add ¼-inch seam allowance to all appliqué pieces.

Templates include ¼-inch seam allowance, except when otherwise indicated

PRIMROSE APPLIQUÉ

* To position appliqué, place seam line of octagon on dotted lines.

234

235

236

237

Template is for ½ of the quilt block.

Add ¼-inch seam allowance.

238

GLOSSARY

Backing: The fabric used on the underside of the quilt.

Baste: Temporarily securing the quilt top, batting and backing together so that they can be handled during quilting.

Batting: The layer between the quilt top and the backing. Gives the quilt its puffiness.

Betweens: Short needles (sizes 8 to 10).

Bias: Diagonal to the grain. True bias is a 45_ angle to the straight grain.

Binding: Enclosing the fabric and batting of the outer border to create a finished edge.

Borders: Fabric used around the outer areas of a quilt to highlight the central area and enlarge the quilt to a desired size.

Cutting Templates: Thick pieces of plastic used for cutting out pattern shapes with the rotary cutter. Examples are Speedies.

Easing: Gently maneuvering two pieces of fabric together to match the seams.

Grain: The direction of the horizontal or vertical threads of the fabric. Will be either parallel to the selvage or at a 90° angle to it.

Hexagon Quilt Block: A six-sided quilt block.

Lattice: Pieces (often strips) of fabric sewn between quilt blocks. Used to add color and to highlight the quilt blocks. Smaller than a quilt block.

Layout: The arrangement of blocks, lattice and borders that make up the quilt top. Also called a set.

Miter: Connecting borders with a diagonal (45°) seam from inner corner to outer corner.

Miterite: Trademark name of an 8 x 24-inch clear plastic ruler with one end cut off at a 45-degree angle. Manufactured by Holiday Designs, Mineola, Tex.

Octagon Quilt Block: An eight-sided quilt block.

Piecing: Stitching small pieces of fabric together to form a quilt block.

Pin-baste: Basting with safety pins. Holds more securely than thread.

Quilt Block: A design unit that is repeated to make the quilt top.

Quilt Center: The pieced quilt before borders are added.

Quilting: Stitching the three layers—quilt top, batting and backing—together.

Quilting Lines: Lines that you mark on the quilt top. Used as guides for sewing the three layers together.

Quilt Set: The arrangement, or layout, of quilt blocks, lattice blocks, edge pieces and corner pieces composing the quilt center. Quilt design.

Quilt Top: The piece of the quilt comprising the quilt blocks, lattice blocks, edge and corner pieces and borders.

Selvage: The woven edge along the length of the fabric.

Set-In: Any piece that must be sewn into a corner formed by two or more other pieces.

Sharps: Hand-sewing needles.

Speedy: Clear plastic cutting template available in various sizes and shapes. Manufactured by Holiday Designs, Mineola, Tex.

Tie: To tie the layers of the quilt together. Fast alternative to hand- or machine-quilting and especially effective for puffy comforters.

Value: The lightness or darkness of a color.

SOURCES

Please check your local quilt store for items mentioned in this book. They are available to the store through these wholesale sources:

Miterite and Cutting Templates (Speedies)

Holiday Designs
Rt. 1, Box 302P
Mineola, Tex. 75773

Rotary Cutters and Mats

Fiskars, Inc.
7811 West Stewart Ave.
Wausau, Wis. 54401

Quilt Batting

Hobbs Bonded Fibers
PO Box 2521
Waco, Tex. 76702

Fabrics

Gutcheon Patchworks, Inc.
917 Pacific Ave., Room 305
Tacoma, Wash. 98402

Mail-Order Suppliers

Check the quilting and sewing magazines for current mail-order companies. Here are some good ones:

Clotilde
2 Sew Smart Way, B8031
Stevens Point, Wis. 54481-8031

Connecting Threads
5750 N.E. Hassalo
Portland, Ore. 97215

Dover Street Booksellers
39 E. Dover St.
PO Box 1563
Easton, Md. 21601

Hard-to-Find Needlework Books
96 Roundwood Rd.
Newton, Mass. 02164

Keepsake Quilting
PO Box 1618, Rt. 25B
Center Harbor, N.H. 03226-1618

Quilts & Other Comforts
1 Quilters Lane, Box 4100
Golden, Colo. 80402-4100

Nancy's Notions
PO Box 683
Beaver Dam, Wis. 53916-0683

Quilting Books Unlimited
1911 West Wilson
Batavia, Ill. 60510

Tole Americana
5750 NE Hassalo, Bld. C
Portland, Ore. 97213

Treadle Art
25834 Narbonne Ave.
Lomita, Calif. 90717

BIBLIOGRAPHY

Campbell, Patricia B., and Mimi Ayers. Jacobean Appliqué. Vol. 1, bk. 1, Exotica. Paducah, Ky.: American Quilter's Society, 1993.

Fanning, Robbie and Tony Fanning. The Complete Book of Machine Quilting. Radnor, Pa.: Chilton Book Co., 1994.

Hargrave, Harriet. Heirloom Machine Quilting. Martinez, Calif.: C & T Publishing, 1990.

Johannah, Barbara. Barbara Johannah's Crystal Piecing. Radnor, Pa.: Chilton Book Co., 1993.

Ollard, Caroline. The Complete Book of Needlecrafts. Radnor, Pa.: Chilton Book Co., 1990.

Poster, Donna. Speed-Cut Quilts. Radnor, Pa.: Chilton Book Co., 1989.

———. The Quilter's Guide to Rotary Cutting. Radnor, Pa.: Chilton Book Co., 1991.

INDEX

Angles, 53-56
Appliquéing
    hand, 57-58
    machine, 58-59
Attachments, sewing machine, 30

Backing
    color of, 19
    preparing, 66
    yardage calculations for, 131
Basting layers, 66
Batting
    preparing, 66
    purchasing, 28
    sources, 178
Bias, handling, 12, 48-49
Bias strips, 36-37
Binding edges
    borderless edges, 70-71
    straight edges, 69-70
Block design, choosing, 14-15. *See also*
    Hexagon quilt blocks; Octagon quilt blocks
Borderless edges, binding, 70-71
Borders
    adding, 61-63
    choosing, 15-16
    cutting, 36
    measurements for, 129-130
    mitering corners
        speedy method, 62-63
        traditional method, 63
Border strips, 130

Caring for quilts, 73-74
Chalk pencils, 30, 65
Colorfast fabric, 31
Colors of quilt
    backing, 19
    choosing, 17-18
    color family and, 18
    color scheme and, 19
    color values and, 18
    flexibility about, 19-20
    importance of, 17
    print, stripe and solid combinations, 18-19

Combinations of quilt blocks
    hexagons, 140-146
    octagons, 147-153
Construction process, basic, 12
Copying, cutting and pasting, 5, 132-139
Corners, mitering
    speedy method, 62-63
    traditional method, 63
Cutting borders, 36
Cutting fabric
Donna's speedy method, 37-43
    guidelines, general, 32
    like pieces and, 32
    mirror pieces and, 32
    rotary-cutting method, 33-37
    shapes of, various, 38-43
    traditional method, 32

Designing quilts, 13-16, 132-139
Drying quilts, 74

Easing during machine piecing, 49
Eight points, joining, 55
Embroidering, 59

Fabric
    bleeding of, 31
    cutting
        Donna's speedy method, 37-43
        guidelines, general, 32
        like pieces and, 32
        mirror pieces and, 32
        rotary-cutting method, 33-37
        shapes of, various, 38-43
        traditional method, 32
    loft in, 50
    prewashing, 31
    print, stripe and solid combinations, 18-19
    purchasing, 27-28
    sources, 178
Fabric sizing, 30, 31
"Factory" method of machine piecing, 50
Feet, sewing machine, 30, 67
Frames, quilting, 29-30
French knots, 59

Glossary, 175

Hand-appliquéing, 57-58
Hand-piecing, 56
Hand-quilting, 66, 67
Hand-washing and -drying quilts, 74
Hexagon quilt blocks
    combinations, 140-146
    designs for and construction of, 76-95
    optional lattice blocks for, 128
    sets, 15, 116-121
    using this book's, 4

Irons, 30

Labels, quilt, 30
Lattice blocks, optional for hexagon and
    octagon sets, 128
Laundering quilts, 74
Layers, basting, 66
Layout page, 21-22, 26
Like pieces of pattern shapes, 32
Long strips in machine piecing, 50

Machine-appliquéing, 58-59
Machine-piecing
    angles and, 53-56
    bias and, handling, 48-49
    easing during, 49
    "factory" method of, 50
    long strips and, 50
    matching seams and, 51
    1/4-inch seams in, 49-50
    pinning for, 49
    points and, 53-56, 132
    pressing seams in, 51
    set-ins and
        basic method, 51-52
        fast and easy method, 52-53
    sewing machine adjustments for, 48
    starter seams and, 51
Machine-quilting, 67-68
Machine-washing and -drying quilts, 74
Mail-order suppliers, 178
Maintenance of quilts, 73-74
Marking pens, 30, 37
Marking quilting lines, 65-66
Matching seams, 51
Mats, cutting, 28, 178
Mirror pieces of pattern shapes, 32
Mitering corners

speedy method, 62-63
    traditional method, 63
Miterite ruler, 29, 33, 37, 38

Needle plates, 48
Needles, 29, 48, 56
Notebook, creating, 7-8

Oaktag, 30
Octagon quilt blocks
    combinations, 147-153
    designs for and construction of, 96-115
    optional lattice blocks for, 128
    sets, 15, 122-127
    using this book's, 4
Outline stitch, 59

Pencils, chalk, 30, 37
Permanent marking pens, 30
Piecing. See also Machine-piecing
    hand, 56
    neatness in, 47-48
    overview of, 47
    ripping out during, 47
    successful, 48
Pinning for machine piecing, 49
Pins, 29, 49
Planning pages, 116-128
Play pages, 134-139
Points, 53-56, 132
Practice exercises, 11-12
Pressing seams, 51, 56
Prewashing fabric, 31
Prints, combining with stripes and
    solids, 18-19

Quilter's tape, 30, 65
Quilting
    hand, 66, 67
    machine, 67-68
    tying, 67, 68
Quilting lines, marking, 65-66
Quilting stencils, 30
Quilt labels, 30
Quilt sets. See Sets, quilts
Quilt top, 66

Ripping out during piecing, 47
Rotary cutters, 28, 34, 178
Rotary cutting
    fabric cutting and, 33-37

supplies for, 28-29
Rulers, 29, 33, 37, 38

Scrap quilts, 19
Seam ripper, 30
Seams
    $^1/_4$-inch, 11, 48, 49-50, 56
    matching, 51
    pinning across, 49
    pressing, 51, 56
    starter, 51
Selecting quilt to make, 13-16
Set-ins
    basic method, 51-52
    fast and easy method, 52-53
Sets, quilt
    choosing, 14-15
    hexagon, 15, 116-121
    octagon, 15, 122-127
    optional pieced lattice blocks for hexagon
      and octagon sets, 128
    using this book's, 5
Sewing machine, 30, 48
Sewing tools, 30. *See also* specific types
Size of quilt, 15, 116-128
Sizing, fabric, 30
Solids, combining with prints and
    stripes, 18-19
Sources, 179
Speedy templates, 29, 33, 37, 38
Spray starch, 30, 31
Starter seams, 51
Stencils, quilting, 30
Stitches, embroidery, 59
Storing quilts, 74
Straight edges, binding, 69-70
Stripes, combining with prints and
    solids, 18-19
Strips
    basic, 34
    bias, 36
    border, 130
    long, 50
    multiple, 34, 36

Supplies
    copying, cutting and pasting, 132
    general, 29-30
    rotary-cutting, 28-29
    sources for, 178

Tape measure, 30
Tape, quilter's, 30, 65
Taping and cutting, 38-43
Template plastic, 30
Templates
    full-size, 156-176
    shapes, cutting, 38-43
    Speedy, 29, 33, 37, 38
    types of, 29
    using this book's, 5, 33
    yardage table for, 5, 154-155
Tension balance, 48
Thimbles, 30
Threads, 30, 48, 67
Twelve points, joining, 55-56
Tying, 67, 68

Values, color, 18

Washing quilts, 74
Water-soluble marking pens, 30, 65

Yardage calculations
    for backing, 131
    example, 22-24
    layout page and, 21-22, 26
    method of, 24-25
    for quilt sets, 116-128
    table for templates, 5, 154-155